Premium by Design

Premium by Design

How to Understand, Design and Market High End Products

MARCO BEVOLO
PhD Candidate, Eindhoven, The Netherlands/Turin, Italy

ALEX GOFMAN
PhD, White Plains, NY USA

HOWARD MOSKOWITZ
PhD, White Plains, NY USA

GOWER

Published by
Gower Publishing Limited
Wey Court East
Union Road
Farnham
Surrey, GU9 7PT
England

Ashgate Publishing Company
Suite 420
101 Cherry Street
Burlington,
VT 05401-4405
USA

www.gowerpublishing.com

British Library Cataloguing in Publication Data
Bevolo, Marco.
  Premium by design : how to understand, design and market
  high end products.
  1. Luxuries--Design. 2. Luxuries--Marketing. 3. New
  products. 4. Social responsibility of business.
  I. Title II. Gofman, Alex. III. Moskowitz, Howard R.
  658.5'75-dc22

  ISBN: 978-1-4094-1890-0 (hbk)
  ISBN: 978-1-4094-1891-7 (ebk)

Library of Congress Cataloging-in-Publication Data
Bevolo, Marco.
  Premium by design : how to understand, design and market high end products / Marco
  Bevolo, Alex Gofman, Howard Moskowitz.
    p. cm.
  Includes bibliographical references and index.
  ISBN 978-1-4094-1890-0 (hbk) -- ISBN 978-1-4094-1891-7
  (ebook) 1. Luxury goods industry. 2. Luxuries. 3. New products. 4. Product design. I.
  Gofman, Alex. II. Moskowitz, Howard R. III. Title.
  HD9999.L852B48 2010
  658.5'75--dc22

                                                                          2010033174

MIX
Paper from
responsible sources
FSC® C018575
www.fsc.org

Printed and bound in Great Britain by the
MPG Books Group, UK

Contents

List of Figures

List of Tables

Notes on Contributors

This book is the collaborative effort of three authors with input from many professionals in the distinct worlds of research, creativity and publishing. We want to underscore that this book is not a small choir of "*a cappella*" singers, but a huge stage with more than 75 voices. All of them were fundamental in making it happen. Their generosity in contributing their time and sharing ideas through interviews and discussions is greatly appreciated.

We interviewed our experts in successive waves. We started our quest with a pilot round to test our research approach in January 2007, through a standardized format of dialogue across the spring and summer, to finish with highly personalized interviews in the winter of 2007/8. You will meet our experts, their ideas, their expert visions and their insights about today and the future, about high end and luxury, about business and life. Our sincere gratitude goes to the experts and industry leaders listed below in a random order.

Note

A number of our 75+ contributors have changed their position, their job title and/or their company since the time of our research. The authors have indicated their formal status at the time of interviewing with the specification of "fr." – this stands for "former" and indicates that the thought leader/expert in object is now no longer in that position.

PILOT INTERVIEWS (PRELIMINARY QUALITATIVE QUESTIONNAIRE)

Shari Swan, Founder and Principal, StreativeBranding, Amsterdam

Lisette Heemskerk, fr. Publisher, Sanoma, Amsterdam

Mark Whiting, Head of Market Intelligence, Moet Hennessy, Paris

Kate Ancketill, Managing Director, GDR, London

Patrizia Beltrami, Director of Communication, Alcantara, Milan

Gary Chang, Founder, EDGE Design, Hong Kong

Steven van der Kruit, Creative Director, Perfumery Division, Firmenich, Geneva

Luciana Stein, formerly editor at Valor Economico, Sao Paulo, Brazil

Gilbert Lee, Client Services Director, Research International, Guangdong, China

Philip Verhagen, fr. Marketing Director, Umbra, Toronto

Ron Pompei, Founder, Pompei AD, New York, formerly CNN Principal Voice

Mark Tungate, Author and Journalist, Paris

Roger Tredre, Consulting Editor, WGSN, London

FINAL INTERVIEWS – EUROPE (FINAL UNIFIED QUALITATIVE QUESTIONNAIRE)

Francoise Sackrider, Director, Institut Francais de la Mode, Paris, France

Torsten Hochstetter, Global Head of Design App./Acc., Herzogenaurach, Germany

Stoyan Kamburow, Director, TNS Infratest, Bielefeld, Germany

Roland Heiler, Managing Director, Porsche Design, Austria

Elisabetta Tangorra, Director, Luxury Box Unit, McCann Erickson, Milan

Catherine Jubin, MD, International Luxury Business Association, Paris

Patrice Muller, Founder, Ipolitis and Hubertus, Geneva

Babette Wasserman, Founder and Director, Babette Wasserman, London

Uche Okonkwo, Director and Founder, Luxe Etc., Paris

Thierry Maman, Managing Director, Berluti, Paris

Karen Moersch, Founder, The Hasley Group, Warwick, UK

Alex Berger, Principal, MMandI, Paris

Lauren McBride, Account Director, DCG Media, London

Max van Lingen, Director Interactive Brand Marketing, Mexx (part of Liz Claiborne), Netherlands

Adjedj Bakas, Founder, Dexter, Amsterdam

Nick Compton, Features Editor, Wallpaper, London

Stan Stalnaker, President and Creative Director, Hub Culture, LDN SGP NYC

Carmen Chin, Department Manager, Burberry, London

Joe Ferry, Head of Design, Virgin Atlantic, London

Clara Salmeri, Qualitative Research Manager, Doxa, Milan

Ben Wood, Added Value, London/Paris

Rogier van der Heide, fr. Director and Global Leader, ARUP, Amsterdam

Ken Grier, Managing Director, The Macallan, UK

Florian Koehler, Architect and Principal, Koehler Kobusch, Hamburg

Stephen Gray, Managing Director, Clive Christian, London

Mette Kristine Oustrup, Founder, Qi, Singapore

Sher Ren Chua, Business Development Manager, CIAO, Paris/Shanghai

Joop Verloop, Partner, Verloop Innovatie, Amsterdam/Los Angeles

FINAL INTERVIEWS – USA AND BRAZIL (FINAL UNIFIED QUALITATIVE QUESTIONNAIRE)

Marco Susani, fr. Design Director, Motorola, Chicago, USA

Eddie Roschi, co-founder, Le Labo (www.lelabofragrances.com), New York

Scott Williams, Executive Vice President, CMO, Morgans Hotel Group

Marianne Castier, Principal, Sterling International Executive Search, New York

Ian Lewis, fr. VP Research and Insights, Time Inc., New York

Evan Oster, fr. Director Market Research Americas, Bacardi Global Brands, USA

Gianluca Siciliano, Marketing Director USA, Lamborghini, NY, USA

Theresa Tran, Principal, Tease Marketing, Portland, USA

FINAL INTERVIEWS – ASIA PACIFIC (FINAL UNIFIED QUALITATIVE QUESTIONNAIRE)

Mineo Sato, fr. Head of Design, Marantz, Tokyo

Davide Quadrio, Founder, ArtHub, Bangkok, Thailand/Shanghai, China

Lorraine Justice, Head, School of Design, Hong Kong Polytechnic, Hong Kong

Freeman Lau, Chairman of the Board, Hong Kong Design Centre, Hong Kong

Lisa Yong, co-founder, YStudios, USA, and Red Network, Hong Kong

Joseph Chui, General Manager, Research Pacific, Hong Kong

Rita Soh, Past President, Singapore Institute of Architects

Rieko Shofu, Executive Manager, Corporate Design Dept., Hakuhodo, Tokyo

Matthew Wang, MAP, Shanghai

Bianca Cheng, Director, Jade International Capital Partners Ltd, Beijing

ADDITIONAL INPUT (NON-STRUCTURED ACCORDING TO QUESTIONNAIRES)

Atto Belloli, Chairman, Istituto Internazionale Studi sul Futurismo, Milan

Jem Bendell, Director, Lifeworth / Ass. Prof., Griffith Business School

Mary McGuinness, Partner, Sputnik, New York

Greg Furman, CEO, Luxury Networking Group, New York

Guy Salter, Deputy Chairman, Walpole British Luxury, London

Olivier Lapidus, Couture Designer and AD Tex for Carrefour, Paris

François Russo, AD, Designer, Bangkok, Thailand

Paul Levy, CEO, City Centre District, Philadelphia, USA

Thomas Houlon, Innovation Director, Tag Heuer, Switzerland

Alex Moskvin, fr. VP, IFF, BrandEmotions™ Agency, New York

Mark Dunhill, CEO, Fabergé, London

Sian Davies, CEO, The Henley Centre, London

Marc Cohen, Founder Director, Ledbury Research, UK

Massimiliano Benedetti, Global Sales and Marketing Director, Yoox, Italy

FINAL VALIDATION INTERVIEWS (PERSONALIZED STRUCTURED QUESTIONNAIRE)

Rattan Chadha, Entrepreneur, founder of Mexx, Voorschoten, Netherlands

Rita Clifton, Chairman, Interbrand, London

Graziano De Boni, fr. CEO and President, Valentino USA, New York / Milan

Luca De Meo, fr. CEO Alfa Romeo and fr. CMO FIAT Automotive Group, Turin, Italy

Markus Langes Swarovski, Member of the Board, Swarovski, Wattens, Austria

Concetta Lanciaux, Luxury Strategy Advisor, Montreux/Paris

Bessie Lee, CEO, GroupM China, Shanghai, PRC

Richard Lee, CEO, WKH Group, luxury brands building and distribution, Hong Kong

Federico Marchetti, CEO, Yoox, Italy

Karen Moersch and Simon Wilson, Founders, The Hasley Group, UK

Paul Nunes, Executive Research Fellow, Accenture Institute, Boston

Andrea Ragnetti, fr. CEO, Philips Consumer Lifestyle, Amsterdam

Karl Schlicht, VP Lexus Europe, Brussels, Belgium

Peter Sosnkowski, Former Chairman and CEO, Rémy Associés Worldwide.

WITH SINCERE THANKS TO:

Sophie Rheims, Consultant, Paris

Lieran Stubbings, fr. Global Luxury Forum 2007 director, Eventica, London/Russia

Rhiannon Bryant, fr. ESOMAR Luxury Forum 2007 event director, Amsterdam

The organizing team, FT Business of Luxury 2007 summit, Venice (Italy)

Foreword

Dr. Stefano Marzano
CEO and Chief Creative Officer, Philips Design

Whether in booming economies or recessions, in whatever region or continent, beyond race or religion, most people have always the aspiration to improve the way they feel about themselves. One might say that this is a natural tension towards bettering one's quality of life that is simply embedded in our minds: in our DNA as humans. Even – or perhaps especially? – in these times of financial crisis, people keep such aspiration as they do aspire to new hope, and if they do not do so for themselves, then they earnestly want it for their children and their beloved ones. Through the eyes of creative talent, such natural need for hope translates into the power of dreams: why else did people line up to spend their hard-earned dimes to watch wonderful musicals during the depression era? Just look at Fred Astaire and Ginger Rogers or Busby Berkely's beautiful dancers in the very heart of the 1930s Great Depression. Right at the edge of the current economic distress, Marco Bevolo, Alex Gofman and Howard Moskowitz explored the fine texture of brands, products and services that might help companies to generate premium margins, by making people happier. They are not addressing the mass market and its sometimes suicidal rush just to cut prices. Nor are they talking about that magnificent trip in a class above First Class that most of us will never manage to afford during our lifetime, with its in flight private-shower facility, its front-cabin suite and its fitness exercising program. The authors look at luxury instead as a source of insights, wisdom and sometimes even wit, in order to gain knowledge about how business uniquely works where premium margins are generated. They do so in order to unveil to the reader a world of achievable aspirations. In this world, the talent of designers and the science of market research join forces, resulting in propositions that anticipate and resonate with people's dreams and ambitions. In this world, the relationship between people and purchase results in emotional enrichment. In this world, the richness of sensorial experiences is complemented by the power of longer-term sustainability. This is the world of the new premium, or of the High End, or – as the authors call it – the world of "Hope at Check Out". Mind you, this is a business book with actionable tools and replicable methodologies at its very heart. Bevolo, Gofman and Moskowitz did not write an essay in social history or a theoretical dissertation on design. And their focus is not on depression times or boom times in terms of economic cycles, or on the micro-economics of selling and buying. Rather, you are holding in your hands a more practical book, one directed towards you. It is a book born with the promise to share with you how to understand this new world of different aspirations, on every level of income. It is a book about how other business leaders succeeded in achieving margins by design. It is a book about how you, the reader, might succeed in it as well, thanks to original tools and processes. Simply, this book is about BETTER, even if it is not always best, just better, but reachable and real products and services. And this book has the charming feature to be built on the marriage of insights from the world of customer science with design research, of future studies with creative industry practices, of precise statistics with the inspiring opinions of thought leaders. This book was written by getting in touch with the people who made this world of High End already happen, for those who will bring it to the next level of success. So, with that I invite you to join the authors as they go on their trip of knowledge and experience. Be ready for business success and failure stories, for scientific analysis and design leadership, and most of all for those visions and tools that will help you to get there.

Stefano Marzano, Eindhoven, The Netherlands, April 2010

Preface

Hundreds of millions of years ago the Earth was different, a huge mass of land known as Pangea. Then the continents separated, and began to move apart further, leaving vast oceans in their wake. Following this analogy, minute by minute today's modern, ever-so distinct continents of mass-produced products and luxury are moving apart. Ever more products become cheaper and more accessible to the public because economics demands that their margins be squeezed to the limits, while, in an almost disdainful manner, extreme luxury flies into the stratosphere of unimaginable excess that could be afforded by very few.

Our world of products, of stores, of buyers differs, however, from the geological example. Do not look for an empty ocean to fill the space left by the disappearing landmass. Rather, just off the shores of luxury, there is a huge, fast growing land of premium value which inspires people to get there, even if they need to stretch their budget. In this new land, the emotional bond with customers translates into premium margins so ardently desired by business. Unlike luxury affordable only by the rich people with many zeros in their accounts, this land does not discriminate. It welcomes virtually everybody with a wide range of incomes. For some, an iPhone might be an aspiration, for others – a Mini. The land of High End has a place for everybody to create his or her warm feeling, and grab hope at checkout.

And the future? The authors believe that the future might be bright, no matter how dark the noonday sun might be. A recession cannot kill optimism, however painful and hard it is. Demography is destiny: in countries like India and Brazil, young talents are emerging in masses; in China, the middle class is growing, and its appetite exploding for exclusive and exciting yet reasonably affordable products and services, with a rapidly growing interest for "eco-chic" and sustainability too. Whereas there are many made-up, zippy, sociologist-inspired names for the trend (among them "masstige" – a term created from merging the words "mass" and "prestige", meaning mass affluence, premium, and new luxury), we, along with many of the experts we interviewed, like to call this new promised land the world of the High End. Much like its analogous "the land between", High End has many inhabitants, and plenty to keep them occupied.

This book will bring you on a journey to and around High End land. It will describe its inhabitants showing their origins, successes and failures. It will show you ways to become a rightful citizen of the land giving you proven tools enabling a successful competition for your place under the sun.

Relax and enjoy.

M. Bevolo, A. Gofman and H. Moskowitz

Acknowledgments

I would like first of all to thank each of the contributors for the generosity and passion that made this book emerge into a business reality. Thank you for the constant patience and support. Of course, my wife Keiko and my mother Sara cannot be praised enough for their constant presence and patience during the intense times that saw this book come alive. As all we do is the concrete realization of the dreams of those who came before us and hopefully the inspiration for those who will follow us, this second book of mine is once again dedicated to the precious memory of my father, Carlo Bevolo, and to the brilliant future of my young family members, Masaki and Ayato, nephews of my beloved wife, Keiko.

Marco Bevolo

The joy of writing could only be possible with the support of the family, but it comes at an undeniable cost – missed soccer games, school concerts, postponed nights at the opera or just skipped time together. My sincere and profound gratitude goes to my family – thank you for your support and encouragement! Irene, Alli, Matt – I now will be more frequently warmed by your smiles than by the mysterious waves of an LCD screen. This book is dedicated to you and to my mother, Revekka, and the memory of my late father, Jacob.

Alex Gofman

No book gets written by itself. That said, a much beloved Jewish proverb in the Ethics of the Fathers teaches us "From all my teachers I have learned ... but from my students I have gained wisdom." So let me first acknowledge my students, each of you around the world, from Beirut to Beijing, from Rosh HaAyin to Lausanne, and beyond. Dear students, you shape my thinking, and sharpen my mind through your questions, discussions, insights. Beyond that, to my co-workers at Moskowitz Jacobs, Inc., and to my long-term colleagues and friends in psychophysics and market research. Most of all, to my family. Individually, each of you inspires and strengthens me to continue thinking, creating, publishing, and applying these ideas. Thank you.

SSI (Survey Sampling, Inc.) has been a most helpful partner in our efforts to bring RDE (Rule Developing Experimentation) to the world of the High End. Survey Sampling International is the premier global provider of sampling solutions for survey research. SSI offers access to consumer and business-to-business respondents via Internet, telephone, and mobile. Additional services include survey programming and hosting; data processing, and sampling consultation. SSI serves more than 1,800 research clients, including nearly three-quarters of the top researchers worldwide.

SSI provides access to more than 3.5 million research respondents in more than 70 countries via proprietary communities and managed affiliate relationships. Founded in 1977, SSI has an international staff of 335 people representing 50 countries and 36 languages. The company is based in Fairfield, Connecticut, with additional offices in London, Paris, Rotterdam, Stockholm, Frankfurt, Madrid, Beijing, Shanghai, Sydney, Tokyo, Toronto, and La Quinta, California. For more information, visit www.surveysampling.com.

We thank SSI for providing access to their high-quality on-line panels for quantitative research in the USA, UK, China and Italy.

Howard Moskowitz

About the Authors

Marco Bevolo is a Lecturer in International Leisure Management/Sciences at NHTV University of Applied Sciences, The Netherlands, and the founder of Marco Bevolo Consulting, formerly a director at Philips Design in 1999, assuming responsibility for the cultural trend research program. He was instrumental in the creation of CultureScan, an trend forecasting research project investigating cultures and aesthetics at the regional and global level.

Prior to joining Philips Design, Marco's work focused mainly on publishing and marketing communications. His professional career started at Italdesign Giugiaro in 1990. He was subsequently editor-in-chief for "Intervista", an Italian lifestyle magazine, then worked as copywriter with Armando Testa with clients such as Procter and Gamble and Bolton. He joined the Euro RSCG Milano agency in 1998.

Independently, he published in 2009 *"The Golden Crossroads"* with Palgrave of the UK. His areas of expertise span from strategic design consulting to event design, with a world-class track record in researching and analyzing aesthetics, architecture, automotive, advertising, fine arts, and the world of premium value, including the rising concept of "sustainable luxury".

Marco graduated from the University of Turin with a degree in the Psychology of Communication. He lives in Turin, Italy, and Eindhoven, the Netherlands, with frequent traveling to Tokyo and the rest of Japan.

Alex Gofman, PhD (www.alexgofman.com), is Vice-President at MJI, a strategic marketing research company headquartered in White Plains, New York, USA, which he joined in 1992. Mr. Gofman is an accomplished technology-oriented marketing research executive with a strong portfolio of successes researching, designing and managing web-based marketing and market research technologies, innovation, consumer insights and analytics for major global clients. Dr. Gofman is widely published and recognized internationally for contributions to consumer research and product development, Web pages optimization, marketing intelligence and related Web technologies, consumer insights, conjoint analysis, segmentation, online marketing, consumer driven dynamic advertisement optimization, and so on.

Alex has authored over 100 papers and patents, and presented at multiple international conferences. He is a co-author with Dr. Howard Moskowitz of *Selling Blue Elephants: How To Make Great Products That People Want Before They Even Know They Want Them* (Wharton School Publishing, 2007). A best-seller on several international lists, the book is currently translated into 15 languages.

Dr. Gofman is an adj. associate professor of marketing teaching graduate courses at Pace University (Lubin Business School). In addition to multiple academic publications, his articles appeared in *Financial Times Press*, Wharton School Publishing and *Marketing Research* magazine along with his regular contributions to the *Daily News* and *Analysis and Research World*.

Howard R. Moskowitz, PhD, is president and CEO of Moskowitz Jacobs, Inc., a strategic marketing research company headquartered in White Plains, New York, USA, a firm he founded in 1981. A well-known experimental psychologist in the field of psychophysics and an inventor of world-class market research technology, he is widely published in the scientific press. A leading thinker and creator of advanced research technology in the area of new product and concept development, his extensive speaking engagements span both scientific and market research conferences, as well as guest lectures at leading business schools. He lectures in the USA and abroad and serves on the editorial board of major journals.

Dr. Moskowitz has been the recipient of numerous awards, including the 2010 Walston Chubb Award for Innovation, to honor and promote creativity among scientists and engineers; the David R. Peryam lifetime achievement award by the American Society for Testing and Materials; the Charles Coolidge Parlin Award from the American Marketing Association, considered to be the "Nobel Prize" of market research, for his lifetime contributions to the field, ranging from product work to the optimization of consumer concept and package designs; and the 2006 ARF Innovation Award for the development of the most innovative research idea. From November 2004 to November 2006, Dr. Moskowitz appeared weekly as the *"Food Doctor"* on ABC *"NewsNow"*, where he anchored a live program, featuring food and beverage entrepreneurs. He is the co-author with Alex Gofman of *Selling Blue Elephants: How to Make Great Products That People Want Even Before They Know They Want Them* (Wharton School Publishing), which was on international best-seller lists, had been endorsed by top universities and corporations, and enjoyed wide media coverage. The author of 20 other books and several hundred papers, Dr. Moskowitz is a frequent contributor to business and scientific journals on topics of messaging, product optimization, and now the newly emerging area of psychophysics and the law.

Visit our website www.PremiumByDesign.com for more information about the book, contributors and updates.

Reviews for
Premium by Design

I found this book to be a very useful and readable guide to what the luxury market is and what it will become and a very good primer on how to anticipate the luxury market of the future.

Arnold Brown, Chairman, Weiner, Edrich,
Brown, Inc., New York

Marco Bevolo, Alex Gofman and Howard Moskowitz show us the way to tomorrow's High End by talking to experts from around the world to learn from them, listen to consumers to practically evaluate what it means and deliver the insights to all of us to get started today. Known as Industry experts and innovators around the world, the authors accelerate our learning and practically invite us to a better world for all, by design ... Enjoy!

Laurent Flores, CEO, CRMMetrix, Paris, France

Status brands are at a turning point. This thought-provoking book explores new luxury paradigms for a changing world. As materialism, hedonism and indulgence are swiftly being replaced by decency, depth and substance, status, moneyed brands have a unique chance to create change, to connect with the soul and positively impact our civilization. The arguments and research Bevolo, Gofman and Moskowitz present here shed light on how to manage this transition.

Herwig Preis, CEO, SelectNY,
New York/Berlin/London/Paris/Geneva

How to get customers? How to lose customers? How to create a new brand from one hundreds of years old or a new idea? This and much more makes Premium by Design *a literal playbook for senior management and marketing personnel for companies large and small. The real life examples bring the lessons to life, anybody who reads this book will come away with numerous ideas they can use in their businesses.*

Doug Gollan, President and Editor in Chief,
Elite Traveler, New York

Premium by Design *offers a provocative challenge to conventional thinking about High End. The authors' conversational tone makes this a good read and the liberal use of verbatims from contributors adds rich dimension to this important topic.*

Denise Lee Yohn, Founder, Denise Lee Yohn, Inc.;
"Brand as Business™" consulting partner and former VP Brand
and Strategy, Sony Electronics Inc. (USA)

Premium by Design *is an excellent source of insights and learning about the increasingly important but little understood mass luxury market. It's that rare sort of book that combines rigorous research with thought provoking views on the future while wrapping it all together in a thoroughly engaging writing style. The authors also deserve credit for including China in their analysis as it will likely be – if it's not already – the primary battleground for tomorrow's high end spending.*

Jim Sailor, Managing Director, TNS Greater China, Shanghai

The physics low of "connected vessel" will transform the economic world in the 21st century. Old terms of High and Low are going to change forever. Premium by Design *is a unique attempt to reveal the complexity of the ever-changing "equalizer" of the "High-End Luxury" definition for the new markets. It is not just an impressive theoretic analysis but also a fascinating global "navigation system" into the 'alchemy' processes of designing new products.*

Ezri Tarazi, Professor, Bezalel Academy of Design,
Jerusalem, and Designer (EDRA, Italy, and more)

Premium by Design *is a thoroughly researched, well argued and well-presented study that combines a rigorous identification of important trends for the future, with new insights. As a result it is a must read for anyone in this market, or aspiring to it. While the emphasis on sustainability is commendable, the key challenge for the world today is how sustainable is the underlying process that is driving this apparent desire for more and more indulgent material possessiveness? This book might not have all the answers, but it will likely provoke and trigger a long overdue debate in the premium and image driven industries about tomorrow's values.*

Bruce Lloyd, Professor Strategic Management,
South Bank University, London

You are a professional or an expert in marketing, you think you know it all, this book might still give you a few others ideas. Clear, easy and methodic, it could easily become a reference when it comes to "High End"

Nicolas Delarue, Founder, AtLarge, Paris

Solid research and geographic analysis of experts around the world has created a High End Toolbox to guild creation of new products for a better future.

Jerome C. Glenn, Executive Director,
The Millennium Project, UN, Washington

The book integrates not only the insights of 70 experts, but also cleverly refocuses our attention on the end-users – the people that are attracted to the High End – by means of their stories, aspirations and preferences, thereby allowing the authors to articulate a new, experience-based vision for the future of the industry. A must-read for anyone conceiving, developing and marketing higher-end consumer products and services!

Michele Visciola (President), Mark Vanderbeeken and
Jan-Christoph Zoels, Experientia, Turin

The Western world has developed to a point where affluence is the mass-democratized gold standard. Luxury is less defined by what one has than by what one perceives others to desire and leaves us ultimately unsure of the lines between luxury as a concept and luxury as a product. Premium by Design *can help us understand, in clarified terms the implications of Masstige as the new marker of a High End value system and that the emotional value is not in fact in the level of the luxury but the appreciation of the prestige.*

Sara Berman, Managing Director,
Sara Berman Design, London

A valuable book offering a unique insight, exploring case histories and various expert view points with actionable tools to achieve Future High End success, making this an easy read appealing to a wide audience. Highly recommended!

Pascale Emalan, former Marketing and Market Research
Director,Takasago, Paris

In view of the "trading down" from Luxury to commodity which the fragrance market has been experiencing for some time now, this book is of the utmost interest to the fragrance industry. It provides an understanding of luxury, from the points of view of both consumers and professionals, as well as valuable insights into how we can reinvent High End for fragrances, and start once again to create intriguing and appealing new concepts.

Barbara Busch, Chairman Analysis Scent International,
Zug-Paris-New York-Frankfurt

Inspiring like delicious tapas from the molecular kitchen – this book contains a bouquet of visionary ideas which contributes to a holistic design experience. It gives us a vivid taste of creativity for more High End substance in our lives.

Wolfgang Mueller-Pietralla, Head of Future Research,
Volkswagen Group, Germany

The definition of luxury lies in the eyes of the beholder – not only in the depth of his or her pockets. Hence pinpointing the meaning of luxury is a matter of mastering sociological, cultural, psychological and aesthetical insights on a global level. Which is exactly what this book does, through a coherent, structured and easy-to-read series of interviews and analysis. A pleasurable read hence turns into a very useful tool for fostering new business creations and for using design and style in a strategic and innovative way.

Laura Traldi, interior design free lance journalist
(Interni, Mondadori Publishers), Milan

Where there is a group of humans, there is a story that binds them together. Premium by Design *tells the story of luxury – authenticity, consistency, exclusivity, innovation and tradition. Luxury brands that ignore the roadmap in this book do so at their own peril. It should sit on the desk of every brand manager and brand marketing manager, and they should refer to it daily.*

T. B. (Mac) McClelland, Jr., President & CEO,
The Luxury Marketing Council (Middle East), Dubai

"Our mission is to offer the best". That's the motto Jacques Arpels, a member of the founding family, designed for the Van Cleef and Arpels Maison. As this is a permanent quest I deeply appreciated the insights, the vision and perspective of Premium by Design. *Indeed, we have to permanently re-invent, to be very creative artist, as the 21st century will not be a replication of the 20th.*

Stanislas de Quercize, CEO, Van Cleef & Arpels, Paris

In the 21st century, the ability to experience the best the world has to offer will be more important to a greater number of consumers than ever before in history. Premium by Design *provides useful insights to help understand the complex art of building the high end brands of the future.*

Serge Dumont, Omnicom Group Inc.,
Senior Vice President/President Asia Pacific

From the "Midas' Eye" of today's luxury to an actionable tool to achieve business success in tomorrow's High End, this books takes you on journey that connects Bevolo's direct experience in China or Japan and design visions, with world class statistics by Moskowitz and Gofman. The destination is the qualitative scoping of a promise land for business achievement, and the measurement of the 'High End mind' with a wealth of quantitative data. A rare combination of creative insights and science, for a unique book about the next wave of margin driven success.

Octave Bodel, Managing Partner, CRF Partners,
Beijing/Hong Kong

In all my years associated with "luxury" I have never read a book that articulates so well the business opportunities that are emerging through a systematic approach to developing "high end" propositions. It's abundantly clear that customers want high end. I believe this book will be of real practical help to people who are seeking to make their businesses, brands and products lead in this profitable market segment, rather than follow or get beaten.

Peter Lavers, former Managing Director,
Customer Futures (an Ogilvy company).

Premium by Design *is a very useful and practical mean for companies that want to take a look inside future High End markets and for everybody who wants to better understand where this growing market is going. Thanks to the use of unique case histories and of an easy style this book is a guide through the changing concept of luxury and how this new concept involves design.*

Pietro Piccinetti, President, Gruppo Sintesi, Italy

The authors offer a new slant on the inherent innovations in design – taken to a higher grouping of indices – and how this expands market presence; it's not merely about something being well made, but it is more about the holistic promissary attribute of the evolution of ideas in context. High end design is about new ideas and ideals that are built on uniquely and newly defined insights – experimentation in the comprehension of consumer movement – and finally revelation in new attitudes of design, luxuriously considered, in reaching to the heart and mind of that market. Ideas first, ideals exercised, design (and experiment) – the new high end signature – explicated. It's about a new reach – to a high ground, a exalted visioning – that brings, in design, luxury to all. And what is luxury but a brand with a story – a long-running heart – that is about truth newly told, authenticity in defining experiment and telling experience – to capture the hearts, and sing the emotions, of the audience. The platinum premise: high design, a new high round to branding success.

Tim Girvin, Principal and Founder, Girvin, Inc.,
NYC/Seattle/Tokyo

Premium by Design is a "must-read" for experts looking to update their notion of what luxury means today. From thorough evaluation of premium brands to insightful interviews with luxury brand architects, this unique survey demonstrates the intricacies of the high end market and its transformative nature as it adapts to the fast-paced changes of the 21st century.

Angel Chang, fashion designer, NYC,
Winner of the Cartier Women's Initiative Award

PART 1
Hope at Checkout for Everybody

Achievable Dreams

I believe that High End is simply the most promising market in terms of growth and future.
          Concetta Lanciaux, former advisor to Bernard Arnault, LVMH

So, what is this Cinderella thing called the *High End*, this younger sister of luxury, an affluent older cousin of *ordinary*, and the *purchasable dream* of everyone who has some spare cash? First, where does High End even come from? We can find it at the mall, even in a modestly affluent one. But, before we start with stuff, let's begin with experience, the mother of High End, rather than shopping. We start with travel, its advertisers aggressively promising enticing luxury of a lifetime, if only you take that flight or train, that safari, or simply the limousine service from home to your destination and back again.

Luxury Gives Birth to the High End

Since the beginning of commercial aviation, most passengers have traveled in less than comfortable conditions, often with food choices that made McDonald's food look like a gourmet restaurant fare in comparison. Of course, money talked then as now. A select few, those who could afford a seat in the front section of the plane, were treated much more respectfully, pampered in comfort. Just a few years ago, flat beds in the first class of some airlines were all the rage. The envying business-class passengers did not suffer much either – they had wide reclining (although not flat) seats with a lot of legroom, good meals and a personal DVD player with a tiny screen for entertainment. Nowadays, Emirates airline offers completely first-class private suites to Dubai with an oversized flat-bed massage seat, a personal mini-bar, fine-dining room service and 1,000 channels of entertainment on a high-definition oversized screen in case you tire of looking out the window. And what about business class, the affordable luxury? As for the business-class passengers, the flat beds are becoming standard, with more choices for entertaining, better airport lounges, and so on. In fact, many amenities of the former first class are now standard for

the business class suggesting that one could view today's luxury as a preview
of tomorrow's High End.

Noticed by an Italian philosopher Cesare Beccaria a quarter of millennium
ago, the trend of people to emulate the classes immediately above them is
happily flourishing in the twenty-first century. While mother luxury seeks ever
more, what was formerly luxury migrates to the affordable, to what we call
the High End. Luxury has always to outdo itself not to be swallowed by the
High End. And so the stories of fabled, not-to-be-believed excesses. In Dubai,
you might be one of the lucky few who can enjoy a stay at *Burj al Arab* hotel,
considered by many the best hotel in the world. The hotel is built out of the water
and designed to resemble a billowing spinnaker sail. You are met at the airport
by your chauffer-driven Rolls Royce, for your personalized, well-serviced,
always so discreet check-in. Every floor has its own private reception desk and
innumerable trained butlers, all at your service. The lowest price at the hotel at
the print time was close to $2,000 a day (the rates have not changed much even
in difficult economic situation, although the hotel started offering some free
nights for longer staying guests). Wouldn't you just know it – the Burj is booked
many months in advance – even through the crisis affecting Dubai and the rest
of us. The question is, should we consider such "conspicuous consumption"
lifestyles as the only picture of future premium? We do not think so, and this is
why we wrote this book.

Clearly, a private suite in the air on the way to the seven stars hotel is the
very best. Yet, just below that very best, just below the luxury to be dreamed
of, lies a vast world of *affordable luxury, where business opportunities flourish, and
where future opportunities emerge again and again*. A lot is still possible in the world
that does not involve being jammed into the "cattle" class of an overcrowded
airplane among screaming kids and calorifically challenged fellow passengers,
with that icon of the road warrior, a Motel 6 room waiting at your destination.
Or, in contrast, in that other world where you would go broke after a week's
stay. Even if you cannot afford a stay in a seven stars hotel, there is a good choice
of business hotels offering the amenities considered just a decade ago to be an
exclusive luxury. In fact, there is an affordable whole new world of near-luxury
level experiences and services that mere mortals can and do buy. It's no longer a
matter of being a sultan, a tycoon or a Hollywood star to be able to afford them.
It is now a matter of affordable premium, with the emphasis on *affordable*, and
the emphasis on *premium*. And, for this book, it's a good business. Companies
are making lots of money from this world of premium. This is the High End,
the world between those top luxury prices and everyday commodities that we

explore in this book, with occasional side trips to the land of luxury that make people feel good.

Is it Stuff? Or is it Soul?

Welcome to this expanding world, where millions of new customers now afford services unimaginable to them just a few years ago. People used to keep up in their consumption with their neighbors, or with relatives generally at the same income category. Nowadays, many want to be Trumps or Mittals, or at least live some part of the luxurious life which they believe is the everyday for these media legends. The craze is to differentiate oneself from the masses, to find things that bring with them a sense of pride, yet all within the constraints of their not limitless yet still existing means. And yet, as we will see, for some, this High End differentiation comes from ennobling actions to sustain the environment and society, rather than from conspicuous consumption. For others, it is a matter of a social status. The good and perhaps the not-so-good parts of our human natures all get to play a role.

A couple of years ago, one of the authors (AG) observed a teenager squatting on a corner of a busy street-market in Mumbai. The adolescent boy proudly showed his friends what seemed to be a newly acquired mobile phone. It was not a cheap, no-frills model. Clearly, it was something better than his peers had (or could possibly get). The gleaming happiness of the proud owner reflected the awed faces of his friends. It did not matter whether he needed all the functionality of the product or utilized its quality production – the others saw *him* owning the desired gadget and that made him proud. He was enjoying his High End – quite conceivable, far more so than more expensive but less inspirational items (for him) like jewelry. The joy was palpable.

Desire for differentiation, to taste something from the next level of living, is blossoming everywhere – from the Asian urban areas to New York and Paris, from the countryside and most clearly to the city. The current trend to High End began, as we shouldn't be surprised to discover, in the over-advertised United States where businesses are accustomed to democratizing nearly anything, as long as the numbers on the bottom line can support it. It was in New York, in Los Angeles, in fine shops in other large cities, that Abercrombie and Fitch, Anthropologie, Coach, Tommy Hilfiger, and so on, moved deliberately but aggressively to bring new luxury to the masses, to delight where stores simply once just satisfied. In Europe, Lancia created its city limousine concept of affordable and stylish cars, and top fashion houses launched their second lines for wider diffusion, like Emporio Armani.

This siren call of the High End, the realm of affordable luxury, is universal. Now this trend is burgeoning in Asia where in country after country it has gathered new audiences to seduce. Occasionally it might seem that a walk in an Asian city is a walk from one High End store to another, with shopper after shopper either actively buying, looking, or often just gazing out of hopeful curiosity dreaming about the not so distant day when they can actually buy "it".

With its consumers buying well over 10 percent of the world's luxury goods and services, Japan represents the ever-renewing spring of today's luxury consumption. A stunning statistic shows that 95 percent of young Japanese females own a *real* Louis Vuitton. Is it a luxury (based on the price – it has to be), a mass-product (95 percent sounds quite massive to us) or something in between? The success of a "prestige-brand-within-reach" like Coach in Japan broadcasts the possibility of a third way. This third way beguiles the everyday shopper because it is within the reach of many, although it might be with a stretch. It lies between the basic concept of a brand like Muji, the stylish, low-cost maker of everyday gear, and the European imports of top luxury.

So What is it About the High End?

Price is always important for most of our purchase decisions. Yet an absolute *homo economicus*, rational economic man, no longer rules the roost; a cheap price is not a pre-requisite for commercial success. People look for something that is not readily available to everyone else. Exclusive is a strong siren call. Many shoppers will pay higher prices for newly discovered prestige attributes. Where there is an opportunity of higher prices with higher margins, you will find no lack of companies wanting to jump on the wagon.

And the secret to this High End? The secret lies in a whole new kind of customer, on whom we focus in this book. Challenged by the economy, yet still relatively affluent, many newly middle-class consumers, just getting into the swing of affording what they had dreamt about, are simply not interested in the old-time luxury. This enfranchised class of buyers is looking for new experiences, in part to show others their newly acquired status. The old luxury industry has yet to catch up with them, as they flit from "new" to "new", affording all, buying, experiencing, boasting, or just looking for the next High End to thrill them.

Some older and well-respected luxury brands believe or at least act as if their names would be all that is needed to win the war and prevail in this new movement to the land of affordable luxury. Yet is it that simple? Compare Apple iPhone – a definitive premium product – with Prada/LG phone and Armani/Samsung phones. Despite the intimidating names of the heavyweight competition, iPhone won in most places of the Western world. The iPhone is upscale, albeit at the same time exciting and affordably real. And its competitors? – perhaps every bit as good, but they missed the boat and didn't establish that emotional link, that connection with the customer.

Companies get to the High End in different ways. You do not always need technological breakthroughs to get to the shopper. Sometimes a little quirky creativity helps. An astute marketer Allyson Stewart-Allen chided that MASSTIGE stands for "Marketers Always Seduce Shoppers To Instigate Great Expenditure". The seduction can be simply a raw but effective appeal to the emotional needs of the target consumers. Consider the Japanese company Yosimiya. What could be more basic, less High End than rice? Yosimiya offered shoppers bags of rice printed with a newborn's photo, name and date of birth. Many proud new parents simply could not resist Yosimiya's human touch. The bags were shaped to resemble a baby and weighed *exactly* as much as an infant, giving the consumer the feeling of holding a newborn. The idea felt fresh and different, customized and expensive enough to display exclusivity yet reasonably affordable for middle-class families. And most important, the offer hit the target – the ordinary, Cinderella-like, transformed to High End, and accurately aimed at the customer's emotional side.

In Times of Trouble – High End and High Hopes

As we write this book, a worldwide economic downturn continues to unfold, raising a question – are we writing about the history of hope, in the midst of a nascent depression? It is clear that this downturn has affected the High End. People cannot buy if they do not have money. At least not for long. Yet we believe with Michael J. Silverstein, the "grandfather" of "trading-up", that the trading-up phenomenon is built-in, hard-wired, a characteristic of people everywhere. The desire for dreams, the Busby Berkley of products and services is hope, and, in its deepest heart, recession-proof. People always want something. Even if they cannot have, they can dream. And it is this dream that lasts, and will allow the High End to weather the crisis. And of course at the end of the crisis is the hoped for rainbow of profits, just waiting.

The whole world seems to be reaching for the higher end of life. Despite low incomes, despite hardships, and expenses that occasionally seem unbearable, people want *their* piece of a better life, and *do* pay extra for it – sometimes, even when to do so they cut back on their necessities. We see our neighbors, friends, colleagues, and by extension the world in general, moving towards upgrades, seeking experiences and services that were noticeably better. It is built in. All people with some smattering of hope in their hearts want to share in this universe of better, which until recently was not even part of the dream of newcomers from the developing world. This is why we see the High End as one of the possible engines of growth and rebirth for our economies, well above and beyond pure "conspicuous consumerism".

Whether you are an established luxury corporation or operate in a mass-products area, you cannot afford to ignore this exploding market of high-end/high-margin products. Otherwise, you could be drowned in the surrounding waters of competition. If not now, then soon.

Our Vision

In our effort to peek into the future, we are going to move beyond the plain, beyond stuff, beyond services, and beyond luxury. We do not dismiss material goods: we love them. However, to find this new land requires us to look more deeply, beyond cute design and growing functionality, into the new categories and industries that will be created in the near future by cultural and social changes. These are the opportunities for you that are being born, each day.

As we explore this new world, keep one more thing in mind – Experience as well as Stuff will start to matter in this world of "more and better". We kept hearing and now see growth in the demand for *experiences* and *ennobling emotions* that define this better quality of life. More and more people are looking for sustainable solutions, stepping above the egocentric ME, I, MINE. In front of our eyes, in the brutally competitive past world of "old luxury", money, affluence, and competitiveness we find growing another world, of environmentally and socially friendly consumption. That is also the new High End, and it will concern us as well.

We wrote this book with two aims. One is to analyze a social/business force that will affect business and business thinking. The other aim is to guide those who want to understand, envision and create products and services for this new world. We believe in knowledge, but knowledge must lead to meaningful action. We also believe in tools for business and creativity, because it is impossible to go it alone. The tool is our action-driven High-End business toolbox, ready to create that strategic knowledge, and those products and services.

A little more about documenting, because documenting is best done in the thick of what's happening, while the emotions are running hot, while the competition is alive and the threats and opportunities real. We wanted the voice of those who create the future, the experts in business, sociology, and trend-watchers, as well as High End customers. Merging the insights from the top global industry leaders and trendsetters with sociology and with a quantitative peek into the mind of the High End consumer, we hope to make this book unique in the burgeoning market of luxury and High End publications. And a fun read.

We designed this book is for a wide range of people – starting from C-level executives, VPs and entrepreneurs, but moving on to designers and to researchers, all people who will just want to make the High End happen. Academics, students and even non-professionals, who are curious about the topic, could find some tasty mind-food in this book.

In this book, you will move from a broad view of Luxury and the High End to its specifics. You will soon see what is really happening out there, what the trends are, where the opportunities lie, and who is doing it right. Most importantly, you will discover the rules guiding today's design for High End products and services. That is the goal – going from describing to doing.

In Short: Why Knowing About High End Matters

You will not win if you are fighting the price war. At least, not for long. Those who battle in the arenas of mass markets fight the price wars and copycat brands. Contrast that losing battle with High End propositions, which command a higher price because of design, quality, scarcity, constant freshness. These factors help High End goods and services fend off competitors who would commoditize markets by introducing successful spin-offs. And – they create an emotional bond with the customer at the same time. It is harder to lose that way. In today's world you want that edge.

The value proposition to you is what Willie Sutton said when asked why he robbed banks: "Because that's where the money is." The High End inspires people to buy; it is where the margins exist, where the connection with empowered customers finds its glue, and where, if you stay on your toes, you may end up doing very well, even – and perhaps especially – in a time of crisis.

2

Horizons where Aspiration Gazes

The contemporary consumer is very "hybrid". There are no real classes anymore when it comes to consumption. For example, you might have low-income people saving on the electricity but then drinking expensive champagne, or saving all year round to then buy a 5 star holidays in Bali for two weeks of vacation. This is the world we experience today, a world where everything is possible.

Rattan Chadha, Entrepreneur, Founder of Mexx
(now part of Liz Claiborne), Holland

First – Follow the Price

What should be the price of a wooden pencil to delight the buyer, making him gleam in happiness while paying what could well be an outrageous price? Your everyday low-price Wal-Mart shoppers are not ecstatic when paying a dollar for a box of pencils. Faber Castel took the €0.25[1] wooden pencil, made it into an item that could fetch €1–5, and then went a step further. They transformed this humble product into the core of a luxury proposition. And the price for this proposition – a lordly €45 for a gift box of two, to €350 for special and limited gift-set editions that a proud and happy owner will treasure and eagerly show to guests and probably never use. That's the potential of pencils, when seen from a High End perspective.

This is just one example from the increasing number of companies which have taken common products, and moved them to High End, far more exciting, and profitable offerings. Coffee is another example – not necessarily the overly cited history of Starbucks, but rather something more prosaic: coffee at home. Consider Nespresso, a High End solution for home consumption, delivering a cup of coffee as a high margin, good taste, and affordable luxury experience. It is not uncommon to find custom roast coffee being offered at €5–10 per cup,

---

1 Throughout this book we will use different currencies as examples in similar contexts to underline the global theme of the book.

made on a Nespresso machine. People seem to enjoy expensive coffee more, even if in a blind taste test they actually prefer another, far cheaper blend.

As we move through everyday life, the number of such "product" transformations from ordinary to High End will amaze, and then inspire the entrepreneur. The range of such transforms goes from slightly above to far beyond what the product commands when it is sold as mere ordinary. In China you can find an entire sector of cosmetics, from the mass-market propositions of brands like Maybelline, Max Factor or Avon which fetch around $10 to $15. These items are positioned as a semi-luxury or luxury item in emerging markets – quite a lot for consumers who are accustomed to paying a much less for products because they have a lot less money. And here lies the business "promised land".

But Don't Get Too High Lest You Eject Yourself Out of Aspiration

In the automotive sector, you find plenty of offerings that you could call "democratic luxury", priced between €30,000 and €50,000. In Europe, these upscale cars include the Italian mass-luxury Lancia brand, with its Ypsilon and Musa "city limousines", Alfa Romeo with its MiTo, and of course the worldwide hit, Mini Cooper S. There are more, such as the BMW 3 Series, the Audi A3 Series, and many others. The High End of cars does not stop abruptly. It is a slippery slope now. Luxury slowly kicks in, this upper neighbor of High End, with cars that range between €40,000 and €200,000, thanks to BMW 5, 6, and 7 lines, the Mercedes E and S Series, or the Audi A6 or A8 series. We are moving out of relative affordability into fantasy, and losing aspiration to unrealizable yet delightful dreams. The High End is a memory as we move to the rarified world of cars that cost €200,000 or more, such as Rolls Royces and Bentleys. It is not with those legends that we deal. They are not the attainable dream at checkout. So, if you are going to sell the High End, don't be seduced. It's the promised land, but not a never-never land.

Fashion also can seduce with this movable border. Of course, you easily find the domain of "democratic luxury" with the key players such as H&M, Zara, Mexx. They feature achievable elegance and luxury with their "instant knock offs" of new prestige designs and styles, and featuring these offerings at an affordable $15–300. Let yourself fantasize, and soon you find yourself looking at Chanel, Dior, Gucci and similar brands, priced anywhere between €2,000 and €30,000. And then, of course, there is the extreme luxury: designer haute couture lines, often hand-made with a price tag possibly varying between €30,000 and €150,000 per piece.

It's Not Price Alone

The above examples of the High End, Luxury, and the slippery slope between, emerged out of a lively dialog with luxury market analyst Professor Peter Sosnkowski of France's ESSEC Business School. In the past, people used the EVA, or Economic Value Added, to assess the economic performance of a corporation.[2] To understand High End pricing, Sosnkowski created an index ratio he calls IVA or Image Value Added. *IVA measures the extent to which image-driven, premium pricing exceeds the higher costs (design, materials, product quality, packaging, merchandising and more) which come naturally with the goal to move up-market.* So, according to Sosnkowski, the High End is more than image – it is grounded in an economic definition powered by emotions. And the practical aspect – IVA gives you a sense of where the new margins are hiding, waiting to be found.

So, what is the High End? People worldwide want this connection with the "something more". This search for that "something more", that world of "BETTER" is hard wired into our human DNA. Searchers for More, for Better, are to be found everywhere, as the movement to the High End increases its pace, and builds its head of steam. And so the business opportunity presents itself, in ways that you expect (stuff), and in ways that you may not expect (ennobling experience).

Here is the way we define this new old trend to Better:

> High End is the aspiration around the offering (either product or service), and a strong emotional connection with people. Across both mature and emerging economies, High End generates higher margins at a price that lies comfortably "within reach".

---

2   EVA is a corporate financial performance analysis approach measuring the extent to which the profit parameter exceeds the cost of capital.

The High End is the Natural Strategy to Focus on Value By Anticipating on Trends

Before getting into the details of what makes the High End, let's look a bit more deeply into four mega-trends which move today's people around the world beyond subsistence or even the ordinary, into a passionate desire for "More" of this High End:

THE WORLDWIDE RENAISSANCE OF LUXURY BRANDS, WHICH EXPLODED IN THE EARLY 1990S

High End comes out of this renaissance. Despite downturns in the economy, people continue to aspire. Nobody can change that. Even in tough times, the demand is there, but suppressed because of economic realities. Unless forced to, people usually do not regress. And even if people regress under pressure, they do so only for the moment, until the pressure is removed and the opportunity comes again. In the next chapter, we will see how the sea of aspirations fuels the High End stemming from the world of luxury.

IT IS IN THE CITIES WHERE YOU FIND THE OLD ROOTS AND THE NEWEST BRANCHES

Historically, cities have been seedbeds of cultural innovation and lifestyle engines. Cities remain the power-giving engines of lifestyles behind High End success. It is natural to find the first shoots of new trends by sniffing around leading urban regions (USA, EU), active cauldrons where the High End evolves and grows.

EMERGING ECONOMIES ARE PUTTING EVEN NEWER SPINS ON THE HIGH END

New urban regions are emerging, with diffused wealth translated into aspiration. The emerging BRIC economies (Brazil, Russia, India and China) now experience exploding demand for luxury, and specifically luxury compatible with their more traditional cultures. The demand from these new customers challenges markets to satisfy their desire for both super-premium products and their more reachable counterpart, the affordable and reachable High End.

DEMANDS FOR HIGHER QUALITY OF LIFE ARE GOING BEYOND JUST LUXURY PRODUCTS TO THE "SPIRIT", THAT MORE NOBLE ASPECT OF ONE'S VERY BEING

High End is not at all about stuff that one buys, or about experiences that one has. Far more profoundly, it is about improving quality of life and making sure that our world continues to grow in prosperity.

Cliff Notes to the High End

For those who were not exposed to the tricks of college students, the Cliff Notes are a legend when it comes to a quick study for a course. Rather than reading the book, one could literally buy the summarized version of the book in the university bookstore, printed in an attractive yellow and black, softbound pamphlet – the famous and eagerly sought Cliff Notes help us to navigate through the information overload. We have these notes today in a variety of different formats, such as Business Book Summaries®. But none have the emotions attached to our youth.

So, here is our version of Cliff Notes to the High End. Although our respondents described their ideas in different words, occasionally with stories, five clearly distinct building blocks for the High End kept emerging. In fact, during the course of the interviews we began to think in terms of these ideas because they made a great deal of sense.

The five recurring components turned out to be:

1.   Perceived exclusivity, the basis or "Degree Zero" of the High End

2.   Aspiration to the world of "More and Better", and even to the edge of luxury

3.   A superior emotional bond with customers

4.   Price as a signal

5.   Design as strategy.

THE "DEGREE ZERO" OF THE HIGH END: PERCEIVED EXCLUSIVITY

Recall our description of the proud Indian boy with an upscale phone admired by his peers? By now, it might sound obvious. The High End is not only about the "thing" itself, or the service, but rather what others *say* or *think* when they see it. It might seem a bit strange that exclusivity can be bought even with a little money, but that is how things work in the High End. Here, aspiration is the driver. And luxury – luxury is simply the mother of all aspiration, pure and simple.

ASPIRATION TO THE WORLD OF MORE AND BETTER, TO LUXURY

A good driver does not simply look at the immediate road at front of him – he scans it farther ahead and to the sides anticipating what might happen. Scanning aspirations to luxury around the world lets us peek at the High End world of tomorrow, that world where a moderate amount of money might buy what today consumers perceive as luxurious and perhaps almost-impossible-to-afford.

A SUPERIOR EMOTIONAL BOND WITH CUSTOMERS

In the emerging markets, the ever-changing status of stuff, of things, of service, needs an anchor and its own rules. Life evolves too quickly; what's "in" today is "out" tomorrow, not even talked about and merely discarded. Go to China to see what they do there. A High End product in China must be visually distinctive with unique and refined design and features, widely endorsed in the market as being premium, projecting an aspiring image that shows "*I belong to an elite group; my life is better than many others and I have a more discerning taste*". The anchor here is the emotion. The emotion links products to one's own self-appreciation that comes into play after the purchase. But these wonderful emotions have to fight, to "duke it out" with another powerful player in the equation – the price.

PRICE AS A SIGNAL

In the High End of aspiration you encounter yet another replay of that ever-present "tug-of-war" between emotions and price differs from commodities, where the rational side, *homo economicus*, settles for a trade-off between what's being gotten and in turn what's being paid. The High End lies beyond comfort and safety, like the most desirable fruit hanging a bit too far on the tree. The fruit is impossible to reach without stretching beyond a comfortable balance zone. Once the purchase is made, however, initial angst transforms magically into a proud feeling, a rush that makes buying customer experiences, something very special and memorable, and well worth the price over the long run.

DESIGN AS STRATEGY

Target stores manage to reach, acquire and retain customers whose average annual income is $58,000. As a point of comparison, K-Mart stores attract customers with an average income of $38,000, and Wal-Mart attracts customers with an average income all the way down at $28,000. How did Target attract these well-heeled, or at least better-heeled buyers? The answer is through collaboration with designers, a winning strategy for Target. In collaborations with Izaac Mizrahi and Cynthia Rowley, Target invested in image-building product designs. The strategy won and continues to win, in the form of customers, but also in the form of design awards and public recognition.

So what is the secret sauce here? Many think that it is all a matter of price, all an issue of economics, and little else. Of course, emotions enter in, but it really looks like price, price, price. Or better formulated: price, to achieve margins, price to get to where the money is. However, read between the lines to see the full picture. There is more than mere price working here, more than economics with high added value. High End means a feeling of connection to an original brand. What does this connection mean? Well, at one level it is a sense that this High End excites customers, touches them, sometimes grabs them in their souls, and relates. And it's not an issue of brand only. What about experiences? That works as well. And, the *summum bonum*, goodness of soul that emerges from sustainability, from caring about the planet, or in other words, do well by doing good. That too is a feeling of connection, and excitement, of being in touch with the nobler part of one's aspiration.

It is not easy to understand the magic of the High End. The High End has so many facets of one's existence, from stuff to experience, from oneself to one's world, from the joy of possession/consumption to the nobility of one's ideals. But we have to begin somewhere, and that somewhere is at the top of the world of "stuff". We will start with the richest part of the market, the world of Luxury that gives a sense of what can be done to upgrade from the ordinary towards that promised land of High End. Here, the winds of luxury blow, even if luxury itself is, once again, unattainable, like a dream, or like a Fata Morgana, the legendary and romantic ghost of King Arthur's sister, Morgan Le Fay. And this *mirage* is what our next chapter is about.

3

Luxury – Aim High for a Strong Head Start

Over time, the generational cohorts have changed from looking at Luxury as inner directed and self-indulgent, to a feeling that Luxury boosts their confidence and positions them to the outside world. That different way of looking at Luxury often leads them to interpret the delivery of the brand promise in a different way. The market opportunities lie in taking advantage of this change.

Karen Moersch and Simon Wilson, Founders,
The Hasley Group, UK

Read enough books about business management and you eventually come up with the phrase "stretch goal", or some other phrase, sometimes inspirational, sometimes blather. But the idea is the same – be all that you can be, go beyond, reach for all the gusto. So, as we voyage through the world of aspiration, let's start at the top, at luxury, where some people live all day long, but about which the rest of us just like to read. Luxury makes great fun reading. And, if you're serious about business at the High End, better look at part of the "mother lode"; which inevitably will trickle down in a few years to be part of your High End.

Dreams of luxury warm our souls from early childhood. Even in urban slums, boys and girls happily smile as they wander in their innocent sleep in castles as princesses in priceless dresses, or noble warriors in golden armor … or driving glamorous sports cars or living in penthouses as rap stars. Dreamily intangible or brutally materialistic, the incarnation of luxury as we see on TV, read in media, dream about or just hear as urban legends shapes our ambitions, goals and aspirations. This might explain why so many children of the ultra-rich fail miserably to live up to expectations – they *live* in a dream already, having everything possible and impossible at their disposal. Not much to dream about!

Growing up pushes reality right into our faces. We eventually realize that our childhood dreams are not very likely to materialize any time soon. Yet most of us never really stop secretly dreaming about this unattainable luxury. And when an opportunity arises to get that designer dress (never mind that all your friends have exactly the same already) or a coveted limited edition hot mobile phone, craving to get it overrides the rational part of the mind. The desire to get closer to this dream luxury world, even a tiny bit closer, inspires us to forget about the necessities and buy "that" instead. Mentally, we move a small but important step towards this aspirational world. Even reading about BETTER and attainable luxury creates our illusion and warm feeling that we are better today than yesterday, that there is a reason to work hard, to push ourselves. And that's your touchstone for the High End.

If you want to "make it" in tomorrow's High End, and catch the wave, it's good to know how luxury works. It is really simple. Contemporary luxury inspires consumers, even when affordability is out of the question. Today's luxury is the mother of tomorrow's High End. Luxury often becomes the source of trends, the mother of opportunities. Luxury is the basis for developers who make it affordable, so the once-impossible becomes a touchable dream that can now be truly HAD, at least for a little more money than one is accustomed to spend.

The features of luxury inevitably migrate, trickling down to more accessible market strata, in one form or another. The barrier between luxury and High End is porous. And the truth of the matter is that people just want. That is how they are constructed. People everywhere aspire to luxury. So contemporary luxury perhaps provides the BEST showcase window for tomorrow's High End. Company after company, artisans galore, and the always on-the-prowl media work their alchemy on luxury because it pays to do so. So, the more we know about how luxury works, the better we will make the High End, and of course the more we can recapture business margins that keep getting pushed towards commodity levels.

Getting Grounded – What You Need to Know About the Meaning of Luxury

---

Definitions:

Luxury is the ability to experience/own the best exclusively attainable.

Luxury is undergoing an evolution now – from "yesterday" (material possessions) to today (services and experiences) to tomorrow (time, space, balance).

So, now you are looking to the High End for business, and you're in the world of luxury, the mother lode. What do you need to look for? What is the wisdom you need to gain? You only have to read a few magazines chatting about luxury before the superlatives start to inundate. Stories about the world of luxury are surfeited with these superlatives such as charisma, allure, and that ultimately inexplicable word "appeal". So here we are already getting a sense of some intangibles that you need. But that's not all. Scholars, with their more analytic and occasionally jaundiced view, look at luxury differently, in a way that can educate and actually inspire. The classic definition of the "idea of luxury", according to Christopher Berry of the University of Glasgow, incorporates the traditional domains of luxury – sustenance, shelter, clothing and leisure. Those are the ideas that come to mind, and they paint word pictures if we just stop and think. By themselves they are ordinary, the very fabric of life. Yet, by means of money and taste, they can be elevated from *function to finesse*, from *doing to delighting*. This is the first lesson from luxury to inform your business efforts.

But it's not just stuff, elegance, delighting. There is more. In a world where money and prosperity do not always increase linearly over time, "more" is going to become BETTER, and BETTER itself is going to morph into *stuff* on the one hand, and into *spirit* on the other.

Today's luxury is inexorably shifting towards the non-material dimensions of spiritual and mental self-fulfillment. Luxury is winning its soul, or perhaps regaining its soul after playing in the overly material world. A luxury brand should act on our souls the same way as we experience the special moments of life. The brand can make life softer and subtle to you – like a hotel that serves high tea by the Victoria Falls in Zambia, making you feel happily far away from where you are. It can make you feel life in a more intense way – like giving you access to a tribe that is nearly extinct. What is happening to you in this new dimension of luxury? *You sense, you enjoy, you experience.* This could be the new luxury. Material things are usually reproducible. Experiences, by contrast, might be unique, and intimately your own.

There are, of course, psychological mechanisms driving this change from stuff to soul. Although people need the basics, we aspire at the very highest level to self-actualization, to become who we are. In the world of luxury, we deal with people who can afford almost anything. As they get everything, whether stuff or power, comfort or anything wealth brings, they stop wanting stuff. A strange and often wonderful transformation occurs. These stuff-surfeited people stop wanting more and more. Now they want to serve, they want to leave their mark; they want the luxury of the soul, and not the luxury of matter. Just look at Michael Bloomberg, mayor of New York City, a self-made billionaire. He cannot spend his money, so he serves the city. This pattern of change teaches us how to capture the High End for business opportunities. We ought not stop at the world of stuff, but look to the new avatar of aspiration, personal authenticity and external sustainability. The top level is self-actualization, which luxury reaches because it can buy everything else. But we get ahead of ourselves.

Let's Learn From Contemporary Luxury – Five Dimensions and Shortcuts

From our dozens of interviews with the top thinkers and players in the luxury industry we learned some key lessons to guide business. They will be foundational for our analysis of the world(s) of aspiration. The interviews painted five key intrinsic and essential qualities (dimensions) of luxury: authenticity, intangible value, price and residual value, tradition and origin, and foundation tale. They must be present for something to be considered luxury. These key ingredients cannot be missing. Despite the fact that luxury seems to be out of reach, the truth is that these five dimensions are the High End. Not now, but probably in the very near future. Luxury is worth dissecting, just for that.

DIMENSION 1: AUTHENTICITY

Just a few years ago, authenticity was not as much a legal term as one of pedigree backed up by scholarship. If the item came from the right place, the right creator, and could be traced with reasonable confidence, it was authentic, and had a chance of making it into the world of luxury.

To understand how authenticity drives true luxury, take a good look at its predatory adversary, counterfeiting, that bane of luxury players, an unconscionably common crime that keeps them in court, and all too often in choleric fits. In today's world the term authenticity has, for the most part, evolved into the law enforcement task of "brand protection."

Today's technology can replicate products with astounding accuracy causing an avalanche of copycat experiences at "everyday low prices". Rolex, this traditional paramount of old luxury, first comes to mind when talking about fakes. As it is quite possible that there are more "Rolexes" sold in Shanghai by peddlers every day than any other "brand" of watch, it is no wonder that the allure of "true" authenticity has grown under pressure of proliferating fakes.

People with "reasonable incomes" do not steal the ordinary. If one makes the effort, it is better to steal high than steal low. Otherwise, why bother? People go to where they can find aspirational icons, things that mean something socially, things that signify much better – upper crust, "you have arrived". Fake Gucci clothes and Rolex watches are offered daily by the unscrupulous peddlers on the crowded streets of major cities, where it is virtually impossible to avoid these symbols of luxury sold for relative pennies. One virtually trips over these counterfeits, lining the street, earnest seller after earnest seller, offering that which is worth a king's ransom for just a few dollars. It is the same with being a poseur. People do not present themselves as ordinary. There is no news there. People present themselves as better than that of which they are stealing the identity, which they aspire to, not that which they reject or ignore.

Counterfeiting is so prevalent today that it is an inseparable part of luxury. Retail specialist consultants Radha Chadha and Paul Husband devoted an entire chapter of their book, "*The Cult of the Luxury Brand*" to what they defined as the "advent of the *genuine fakes*", analyzing this all-too-well-known parallel market of finely crafted knock-offs.

Lessons to the High End from authenticity in luxury

The world of luxury shows us that when something is worthy of aspiration it's worthy of counterfeiting. And unfortunately, like its mother, luxury, the High End is not sheltered from counterfeiting, just because it is attainable. The High End is aspirational as well. It's only a matter of time before the counterfeiter discovers the particular High End offering, and fabricates the knock-off. So, the lesson to take away is – it is crucial for High End players to design their brands and products as powerful icons, and then prepare for the inevitable downside effect of this success – counterfeiting. Perhaps the counterfeit is the signal of "having arrived". Imitation is truly the most sincere form of flattery.

DIMENSION 2: INTANGIBLE VALUE

There are no units of "craftsmanship". Yet the connoisseur knows when an item is a good example of craftsmanship or, unhappily, a poor example. Top luxury brands have this characteristic, which must be intuited. Certainly, there are critics who can point out specific aspects of the craftsmanship for particular items, but in reality it's an intuitive sense of *luxe*. And a corollary rule is that the truly top luxury brand will switch from providing mere "logoed stuff" to enhancing the process of self-actualization and self-expression.

If intangible value is so important, then why are luxury fashion brands going mass? Certainly, this is not the correct way to impart the intangible … or is it? Mass does not confer intangible value. It confers … well, mass. How can conglomerates and their brands respond to this move to mass? The answer is obvious. By going small again, at least for the part that is chosen to maintain its *luxe*. From the vantage point of those intangible qualities that define exclusivity, we might guess that small-scale businesses are getting back into the business of providing experience (personal attention) and uniquely customized stuff (products that best fit the luxury paradigm). Businesses should flourish when they make their customers feel proud to be selected for a special treat by the brand of their choice acting as a personal craftsman.

Lessons to the High End from intangible value in luxury

As in luxury, the High End proposition will have to transmit a sense of intangible value. Yet, and paradoxically, here's the rub. The High End is not the outcome of unique craftsmanship but rather mass production – mostly in outsourced capacity, in emerging countries that possess neither legacy nor reputation in terms of *finesse* of production. High End business has to deal with this handicap and, perhaps by the alchemy of advertising and positioning, convert the negative into a positive. We will elaborate on this topic in our treatment of Tradition and Origin.

DIMENSION 3: RESIDUAL VALUE, EXCLUSIVITY AND PRICE

One latent does not really announce itself until it is explained. And then, there is the inevitable "aha". This something is *residual value*, a micro-economic criterion that in our age of throw-aways is not even associated with anything except big-ticket purchases, and even then in terms of value loss, like the car you just bought and which lost 20 percent of its value the minute you drove it away from the dealer. True luxury goods do not lose value over time, but paradoxically gain value. Every true luxury product is potentially a collectible artifact. Just think about cars like a Rolls Royce that the owner can turn in, and get as much money back as he paid when first buying it.

Price in luxury is all about better, far better, superior service, a superior product, a superior experience. We keep returning to the world of BETTER, not the mere world of stuff. Read the history of the American ultra rich at the turn of the twentieth century. You soon realize that with all their money quite often industrial magnates and heiresses bought material objects. Only with seasoning did they develop the taste for quality, for objects that would gain in value over time.

Let's think about this notion of losing versus gaining value after the item has been enjoyed over years, sometimes over generations. We repeat the truism above that most cars depreciate the instant they are driven away from the dealer. This seems like a universal truth. But is it? Meet Richard Lee, the importer of the first Ferrari into the People's Republic of China in the early 1990s. Now Lee represents Ferrari–Maserati brands in Hong Kong, Macau and Dalian. Lee fervently believes that residual value can become a major selling point for his customers, even for cars. And Lee puts that belief into operation. When a customer complains that he is bored (!) with the prize Enzo or Challenge Stradale, Lee publicly invites the customer to sell the car back, paying enough profit to cover the inflation and more. And the effect – true luxury to be enjoyed and not disposed of when finished, but rather treasured more and valued more as time goes on.

Looking at museum pieces, at art galleries, and at the very rare cars we have just described, we learn a lesson that will apply to the attainable High End. The "right" objects can keep or increase their status of uniqueness, and monetary value with the passage of time. Furthermore, and perhaps delightfully unexpected, residual value itself might link stuff and a better world. Residual value means less stuff, less waste, more personal and emotional comfort, more treasured stuff, less discarded junk. In other words, residual values open up a new facet of the world of aspiration, and for business a new opportunity in the High End.

Residual value does not come cheap. No one can sell just one item and stay in the marketplace, at least for very long. A company has to sell a lot of the item, a luxury service has to be offered and paid for many times. And so we witness the ever-changing dance between "how much to survive" and "how little to preserve the exclusivity of the brand".

Lessons to the High End from residual value in luxury

Creating products with high residual value is, perhaps, the most promising future for the High End brand. Thanks to specific marketing engineering and an intelligent use of design, you can transform relatively humble and lower priced everyday objects into collectibles, and so bridge the gap between stuff and soul, both critical for the new High End.

DIMENSION 4: TRADITION AND ORIGIN

Traditions and heritage, *noblesse oblige and pride of place*, constitute the calling card, the cornerstones, and the guardians of luxury. Tradition and heritage invoke the respectability of ancient names and the grandeur of blue blood, or at least try to. For a brand or an experience to become the *crème de la crème*, a respectable provenance is a must. And, of course, like a title in the nobility, the older and more hallowed the better. The origins of brands, materials and goods and the location of shops are and remain a vital pre-requisite. Think of Breguet that was already a leader in luxury watches at the time of Napoleon. It's hard to choose one's ancestors properly, but those fortunate enough to have noble ones ought not to discard the advantage they confer.

Nowadays just a few countries are traditionally considered to be a source of *believable* luxury propositions. Rounding up the usual suspects, Japan, the USA, the UK, Italy, Germany, France and Switzerland constitute one global circuit of creation, production and consumption of luxury in its strictest sense. Of course, there will be others, as wealth manages to buy even provenance.

We are accustomed to luxury from the European countries with a heritage of high quality and provenance. Can luxury come from the new economies, which are not usually associated with luxury, such as emerging BRIC markets –

Brazil, Russia, India, and China? Of course, there is no single right answer to this question. Certainly, Russia, India and China have long histories with glorious periods where art flourished, and where precious items, stuff of luxury, were created by master artisans. They have provenance, to be sure. Brazil has wealth, opportunity, glorious forests, natural treasures, and a young population who will become wealthy some day because of their youth and resources. Can Brazil be a source of luxury?

It is likely that these BRIC countries will, in their own way, redefine some of the world of luxury. The luxury may look different, or may be just a recasting of traditional luxury. The answers will depend upon the specific market, and what one looks for in the world of *luxe*. India is very strong with gold, for example, and one can expect that India will create its own mark by exporting an increasing amount of luxury jewelry to advanced economies.

Russia is also a looming presence. While never losing the attention of fine collectors, the rebirth of Fabergé could return the historical Russian jewel maker to wider audiences. But it will be a different Russia, perhaps not altogether in Kievan Rus, the ancient homeland of the Russians. The *new* Fabergé, Russian icon of luxury, is, in fact, the London-based, Richemont-owned brand under the leadership of luxury veteran CEO Mark Dunhill. Dunhill may well return Russia to the world of luxury brands.

However, it is Brazil that might surprise and it is China that might explode with their production capability. In Brazil, where the luxury has always been a foreign affair, top retailer Daslu developed an in-house luxury style. Now Brazil exports its Daslu brand to Europe, where it finds its way to the flagships of continental luxury, including Parisian boutique Colette, making Daslu truly unique.

China is another story. Top brands in China still come from the foreign countries. Led by Chinese *ubertalent* Joanne Ooi, Shanghai Tang, the all-Chinese aesthetics brand of the Richemont Group, is a noteworthy exception to the rule. Greg Furman, CEO of the Luxury Council of New York, predicted that China is expected to become the most important market for luxury makers of the world, with the potential to surpass the USA. With thousands years of heritage in high taste and ultimate luxury, China can be expected to lead the world once again. Demographics are destiny, and demographics, and with willpower, demography becomes virtually unbeatable. This time, however, China will not lead by chance, but by design. We will talk further about how design will contribute to the renaissance of Chinese High End in Chapter 10, and we will share our empirical research about the Chinese vision of the High End in Chapter 11.

Lessons to the High End from tradition and origin

This is perhaps one of the dimensions where High End brands cannot imitate the royalty of luxury players, except perhaps by the artful dodge, or perhaps more diplomatically by creative invention. Furthermore, many High End products will be most likely produced through outsourcing. (Actually so are a number of actual luxury products as well, although this still remains a fairly well-hidden secret.) It seems logical that an effort to build a good reputation is about as far as the typical High End marketer can go – unless, of course there is some form of historical depth behind the brand that can be exploited in a creative, oblique manner.

DIMENSION 5: THE FOUNDATION TALE

A. Lange and Sohne, an established and well-respected luxury watchmaker before World War Two, practically disappeared from the luxury world during the turbulent, hyper-competitive second part of the twentieth century. It took the fall of the Berlin Wall to revive A. Lange and Sohne, this time through a story: *Now … the old, beloved, reversed brand was renewed, models were updated and restyled, and its back*! The happy result? Now A. Lange and Sohne has again become a sought-after luxury brand of watch. What is this all about? Do fairy tales really come true?

The public wants something special, something exclusive, something not everybody is wearing. Yet, just as much as the "stuff", the public loves stories which come from history or perhaps legend. The story lends the cachet, the special magic that makes the ordinary special, and makes the special memorable. At the most superficial level, stories provide a narrative flow, featuring the hallmarks of classic advertising and orchestrated PR. At a deeper level, however, psychoanalysis tells us that the story weaves together the specific content of a single campaign with the brand's origins and essence. Here a story celebrates the roots of the brand. The narrative provides a unique foundation tale, almost biblical in nature, sometimes holy, and always inspiring.

Foundation tales are powerful narrative mechanisms. They work. And perhaps when all is said and done these wonderful stories become the most effective tools available to those who manage and market luxury brands. The memorable story, a legend, something that confers a sense of awe, separates true luxury players from mere *wannabes*. Look into the eyes of the teller and the listener to see the impact. The result is magic – that *je ne sais quoi* which divides the birth of a myth from the more ordinary great idea proposition. It is no wonder that Homer got his start in story-telling; that the itinerant European poetry reciters were so popular, and that stories from the Bible never stop being used as guides to daily life.

Once such a level is reached, the next step is, of course, to preserve the myth in good times and, more importantly, in bad ones. And there always are bad times which injure the brand. There is a cost to that preservation. The story has to be guarded. The value of the story is priceless, embellished in the retelling, becoming the ambassador to the world, always ready with proof because the story simply is "what is". And the story penetrates deeply. People like stories, believe the stories, and act because of the stories. We can be assured that stories are the engine of aspiration and emotion, hence one of the key pillars of luxury – and by reflection, a key pillar of the High End as well.

Lessons to the High End from the foundation tale in luxury

The foundation tale lies at the heart of creative storytelling. As a newcomer, don't expect to reach the levels of historical richness of stories enjoyed by established luxury leaders like Breguet or Moet Chandon, the brands that were there when the kings, revolutions, emperors and nations were made, and just as often unmade. On the other hand, brands only known for just a couple of generations, such as Prada or Gucci, managed to join the club of fabulous storytellers. Ultimately, it will all be about storytelling, and the ability to express one's inner truth at its best through these stories. The High End player might want to pause here, and think about the way to create a story relevant to the brand's culture, and tug at the hearts and souls of the customer prospects.

Luxury Strategies: How the Luxury Players Make it Happen

Although the luxury products of the best companies have their own distinct characters, the strategies these companies create and deploy are surprisingly similar. The rules are straightforward. Depending on the company culture, the main ways to make a winner are innovation, cultural marketing, celebrity marketing and licensing.

INNOVATION, IN MODERATION, MAKES A DIFFERENCE

Let's go back almost a century to France around the time just before World War I. Haussman's Paris was filled with beaux arts architecture and sand-colored apartment houses; everyday women were reaching for modernity through hopes and magazines, and the past was being slowly kicked to death by artists on the one hand, and designers on the other. Enter designer M. Paul Poiret, a man whose contributions to twentieth-century upscale fashion might be properly compared to Picasso's contributions to art. Upon encountering the ever-elegant Coco Chanel dressed in black, Poiret wittily asked her to whose funeral she was going. Not missing a beat, Chanel looked back and (perhaps too) swiftly replied *"Yours, monsieur."*

For all his genius in style, his elegance, all his intuition about what the truly up-scale people wanted, Poiret had just missed the evolution in culture and costume that moved female audiences and customers out of the pre-World War One era and into modern times. He might have seen the fashionable but helmet-like cloches on the heads of ladies and shop girls alike, realized something was happening, and taken action. But he didn't. And so Poiret's business suffered, and then simply died. We believe that already the aspiration of everyman (or everywoman) to be "king or queen for a day" was in full flower. So what about *Madame* Chanel? Coco Chanel went on to build a business of luxury goods using her intuition and innovative interpretation of the new feminine ideal.

Coco Chanel is remembered because she changed the way we look at fashion. Chanel *is* fashion and luxury. She represented herself, but incorporated the essence of herself into that ever-popular brand which is the quintessence of style and femininity. From the black dress to costume jewelry, with charm and insight Chanel introduced a number of great innovations to fashion and luxury. Her top moments? It's hard to pick one. Perhaps the outstanding one is her creation of the Chanel No. 5 perfume, a true luxury standard, which was destined to become a popular culture icon. More than anything, it can truthfully be said that Chanel was a pioneer, a true *moderniste* and heroine. Chanel was never afraid of being controversial. In the end, her 87 years of mixed creative, entrepreneurial and jet-set achievements embody the stuff of dreams that the luxury industry creates and sells so very well.

Innovation, in fact continual innovation, is one key to success in the lifestyle-driven luxury business. But wisdom has a place here too, as a guide. Businesses simply must anticipate the customer's values, needs and tastes and, with a bit of acumen, try to be just slightly ahead of them. It's seduction, knowing and delivering; timing is everything. The challenge is clear – preserve the tradition and yet embrace the change.

Lessons to the High End from innovation in luxury

Lacking the pedigree of tradition and the centuries old foundation tales, High End makers rely on talent to anticipate people's future dreams and aspirations. Anticipation is not enough. Harness that anticipation to a reality – but make that reality contemporary. Weave in stories, for it is through stories that the modern will become magic. Mix value with imagination, with the special sauce that is contributed by the mind of the customer. The High End must keep up with technology and design. Those twins will produce solutions and make customers happy. Enrobe the future in a welcome, through stories, through technology, but most of all through applied imagination. Customers are ready. They need only to be enchanted.

CULTURAL MARKETING LINKING WITH ASPIRATIONS

Culture is that fertile ground where experience takes place and lifestyles are nurtured. If we could understand cultural values, then perhaps we would uncover the *whys* of experience design, and understand what people want, what works at the luxury level, and why it works. Understanding the relevance of the cultural milieu helps change the marketing thinking along the way. The much maligned, underappreciated, hard-working but déclassé automobile sales tactics do not work in the world of luxury. Subtlety is welcome and it will be equally welcome in the High End. Culture makes a difference, reconciling luxury and marketing in a creative, soul-enriching way.

Let's focus on art, which is deeply involved in luxury, and will be important for the creative aspects of the High End. Or better, let's go to the experience of art, rather than the stuff itself, and in so doing learn some lessons about our goals.

Art is the quintessence of luxury. We need only go to museums to see that for centuries the notion of "art for art's sake" was not popular for a very long term. (Art for art's sake would be created by Michelangelo in his non-finito pieces.) Rich patrons, whether they were nobility or clergy, would commission works for their collections, churches, tombs, and of course for display. But again going to museums in the past was just looking at stuff, not experiencing. And we're talking about cultural marketing strategies for business, for the High End, and not about art appreciation.

So, let's go to "where the business is at". Let's move from the world of the masters, museums, and rarified tastes of aesthetes to the world of sponsoring art. Those who sponsor art are part of a long tradition, coming from the nobility and church. Today they have become part of the democratic nature of the High End. Actually, the strategy of sponsoring art can be traced to the way luxury tycoons involve fine arts and culture in their business. Since the connection between aristocracy and art patronage has been part of our societies for millennia, it seems natural that luxury players have made remarkable, consistent, and now increasingly successful efforts to enter the realm of higher culture. Their almost monomaniacal focus on culture is not a random choice of where to put their spare cash. Rather, culture and art subtly add to the cachet. A good dollop of culture, properly applied, can separate the luxury proposition from mass market, poseurs or, heaven forbid, arrivistes without culture. This complex connection between the worlds of "luxury" and "culture" is central in the book *The Golden Crossroads*, by one of the authors (MB), in research collaboration with AG and HM.

We visit Prada for a lesson in art culture, the High End, and what can be done. Prada has been a pioneer in fine arts and luxury branding. More than a decade ago author MB interviewed Miuccia Prada herself about her commitment to art and her interests in the general field of culture. What was striking was how her art and cultural interests represented so well her modus operandi. Ahead of all Milanese competition, in the mid 1990s Miuccia created an art foundation that rapidly rose to world fame, to solidly position the brand as *avantgarde*. Her ability to manage her cultural policies well beyond tactic sponsoring brought Prada's genius beyond just fine arts: architecture became part of her "mix" too – and architecture at its finest level in the world.

Prada's true genius for luxury marketing seamlessly mixes high cultural engagement with subtle, culturally rich events and marketing-related operations. To help face these challenging opportunities, Prada hired AMO, the research think-tank of Rem Koolhas' architectural firm, OMA (a convenient reuse of the same letters in a different order), led by Reinier de Graf. AMO established a long-term relationship with Prada. They ideate and produce events, shows, and create an on-line presence for this Italian fashion icon. AMO repeatedly proved its ability to push the boundaries of marketing communication by staging unique performances for the Prada brand, such as the recent America's

Cup launch at Valencia's Mercado Central. For one night only, refined Prada products were mixed with everyday's commodities in a nonchalant placement, which added to the natural "radical chic" allure of the Prada brand. Such sophisticated marketing and merchandising show how Prada plays across the cultural distribution of both luxury and mass market. Prada has created the gold standard in premium categories, and done so completely in its own way, merging luxury, highbrow and lowbrow cultures in a unique mix.

Culture confers something special, panache, an exquisiteness that supports the luxury product. This is the stuff that luxury players crave and need the most. The exquisiteness is not available in large amounts, and cannot simply be bought wholesale, at least not any more. We are a century late for that. We missed the robber-baron era. But we still have creativity, and with creativity and vision we have culture flourishing anew in the world of luxury, and rushing into the world of aspiration, our High End.

Lesson to the High End from cultural marketing in luxury

Cultural marketing may be the most difficult domain for High End brands. Luxury brands made substantial progress in the last couple of decades by fitting themselves into the world of high culture and are now warmly welcomed. The happy results are unbeatable gains in terms of reputation, beyond any metrics or quantitative measurement. To truly "play" in this context, High End brands will have to leave behind their mass-marketing roots. High End should make that leap of faith into a whole new approach to what marketing is and what it can become, taking the "right" lessons from its mother, the luxury world.

CELEBRITY MARKETING

> *Recall the role played by Madame Pompadour in establishing the profile of the Moet et Chandon brand … What has deeply changed is the socio-cultural mechanism, and its context. From aristocracy and royalties via top models and rock stars, we have reached the current stage where celebrities are mostly an offspring of the movie industry. The real question is indeed what will come next? Here, Louis Vuitton made a very precise choice by inviting Mikhail Gorbachev as the testimonial of the latest advertising campaign.*
>
> *Concetta Lanciaux, former personal advisor to*
> *Bernard Arnault, LVMH*

Celebrity is the currency of popular culture, the stories that make people dream. Of course, anybody can buy a testimonial, but the truly leading brand does not aspire to what could be purchased at whim. The luxury brand wants to have an authentic relationship with its own evangelists. What the brand wants is the love of their stars.

The relation between a true luxury player and celebrity customers involves a deep, subtle art of engagement. According to Thieryy Maman, the CEO of the luxury shoemaker Berluti, the star athlete Zinedine Zidane deliberately and systematically exposed his Berluti shoes when on TV. He did it at no cost to the company, just for the pride and satisfaction of wearing Berluti. The exposure had to be discreet, because at that time Zidane was under contract for marketing testimonials for another sports shoe manufacturer. Although not directly competing with Berluti, the management of this sports sponsoring brand might have been irritated: however, Zidane took the risk, just for love (of Berluti) only! This positive impact of visibility and endorsement, a tribute to the brand's authenticity, is exactly what is needed in luxury marketing.

Lessons to the High End from celebrity marketing in luxury

Specifics and tactics are everything here. What becomes important is the crafting of the Berluti-Zidane type of affair, that elusive tactic of going beyond the simple, easy-to-buy relation between the brand and the testimonial. We will see in Chapters 7 and 8 how brands like Tag Heuer managed to go even further by establishing and promoting their unique relationships with a legend like Steve McQueen.

LICENSING

The business of luxury is business, of course. Yet we like to think of luxury as a separate world, not affected by economics. And so our next lesson about luxury begins,as we look at the financial realities of our world, and where the money really can come from.

Some hugely popular luxury brand-names suffer split personalities. Think of brands such as Louis Vuitton, Bottega Veneta, and Giorgio Armani. One side of them serves a primarily exclusive clientele with tailor-made, uniquely crafted products. Their other side serves the mass-market, features licenses, the real cash cows. The *why* is simple. Money seduces if you're in business. Sunglasses, perfumes, eyewear and other products can share some of the reflected glory of the mother brand while produced by less well-known companies in an outsourced facility. Licensing is the route to huge margins on rather ordinary products.

To the purists of luxury, extending luxury brands towards wider audiences produces anger, despair, and occasional glee as the profits roll in. The licensing approach as we know it today was created and, as many believe, abused by French 1960s icon Pierre Cardin. The consensus is that Pierre Cardin fell down, however, in a spiral of banalization that eventually occurs when the aspirational businesses "dance with the devil of everyday ordinary". From a brilliant top luxury brand, Pierre Cardin ended up signing every kind of product licensing, without choosing coherent lines that would extend and maintain the image. To Pierre Cardin, the world was a licensing wonderland, filled with economic opportunity extending every way, in every direction, to every product. Not surprisingly, the Pierre Cardin brand image slowly moved from a luxury top brand to a popular brand, sold everywhere.

The Pierre Cardin story, and especially the long and slow decline, teaches the lesson. The fatal flaw was the hubris of brand, no coherent thinking, and the willful loss of consistent strategy. In other words, you could not make up this type of comedy of errors. The Pierre Cardin brand has lost its consumer. In the pall-mall search for profits, the Pierre Cardin brand progressively abandoned its area of competence. The Pierre Cardin extension lines, source of momentary revenue, added nothing to the brand, but rather degraded out of luxury, out of High End, into a hellish somewhere else.

Yet, the story is not entirely sad. The gods do not punish completely. Pierre Cardin might have lost its cachet, but it did not lose the money! From the financial point of view, the picture is not that bad at all, as the brand might be diluted but still quite valuable. The income from licenses for Pierre Cardin is 36 million euros a year. At the age of 82, Cardin set an asking price of 400 million euros for potential purchasers of his brand. The numbers cast a different shadow on this once glorious brand. So at once, we have the loss of cachet, but at the gain of revenue. A tough decision indeed – cachet or cash.

Since Cardin began his efforts to expand revenues, licensing has become a common practice in the luxury industry. Licensing allows the company to cash in on the brand name, while *presumably* maintaining the charisma and the allure to the masses.

But where does licensing really work? At its best, licensing works for perfumes and cosmetics. Let's take a closer look at a few names in this world to better understand. International Fragrance and Flavors, Firmenich and Givaudan are the leaders in the game of creating the actual fragrance. Unbeknownst to the fragrance buyer, a lot of the so-called "juice" comes from these companies. These companies are the silent architects and the indispensable engineers driving the licensing business model. They create what the companies sell, with perfumers on the prowl for the latest trends, the smells of what's in. In a sense, they create and sell/license their works of art, the physical stuff of perfumes, of new car smells, and room fragrances, to name just a few. A similar reality governs the eyewear industry. Consider Italy's Luxottica, one of the most important makers of frames for Chanel, Dolce and Gabbana, DKNY, Prada and a group of other leading brands. The bottom line here is that licensing is acceptable in luxury, and of course at the High End. Without the people who are the real creative artists there might be a lot less to sell. But without the sales coming from somewhere there might be many fewer real creative artists. Licensing feeds the lot.

And of course out of licensing, the bane of exclusivity, we move to its opposite twin, anti-licensing, that is, custom or bespoke services. Here we see the magic appear once again. By customizing a service that is also available to the masses, an astute marketer creates a sense of departure from the ordinary, endowing it with a magic something that elevates the daily to the special. What is the magic here? Of course, for luxury we're not talking about moving downwards, out of licensing. Rather, we are talking about the opposite – making a product that is so upscale it needs no logo, nothing to identify it as luxury. For example, custom-made suits. Bottega Veneta mastered the art of the anti-logo in favor of custom-tailored cloth, to answer the call for exclusivity.

So what are we to make of the business of licensing, of Pierre Cardin, of customizing? What can we learn from the "top" that will make our efforts in the attainable High End attainable? Well, we know for sure that licensing is truly one of the pillars of the luxury giants such as LVMH or Prada. Licensing has become a major strategy in terms of economic trends of this industry. Licensing creates fortunes. But, at the same time, licensing cuts the other way. All the prestige of luxury can go right down the drain, for the wrong licensing arrangement. So here we are, at a tug of war between profits and prestige. And so the need for the remedy for licensing, or at least something that will allow the money to flow while the basic image is left undamaged. Perhaps anti-licensing, customizing the ordinary, will allow for licensing of the new, while not affecting the core. The jury is still out on licensing, at least for luxury, but when it comes to the lesser world of the attainable High End, licensing has a bright future.

Lessons to the High End from licensing

The dilemma faced by the luxury industry when it comes to licensing is simply the loss of charisma. But that's not the case for the High End. Licensing may be effective in moving up from lower down. High End brands must elevate themselves to the higher ground of premium. They have less to lose and more to gain from licensing than luxury does. It is all a matter of where the product is coming from, and to where it is going. Is the sun setting , or is it rising?

Summing Up: Lessons to the High End from Mother Luxury

At the end of our tour around luxury, we now look at prescriptions for the High End. Here is what you should consider when you move from the world of ordinary to the world of aspiration.

AUTHENTICITY

High End players should seek to retain the value of their investments in design and quality by preventing any possible future counterfeiting in a systematic way, making counterfeit prevention part of the DNA of the process, not just a momentary kneejerk response.

INTANGIBLE VALUE

High End players must create the perception of intangible value. Defining and achieving the intangible will remain a challenge.

RESIDUAL VALUE

This is one of the key distinguishing factors of real luxury. High End players can achieve similar effects, thanks to marketing savvy and the long-lasting value of design.

TRADITION AND ORIGIN

Luxury can and does flaunt pedigree. High End players have to be smart here, creatively proclaim the economic benefits of outsourcing. It is up to High End leaders to transform this apparent disadvantage into a plus.

FOUNDATION TALE

High End players cannot go back to aristocracy and fabled beginnings. There are no real tales. Storytelling, not necessarily traceable to blue blood or artistic provenance, will help. Imagination and good narration count here.

INNOVATION

Of course, innovation is the natural lifeblood, the very life force of business success. This is a challenge for luxury players, and a necessity for High End enterprises. This is probably not as hard, since innovation lies at the core of High End, which itself is an innovative offspring from the ordinary, aspiring towards attainable luxury.

CULTURAL MARKETING

The opportunity for High End is in marketing culture, ranging from fine arts to architecture. Just make the marketing effort fit High End. Do not think that cultural marketing means willy-nilly sponsorship.

CELEBRITY MARKETING

A fundamental approach to luxury branding, and can be easily transferred to the context of the High End.

LICENSING

Here is an opportunity for luxury to enjoy even greater commercial success. High End brands should associate themselves with higher ground designer names in order to increase their perceived value.

Putting it all together, we see that Luxury is fundamental to understand the High End. Lessons learned in luxury make the High End happen more smartly, with less effort. Luxury should not intimidate the High End entrepreneur or business leader. On the contrary, discuss, analyze and use the world of luxury as a reference for daily business success. The key "secret sauce" for the High End is the absolutely necessary drive to innovate, and the smart use of ideas like cultural marketing, celebrity marketing and licensing. It is about brains, not aristocracy, and about hope at the checkout, rather than snobbery and fading pride of place.

Conspicuously missing from this chapter is the importance of design in luxury. The design processes for luxury and High End products have many commonalities. Design is so critical that we devote a full chapter to it, showing how the High End can use design in business as a best practice.

4

Business Tool: Deciphering the "Algebra" of Consumer's Minds

The future of luxury lies all in the possibility of simplification. ... digital technologies will be the engine of progress, just like the factory was in the industrial era of the last century.

Luca De Meo, former CEO, Alfa Romeo, and former CMO,
FIAT Group Automobiles, Turin, Italy

Science, Engineering, and Understanding the Mind

For a High End proposition to be successful, people, the ultimate judges, will have to buy it. Sometimes, superior quality and exquisitely designed products find their way to the dusty shelves of discount stores. And in an infuriating turn of events, their inferior competition, like it or not, manages to hit the jackpot.

That being said, over the long haul success has little to do with sheer "luck". Rather, success results from better, deeper insights into the customers' minds, perceptions, preferences and predilections. In this chapter, we give you one path to the customer mind, as a business tool to pole-vault into the High End. When you read it, you will get a sense of what it takes to discover the "algebra of the mind". If you think about tomorrow's High End potential customers, "what makes them tick?" What features should you put in a product to make people want to buy it, even at a higher price? What should you offer in a commodity service to elevate from a nice to a must have? What messages to put in advertising to create the premium feeling? What are the ideas for the stories that could create a buzz? As you might guess, we are talking now in "brass talks", in specifics, and not in theory.

Our approach is straightforward. Yes, it requires thinking and experiments, not just art and intuition. You may want to analyze your way to the High End, read about, even fantasize, but there are hard work and experiments to build the knowledge you need. We will show you how to do these experiments so the High End will open itself up to you.

Our approach is called *Rule Development Experimentation*, or simply RDE. Incubated over decades inside the most innovative and forward-looking global companies, the RDE approach has been formalized and developed by Moskowitz Jacobs Inc. in cooperation with Dr. Yoram (Jerry) Wind of the Wharton School of University of Pennsylvania. The term was initially coined by two of the authors (HRM, AG) in a series of articles and conference papers. The knowledge-building approach for systematic design and developing the rules in various applications was formalized in their book *Selling Blue Elephants*.

So, what is RDE? Rule Developing Experimentation is a systematized solution-oriented business process of experimentation which designs, tests, and modifies alternative ideas, packages, products, or services in a disciplined way using *experimental design*. The outcome – the developer and marketer discover patterns and then rules showing what appeals to the customer, even if the customer can't articulate the need, much less the solution.

RDE for the Emotion-Rich High End – is it Even Necessary?

Yes.

People may not be able to tell you what they want, but they will know it when they see it. Asking people what they want or what might happen in future puts undue burden on them. This task might be too difficult for many consumers. At the same time, there is no lack of ideas in the minds of some people, both insiders and users. Some of these ideas are well formed; others are just notions, floating in the ether, a momentary diversion. The problem is how to sort these ideas out. RDE allows and tests many more ideas than traditional market research "beauty contests", thus expanding your ability to find something new, promising and insightful.

RDE provides another capability – segmentation, conquering by diving in a "knowing" manner. People differ profoundly from one another in what attracts them, in their mindsets. This might be obvious, a truism, and indeed such differences are often trumpeted by marketers. However, for the most part these mindsets look pretty much the same when all of us, the designer, the marketer, the manufacturer, only have information about our customer's age, income, gender, and even products previously purchased. This is the knowledge that can be purchased. But is it the knowledge that the designer needs to create the product, to reach the High End with something that truly appeals?

To see the "reality" of segments of the mind, just go to any food store, and look at the tea section. You are likely to see flavored teas, unflavored teas, herbal teas, regular teas, and a host of new entries. People who live in the same house, married couples or siblings, may have radically different preferences for the tea that they like. We are talking here about granularity, about fine distinctions among products which make up all the difference.

Now let's see how RDE identifies these mindset segments, that is, groups of people who may look the same, but have radically different mindsets, different wants, and of course who will react in different ways to an offering. RDE "clusters" or joins people into groups, based on how they respond to statements about what the High End means to them. Notice that we are not dealing here with who the people are, but rather *how they think*. The process, not surprisingly, is called "mindset segmentation".

Back to basics and standard practice first. Traditionally, marketers like to divide people on easy, but perhaps less useful information such as demographics – gender, age, income, where people live, and the like. The ingoing thinking is that "birds of a feather flock together". Yet people with the same income living in the same neighborhood could differ dramatically from each other. At the same time, their mindsets might be similar to other people with different demographics. Let's look at the world of experience, say the world of opera. In opera, it is not where you sit for an opera series but what particular operas you like. People will have mindset similarities in the music field regardless whether they sit on the upper "bird nest" level or in a premium box. At the same time, patrons sitting next to each other in seemingly homogeneous social groups (that is, similar incomes!) may enjoy drastically different parts of the same opera. In essence, the mindsets unite similar-minded people regardless of their income, occupation, geography and other demographics.

Getting into the Action – Making RDE Work for You – a Primer

Here are the six steps to make RDE come alive for you. Follow these steps, and the world of RDE opens up to reveal "what works" in the High End, and what types of mindset exist. RDE works with "stuff", with ideas that you will eventually present to your customers who participate in the RDE experiment. So – how do you do it? Before you read the steps, think of the next product or service YOU want to offer. Try to fix the idea in your mind. Now that you have it, let's see how RDE will put flesh on it, and help you give it life. Remember that the idea is there, but what are the features, the aspects, the reasons for buying it? That's what RDE will deliver.

Step 1. You're working in a world of attributes, so you need to know what your offering will actually be. Start with your raw materials: begin with silos or groups of features which constitute the target proposition (name, offering, features, benefits, and so on.) This first step is ideation and bookkeeping. Structure the world you will investigate with RDE, and make the components "orderly" so you can easily understand your data. For each silo, identify/create the ideas or elements which belong to that silo. Do not restrict your attention to those elements that you think will "do well" in the test. Go broad and far.

Step 2. People respond to advertisements, to product descriptions, but not to one-at-a-time, disconnected ideas. Create your test stimuli: mix and match the RDE elements according to an experimental design. Regardless of its intimidating name, the experimental design is just like a recipe. The design tells you what specific combinations to create. The combinations are "vignettes" or test concepts. The RDE tool does the "heavy lifting", this mixing and matching, virtually automatically. For technical, statistical reasons the tool ensures that the different elements appear independently of each other, that is, as so-called free agents. The RDE analysis will trace the customer's reaction to the individual contribution of each element. You actually do not have to do this step yourself. Once you have selected the raw materials (elements) in Step 1 and typed in the elements into the RDE "tool", the tool does everything else – from presenting the combinations to acquiring the data to "tracing back" what elements are working for each person.

Step 3. Data, not guessing, is important. A little data goes a long way to show you what works. Run the test: show the test vignettes (or test concepts) to participants, one vignette at a time. Collect the participant's ratings on a rating scale. The scale is up to you. We used the scale "How well does this vignette fit your idea of a future offering in the High End?" (That particular question asks the person to put himself into the "future"). A typical respondent finds this task very easy to do. He or she may begin by trying to analyze every single element in the vignette. However, by the time the respondent evaluates the third or fourth vignette, the person simply responds the way he feels. The bottom line here – you get the true "inner feeling.

Step 4. Statistics work, but you don't have to be a statistician. Create the personal "model" automatically. You want to discover which particular elements "drive" the response. Let's assume for a moment that you instructed the respondent to rate how well the idea of a future offering fits the High End. The analysis uncovers how each element drives that rating. We use a standard statistical procedure called *regression analysis*. For each individual in the study, we discover the specific *numeric contribution* of each element to the general perception of High End. Some of the elements add to the perception of High End (positive numbers), others detract from it (negative numbers), and yet others do not change it at all (numbers close to 0). Hard numbers do not replace insight, but as you will see, numbers give you a better sense of how the elements "work". Since the regression analysis is done automatically by RDE tools and reported in user-friendly terms, there is no need to understand in-depth what happens "under the hood" – unless of course you want to learn more.

Step 5. We're all different. If you know these differences, you can fine tune your offer and hit the "nail on the head". Divide to discover. People differ from each other. You can see how males respond versus females, how high-income people respond compared with how low-income people respond, and so on. When you run the same RDE experiment in different countries, you find out how the countries differ – an insight that adds a great deal to other knowledge about the countries and their cultures. However, there is more – people's mindsets. RDE will reveal these different groups of people, who differ by what they think about for the High End. This way of dividing people diverges very much from the conventional ways that use gender, income, products purchased and the like. The segmentation will reveal business opportunities.

Step 6. The best offering has good components, well combined. So what are they? Improve and even create using knowledge and metrics. "Optimize" the ideas in the vignette. Find the best combination that has the highest sum of RDE impacts. Then using these rules, create *new* High End propositions. Make sure that the new ideas have winning features so that you capture the best of what could be. We will show how to create High End services for banking, and how the not-for-profit world can use RDE to promote High End activities, such as cultural events.

Getting our Feet Wet – RDE Pilot Test to Study "Future Drivers" of the High End

Rather than merely explaining RDE, let us share with you an experiment performed for this book. In that way, we follow the path laid out by restaurateurs and chefs. When they want to please the gourmet connoisseurs of fine food, frequently these experienced restaurateurs and chefs make their first judgment about a food establishment by taking a peek at its working areas. When they like what they see, they proceed to the dining room to enjoy their food. Good restaurants are not afraid to show their kitchen. In the next chapters, you will "feast" on data and insights about high-end consumers from around the world. Right now, however, we want you to feel comfortable with that by inviting you to our "research kitchen".

In our preparations for the much larger, intercontinental four-country RDE (described in the next chapters), we launched this pilot project exploring the preliminary ideas in the USA. Based on what we learned in this pilot study, we enhanced and then streamlined the larger-scale study. Meanwhile, let's now proceed to the pilot, and see what we did, how we did it, and what we discovered.

We first developed five silos ("buckets" of related ideas) that would be relevant for the future of High End (Figure 4.1).

Figure 4.1   Five silos of the US pilot RDE project

Each silo comprises four different elements. For example, elements of Silo A ("Design") appear in Figure 4.2 where we have selected four ideas, and expressed them in short, direct statements. One of the keys here is simplicity, but with a twist. A consumer does not want to read elegantly crafted sentences in a vignette, preferring instead simple statements that get to point and put the message across. At the same time, the consumer wants more than a simple "bullet point". There has to be some "meat" to the message, something of the human touch. Most customers simply do not have the patience for a laundry list of basic ideas. The bottom line – make the elements convey something tangible, a word picture for the reader. It is a fine balance between descriptive art and soulless but simplistic description.

Let's go into a bit of depth to explain what we mean by the notion of simple yet "meaty" phrases. Look at element A1: *Craftsmanship with a personal touch* (Figure 4.2). The statement is terse, yet it paints a real "picture". The notion of craftsmanship goes beyond a simple word combined with *"with a personal touch"* which adds color to the message making it come alive. Contrast that phrase with the "boiled-down", almost sterile phrase "craftsmanship". That one word, craftsmanship, although meaningful, gives no tone, no texture, nothing but a simple word. Of course, respondents will read the word "craftsmanship", but we have not done it justice by one word alone.

A1: **Craftsmanship with a personal touch**

A2: **Multi-functional... beautifully crafted... effortlessly simple to use**

A3: **Beautifully designed ... so simple to operate**

A4: **Limited edition...designer products**

Figure 4.2   Four elements in silo A of the US pilot RDE project

Collecting the Data – Making RDE Actually Happen

We run these RDE studies on the Internet. The reasons are straightforward – it's very easy. The Internet has made it possible to do studies with RDE in a few days, and have all the data ready for automatic analysis without much effort. Indeed, the RDE is a true web tool.

In this first RDE exercise to identify markers of the High End, we invited respondents from a panel of consumers in the USA with 4,000 invitations, out of which 373 members agreed to participate. This is a typical "response rate". It is about 9 percent. A practical note for when you want to run your own RDE project– when you pay the respondents from a panel you will probably enjoy a higher response rate, especially when you make the invitation interesting.

So what happens? The respondent receives an email invitation. If sufficiently intrigued, the respondent need only click on the embedded link, and automatically the next thing to happen is that the RDE tool appears on the screen.

The RDE interview is scripted, formalized, reasonably interesting, and totally automatic. The RDE tool leads the respondent to the interview. The first screen tells the respondent what to expect, and instructs the respondent what to do. This is a very important step; it may seem as if everyone knows what to do, but the reality is that most people do not really feel comfortable in an interview unless the "ground rules" are explained, such as the purpose of the study (without giving away to much), and what the rating scale means.

Having logged in and been instructed, the respondent now evaluates a set of different screens, or vignettes, similar to what we see in Figure 4.3. The actual task is simple; it does not require very much concentration. The elements, that is, phrases, appear in the screen in a centered format, easy to read. We deliberately make the screen user-friendly. The RDE tool mixes the elements into different combinations, according to a recipe, or experimental design.

Each screen is designed to be easy on the eye. The respondent reads the screen, presses an answer, and the next screen appears. The RDE tool simply follows its design, and puts on the combinations, one after another. Each person evaluates a unique set of combinations. Furthermore, each of the elements appears several times in combination with other elements. There is no way that the respondent can possibly be "politically correct" or "game" the system – there are just too many combinations to do that.

Although the respondent does not realize it, there are rules to create the vignette, that is, structure to the recipes. For example, in any vignette, at most one element appears from each silo. Occasionally a silo is entirely absent as required by the RDE. You can think of that as separate recipes of ideas. Each vignette is just another recipe for which the participants must answer a simple question. We do not yet know what works and what does not. We will discover that when the RDE tools do the automatic analysis.

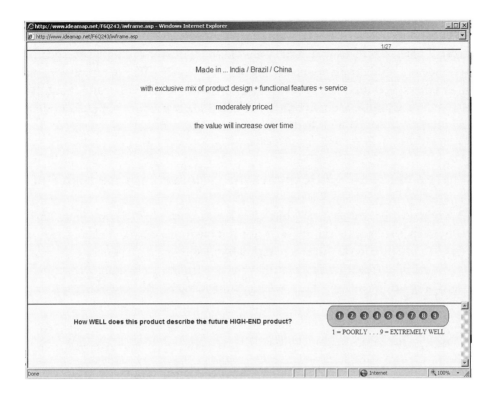

Figure 4.3   Sample test concept in the US pilot RDE project

What the Respondent Sees and Does

In this particular RDE project, each respondent rated a unique set of 25 test vignettes, reading them and rating the entire combination using a simple scale: *"How well does this product describe the future High-End product?"* The respondents used a 4–9 scale to rate degree of agreement. Other scales work just as well. It's just important to make sure that the scale has enough "points" to show differences among vignettes – and as a practical matter, the scale is easy to use. A 4–9 scale can be used with one keystroke.

But there is more – the classification, the "whom" we have persuaded to participate. When we run an RDE study, we usually want to know more about each individual. This information lets us analyze parts of the data, corresponding to different ages, genders, and the like. We really cannot tell much about the person from the list of ratings assigned to the vignettes. To learn more about the person, the respondent must complete a self-profiling "classification" questionnaire, telling us who he/she is, such as his/her age, income, gender, and so on. When it comes to analyzing, we will use this self-profiling questionnaire to divide our study participants by groups based on the demographics or any other criteria included in the questionnaire. The more we can learn about the respondent, within reason, the better we will understand him or her. Complete and relevant information is better than incomplete information.

Where's the Beef? – RDE Shows the "Mindset" for the High End

We worked with the data from a relatively large group of 373 respondents. Each respondent rated a different set of 25 test combinations (also called concepts or vignettes – all three terms are interchangeable). By giving each person a different set of combinations we don't worry that one particular combination of elements works very well together (called synergy), throwing off the results because the elements perform far better together than we would have expected.

As a point of information, with RDE, you need about 100–300 people to get solid results. We cannot get more specific than the range 100–300 because it is a matter of how homogenous are the minds that we deal with, that is, the study participants. If there is not a lot of substantial variation from person to person, then we will be fine with 100. But if we are venturing into uncharted waters, it's safer to test with more people than with fewer. It costs a little more, but the increased "base size" is good insurance.

RDE works differently from conventional approaches. Conventional questionnaires instruct the respondent to rate each element, one at a time. In these conventional questionnaires the elements never compete with each other. Reality is far different, far more brutal. People are confronted with combinations of messages, or features, or both. That's the way the world is constructed, not the nice "one-at-a-time" that's so artificial. Ideas fight each other for attention. Competition is king. In a product it might be brand, price, some statements about how the product is made, what the product is used for, and so on. So, in order to capture this competition among ideas that characterizes reality, we work with vignettes.

So what happens with vignettes? In the mind of a participant ideas compete with each other, and eventually the participant assigns a rating. Most of the time a participant is not even aware of what is happening. First the person reads the vignette. For most people, everything is fast, below the level of consciousness. The person simply gets a "feeling", a "sense", and assigns a rating to the combination. And that's where the magic comes in. *We do not want an intellectualized response. We want an intuitive or gut feeling, this "sense", this "immediacy".*

Now that we have the vignettes, and we know how each vignette scores, it is time to "trace" the rating to the components or elements in the vignette. Regression analysis computes what each of our 20 separate ideas or "elements" about the High End contributes to a person's perception of the *total* "High End". We are going to perform (or rather the computer will perform) 373 separate regressions, one regression for each respondent. Even if a person cannot articulate what drives his or her perception, the regression analysis will show how much each of our 20 elements "brings to the party". It's like Sherlock Holmes first identifying the pieces of a mystery by observing and analyzing a set of seemingly random scenes and objects, and afterwards solving the mystery, revealing the story, telling us with what's really going on. RDE statistical modeling virtually guarantees to discover what works and what does not.

What the Numbers Mean

The numbers you will see from the analysis fall into two types. Both emerge automatically from the regression analysis, and are done using standard statistical methods. The first group comprises only one number, the additive constant or the baseline. The second group comprises an array of 20 numbers, one for each of our 20 elements. These second numbers are the coefficients, or the impact values, one for each element.

The Baseline (additive constant). The baseline is the propensity to judge the vignette as High End in the absence of elements. Of course, all vignettes comprise elements. Nonetheless, it's possible to estimate this baseline statistically, to get a sense of what would be the likely rating of "High End" in the absence of elements.

Let's illustrate the meaning of the additive constant by means of an analogy. In show-business terms, the baseline is like the *general mood of the audience*. Sometimes the audience is very open and receptive to jokes a speaker uses. A good gag makes people laugh hysterically, whereas a modest gag might elicit a giggle or a smile. With this receptive audience, even a bad joke is most likely to be forgiven. Contrast this receptive and happy mood with the hostile or negative audience where no one is prepared to laugh. The general mood is dour. The jokes can be equally good, but with a pretty cold audience to start with, that is, with a much lower baseline, they could do only that much. An experienced comic "reads" the audience. If we are talking about "propensity to laugh", then the baseline is high for the first, receptive audience. In contrast, the baseline is low for the second, non-receptive audience.

In our pilot project, we discovered through the regression analysis that the baseline is +30. What does that +30 mean? What does this number tell us, and what does it mean for business?

This baseline of +30 (or 30 percent) means that *about three out of ten participants are predisposed to qualify a proposition, product or service, as high-end, even when no elements are shown.* Speaking a bit less technically, the baseline (+30) is the expected proportion of test participants who would call the vignette "High End" without any elements. It is a sense of their willingness or predisposition to see the High End in a proposition, just by knowing that the study topic involves the High End. You might call this a readiness factor. We're going to see this additive constant of around 30 repeat again and again. There's something here; it's as if one out of three or four people is predisposed to call something High End, no matter what.

Let's now move to the second part of the regression analysis. We find here a set of impact numbers, one impact number for each of the 20 elements. We see these laid out pictorially as bars in Figure 4.4. *The impact number shows the contribution of the particular element to the High End.* Regression analysis pulls out these individual impacts. The impact number for a specific element shows the additional percentage of participants who would call the proposition "High End" when that particular element appears in the vignette or concept. The way that we set up the RDE study makes this analysis very simple to do by regression modeling.

The actual innards of the method, how regression modeling works, are not of interest here. You can read about them in statistics texts, or user manuals for off-the-shelf computer programs. What you should know, however, is that efforts in setting up the RDE study are geared towards making sure that the regression analysis will work correctly and that we do the analysis on a person-by-person basis.

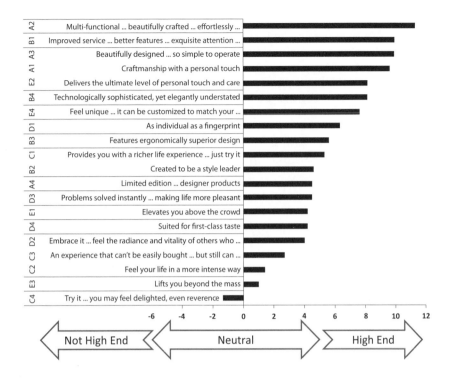

Figure 4.4   **Impact value (performance) of elements in the US pilot project, for the total panel. Each element has the individual ability to push a vignette towards being perceived as High End (high positive numbers) or being perceived as *not* High End (negative numbers)**

The impact value (that is, the regression coefficient) can be positive or negative. The big story is in these impact values, so it's important to pay attention to them. Positive impact increases the proportion of the people who would consider a proposition with this idea to be premium. Big numbers mean that the element is a major driver towards premium. Negative impact means that the element *actually decreases* the proportion of participants calling the vignette High End. Both the baseline and the impact of the individual elements are important.

Now that we have the numbers, what is the story that we can glean from these numbers? It is easy to get numbers from experiments, and very easy from an RDE study. But numbers can go just so far, and no more. What is the story that nature wants to tell? And most important, why are we doing an "experiment" in the midst of the High End, where taste, art and aspiration should run free?

RDE is about understanding nature, digging up the rules, and doing something for business with that knowledge. These rules come out from the numbers, but they are not the numbers. They are what might be behind the numbers. Once we have the story, the big picture suddenly becomes quite clear.

Let us now look for the business story, make the synthesis that we need to and find out what is happening. What works for the High End? What does not work? What should you be thinking about to launch your High End product, your service? What is the story of the High End as we see it unfold in Figure 4.5? Keep in mind the twins: knowledge and application.

We begin with the thermometer scale on the bottom of the figure. For many RDE projects spanning the range from not-for-profit-giving, to insurance, to magazines, to yogurts, and all things in between, we discovered from experience that impacts with values of +6 and above correlate with positive responses by the customer market. Without going into the statistical analysis, the heart of the matter is that when the impact values go around +6 and higher, things begin to happen when consumers are involved. And, even better things happen with the higher impact values of +10. It makes sense. Our mix and match strategy throws lots of information at the consumer participant. Anything that does well in this "torture test of ideas" stands out from the competitors, from the noise; it gets noticed, and gets noticed positively. In Figure 4.5, you see a bunch of good ideas about the High End, ideas that work for you.

Now for some not so good stuff. Not every idea drives the perception of High End, however. There was one element that scored mildly negatively (although in the general neutral area) *Try is … you may feel delight, even reverence.* Except for this one element, which the consumers did not associate with High End, the other ideas were slightly positive to strongly positive.

You might think we are just being lucky here, that people are just ready to ascribe High End ideas to anything. Not really. The reason is homework. The reason for the success had a lot to do with serious thinking. The more you think about what might work, the more deeply you understand your topic. This holds true for ideas that will get you into the High End.

We just did not throw in elements from guesswork. Rather, when we prepared for this pilot test, we read a lot about the High End, got quotes, dissected what experts and consumers, as well as newspapers and magazines, were saying, and proceeded from there. We shamelessly absorbed the wisdom of others as we prepared for the project! Yet even so, we really did not know what to expect when we put these vignettes in front of consumers. Finally, when it comes to interpretation, remember that the impact numbers reveal the customer's mind, meaning new business opportunities.

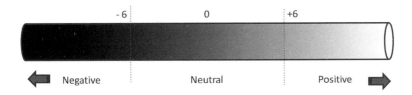

Figure 4.5   How to interpret what the RDE impact means for a specific element

So – What is the High End Going to be about in a Year or Two?

For the interview on the computer, each of the 373 participants evaluated a different, unique set of combinations, similar to the vignette we saw in Figure 4.3. Each vignette comprises a set of phrases that *could describe* aspects of the High End. We realize that people may not be able to describe the future, but they have a "sense", a feeling of "what belongs, what doesn't belong". With this type of knowledge, you can now jump-start your efforts, taking advantage of what the future just might be.

Without asking the respondent to define the High End, in his or her mind, we simply presented the combination and recorded the rating. The analysis tells us the proportion of people who would say each element is the High End if the element were put into the vignette. That is, we can get into the "mind" of the individual respondent, even without requiring the respondent to define the High End. We will "discover" the High End from the customer mind by seeing how the respondent evaluates the different combinations. Knowing this, it's possible now to plan one's new offerings.

What is the "story" lurking inside these data. While we're discovering the story together, you might also want to look at Appendix (Table A1), where we list the impact numbers for the total panel, and for some key groups.

To put matters into perspective, let's first review. We want to discover which specific elements, if any, increase the perception of High End. Think about this for a moment. In essence, we want to discover how to "engineer" the perception of something (artifact, service) as being part of the High End. We are so accustomed to looking at "what is" that often we forget that business is better off when it knows the future, the "what could be". The interpretation is simple – high positive impacts suggest that the element adds to the perception of High End, whereas negative impacts (-6 and below) would indicate that the ideas detract from the perception of High End.

When we do these RDE tests, we are really looking for what works. The worst possible result would be that, no matter how one "cuts the data", all the elements hover around zero. That horrific news would mean that *nothing* we looked at drives the perception of High End. We have to go back to the drawing board. Although this terrible news is not the case here, what if it were? What if all the elements were to hover around zero? No element would drive the perception of High End any more than any other element. The practical next step is to try again, with other elements, and keep doing this until either we convince ourselves that nothing can drive the perception of the High End (meaning we're out of luck), or that we find some vein of ideas, of elements where the High End pokes through (a much happier outcome).

Fortunately, such flat results generally do not happen. Most RDE projects end up with enough different directions that something lights the way. It is not random, however, since the RDE set-up is almost a "torture test" for ideas. Whatever scores well in an RDE project, that is, has a high impact, does so because it works against many different backgrounds, and in competition with many different elements. Our job is simply to discover them, hopefully earlier rather than later.

Usually there are strong performing elements and there are weak performing elements. In our pilot test, there are some elements that truly signal the High End, and other elements that are not particularly related to the High End (Appendix, Table A1). We have the data here for the total panel, for the males and the females, and for the four mindsets that we were able to isolate.

What Really Works?

Let's cut right to the chase, and go to the results. The "devil" is always in the detail, which also happens to contain some interesting discoveries as well.

Let's revisit the data. While you are reading, glance from time to time at Figure 4.4. You may also want to look at the full set of data in Table A1 (Appendix). We can only touch on the highlights here. As you get increasingly involved with the High End, and as your needs become clearer, detailed tables stop being a nuisance space-holder, and become the box holding some treasures.

When you look at what elements drive the High End do not worry about the particular silo. The silo is just a bookkeeping system, to ensure that incompatible elements do not appear together. The analysis treats all 20 elements as equal and independent. The real information about the High End is to be found in the particular element, and more specifically in the meaning of that element. Language, ideas, and the "what" that stands behind them, are what is important, and what should occupy you. Look for the strongest performing elements. Then, try to extract the story underneath the data. That's the real understanding, and the true contribution of RDE. You build up from elements, seeing the big picture from the specifics of the smaller pictures.

Let's move forward to the meat of the RDE exercise. Each of our elements appeared three times against different backgrounds, for each of the 373 respondents. That means each element appeared more than 1,000 times in the study. (The exact number is 373 × 3 = 1119.) Out of this competition, what elements scored well and floated to the top? Whatever wins should be good, since RDE is a true torture test for ideas.

The results are fairly clear. Here is your first key. The four elements listed below are the ones which increase what consumers think the High End will be in the near future. Keep in mind that the odds of such strong performance occurring are virtually 0 if the 20 elements really don't drive the perception of the High End and what we see is the result of randomness.

These four elements score well, and make sense. In the multi-element duel they stand out in an absolute sense. Each element has an impact of 10 or higher, meaning that when the element appears in the vignette an additional 10 percent (11 percent for the element A2) of the participants feel that the vignette describes the High End of the near future:

A2 Multi-functional ... beautifully crafted ... effortlessly simple to use   (+11)

A3 Beautifully designed ... so simple to operate   (+10)

B1 Improved service ... better features ... exquisite attention to details   (+10)

A1 Craftsmanship with a personal touch   (+10)

Stand back now, take stock of what just happened, and think about business. We are accustomed to "science" delivering answers about the way the world and people work. Just look at the numbers. The impact values show which specific elements drive the perception of the High End, and which elements "go along for the ride". But what's the story? That's your task for right now. If you had to tell someone what's happening, what are you learning, then what precisely would you say from the four elements which score well?

RDE Mindsets

People are not created the same, even if they share the same socio-demographics. Two people living in the same apartment house, having similar incomes, similar family structures, similar jobs, might have radically different tastes. Just look at casinos. Gambling casinos do a lot of data-mining, trying to relate the characteristics of a person to the propensity to gamble, which in turn means targeting the person. The best predictor of gambling at a casino is, as you might expect, previous gambling at a casino.

But what about mindsets? Whether we want to promote a casino, or promote High End products, how do we identify these mindsets, these people who are likely to buy from us? How do our RDE data help?

To discover like-minded segments, we are going to "lump together" people who show similar patterns of what they think drives the High End. We will put them in clusters or segments.

Each individual generated for us 20 such impact values. Since our statistical analysis created a pattern of 20 impacts for each person, it is fairly easy to cluster together individuals based on the patterns. Keep in mind that this clustering exercise does not require us to ponder over the data, wondering what the story is. The clustering procedure is a statistical one, run "purely by the numbers". The RDE tool does this automatically.

Of course, we are not totally free. We still owe it to ourselves to name these clusters or segments, to give them some interpretive meaning. We cannot do this naming unless we look at the different segmentation results. At the start of our investigation into the High End we didn't know whether there were two segments, three, four, or even five segments. So, we split the 373 respondents into 2 groups, then 3 groups, then 4 groups, then 5 groups. For each split, we tried to discover whether the splits made sense or told a story. We looked through the different results and sorted the element impacts from highest to lowest. We looked for that clustering solution telling the story that made a lot of sense.

In this project, we found that the four segments solution made the most sense (Figure 4.6), but only after we tried create a coherent story using only two segments, which didn't quite work. We then tried three segments. The story still did not gel. Finally, when we got to four segments, the division made intuitive sense. There was a story to be told. (One rule of thumb here is to aim for the fewest number of segments that allow for the "mother" test – can you explain it to your mother, so she understands it clearly)?

The "trick" to finding the story is simply to sort the elements by the impact scores. Look at what elements do well in a single segment. Then, try to "tell the story". Is there a story to be told? In fact, when it comes to four segments, are there four stories to be told? The answer is yes. Of course some elements score well across all segments – and didn't give us the material for a story. There were other unique elements that won in a specific segment, but lost in the others. These winning and losing elements in a single segment "tell their story simply and convincingly". You can see the impact values for each element, for each segment in Table A1 (Appendix), which was the basis for our interpretation of the segments.

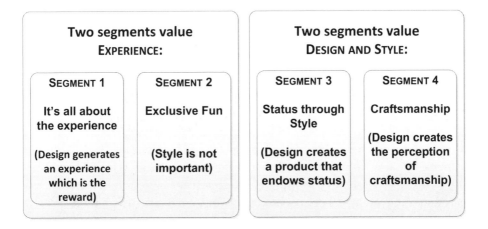

Figure 4.6   Four segments for the US RDE

US PILOT SEGMENT 1 "IT'S ALL ABOUT THE EXPERIENCE"

To convince these people that you have a High End opportunity or product, talk to them about the "experience". That is going to land them, convince them you are really talking about the heart of the future High End. For example, *"Provides you with a richer life experience … just try it"* drives up the perception of High-End by +14 points. Segment 1 also responds positively to statements about design and, to a lesser degree, to statements about styling. At the same time, don't talk to Segment 1 about exclusivity. To Segment 1, exclusivity is not associated with High End.

> Business application – Segment 1 values the "design" as a marker of the High End. But … for them design in merely a step to personal experience. It's not about status. It's about design. That's important to remember. Design for design, not design for status or something else.

US PILOT SEGMENT 2 "EXCLUSIVE FUN"

These people want exclusivity (+10 to +14) and like to hear about the High End proposition in emotional terms (suited for first-class taste, +8). Segment 2 also wants to hear about "Experience" (from +6 to +14 points) but does not want to hear messages about style. To get to Segment 2, focus on exclusivity and experience.

> Business application – For Segment 2, the sense of exclusivity and experience is a marker of the High End. Style is not important at all for Segment 2. And design – at the end of the day design is just a vehicle to boast about exclusivity.

SEGMENT 3 "STATUS THROUGH STYLE"

They appreciate style above all (from +12 to +17 points) as well as design, although to a much lesser extent. Exclusivity drives High End (+5 to +13). At the same time, Segment 3 is indifferent to statements about the experience and emotions. To convince these people of your offering, talk design to them.

> Business application – Segment 3 perceives stylish design as a way to achieve status. Status. There is nothing emotional about that, nor does Segment 3 search for an "experience". What a difference from Segment 1!

SEGMENT 4 "CRAFTSMANSHIP"

They strongly respond to design and style, a sense of craftsmanship. All design statements drive perception of High End, by 12–19 points! Segment 4 likes style (+6 to + 13) and responds to emotion (but *not* experience) statements as a driver of the High End. Segment 4 is indifferent to messages about experience. Emphasize the notion of craftsmanship.

> Business application – Segment 4 values and enjoys craftsmanship through design and style. Segment 4 does not mind feeling a bit exclusive and responds somewhat emotionally, but this is all secondary.

So there you have it – four different groups of minds. Not exact opposites, but rather people with clearly different hot buttons. And, when you look at who these people are, you find that on average they're similar to each other – from the outside, that is. But RDE suggests different ways that their heads work. And, if you know the mindset of a person you meet, you're likely to know what to say, and what to avoid.

Grabbing the "Trade's" Ear

One of the interesting things about a competitive world is the need to crystallize ideas, so that they can be "pitched" in a very limited amount of time. This is the so-called "elevator pitch". If we were pitching a company about the opportunities, what could we say regarding what we have just learned? Certainly, we could not go through the entire RDE process – there is just not enough time, nor interest. But imagine the reaction of the manufacturer or the store if we could just tell them "how the world of High End" breaks out in the United States. And so to the one slide in Figure 4.7. With this slide you may intrigue the manufacturer (Whom do you want to appeal to?), inspire the merchant (Who is this next customer coming in? What should you say?), and challenge the customer (Where, exactly, do YOU fit in this set group of four segments?).

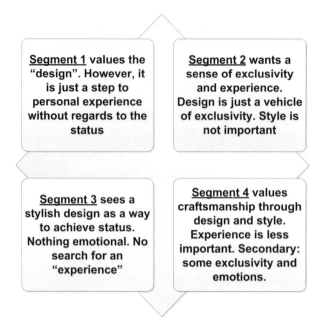

Figure 4.7   The description of the four segments from the US pilot
              project

Do Not Just Describe – *Create*

Learning without application is OK, but business demands sales, results, and profits. Keeping that in mind, how do we go from learning to creating? Now that we have our segments more or less clearly defined, do we make something, and then announce it? What are the practical next steps?

We learned three lessons from our pilot study:

1.   Saying "It's High End" does not make it High End. Content matters.

2.   Gender matters, not so much for mindsets as for the nature of the specific product. In this pilot project, men and women have the same mindset when it comes to the High End. Except for the obviously gender-specific product or service, do not worry about separate High End propositions for men and women.

3.   Minds make a difference. Make or say the right thing and the customer comes to you. Make or say the wrong thing, and the customer runs away. Pay lots of attention to the segments. What one segment likes, another dislikes. The segments really differ from each other.

Even though we know that the segments differ from each other, it is always a good idea to begin at the average. Of course, the average comes from many different groups of people with varying, often opposing mindsets. It is a good idea to "cut out teeth" on the big picture. A lot of critics will be happy because we've begun with the big opportunity first. Look at the best, the highest-rated ideas from each silo. These are the gold, with high potential to get your idea *perceived* as High End. Whatever it is, weave these ideas into it:

A2	Multi-functional ... beautifully crafted ... effortlessly simple to use
B1	Improved service ... better features ... exquisite attention to details
C1	Provides you with a richer life experience ... just try it
D1	As individual as a fingerprint
E2	Delivers the ultimate level of personal touch and care

Now for the mathematics. We begin with an additive constant, which tells us is the percentage of people who would call the proposition "High End", even without messages. So, this is the predisposition to call something High End. Each element then delivers its own individual "payload", that is, the ability to drive the perception of High End. The sum of the impacts of these elements along with the baseline tells you the approximate percentage of people who would consider a proposition to be a High End when they see the particular combination or vignette.

You absolutely want to get the sum to be as high as possible, using as few elements as you possibly can. The only other requirement is that the elements "fit together" or at least they should not contradict each other. That is a judgment call. The bottom-line here is that you learn the "rules", and you can construct your own ideas.

Starting with the baseline, we know from the RDE data that approximately 30 percent of our participants are predisposed to consider a proposition as a High End. Now it is time for the additional elements to do their work, to add to the perception of High End. Look for positive numbers; these are the elements that drive the High End perception you want. Figure 4.8 shows these contributions laid out in the form of bar graphs. The actual numbers are in Appendix (Table A1). One thing is important here – you may begin the process by looking at the group, but as you become more experienced, you will undoubtedly work with tables. With experience, you end up seeing a lot of the story in the table, such as how all the elements contribute.

By taking at most one element from each silo (the highest ranked one), you will end up with a proposition whose sum is 70. This means that 70 percent of the participants would rate the proposition as High End if they were to see the vignette whose individual impacts appear in the left part of Figure 4.8. Again, look closely at the elements to make sure that they work with each other.

This sum of 70 means that 70 out of 100 Americans would perceive this proposition as High End. This value of 70 is considerably more than the baseline or general predisposition, which had a value of 30. The sum is more than double.

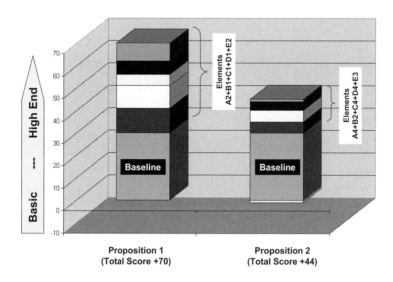

Figure 4.8   **Creating two different High End propositions, and estimating how well they will "perform" when rated as being "future High End" in the US market**

Why did this happen? How did we go from skepticism to a High End proposition? Quite simply, we took the basic predisposition to call a proposition High End (from the baseline), and cherry-picked the strong elements that give the proposition the feeling of High End. We (and so can you) select ideas that create a new, High End proposition. We know what to say. When we know what we are doing, we can select the "right features" that support the vignette. We need something that can be described as "craftsman type work", which gives a "richer experience" that has fine "details", that is certainly "individual and personalized". The bottom line – with whatever you are creating, choose what can support these claims, because then you will have a strong, High End offering.

We have just stacked the deck in our favor by using the best ideas. Now let's look at what happens when you're a little less focused and you happen to choose "bad" (low-scoring negative impacts) ideas from the same table. You might create a vignette with a much lower sum, that is, a much lower perception of the proposition as being High End compared to what we just optimized. Suppose a proposition were to contain the following messages:

A4	Limited edition ... designer products
B2	Created to be a style leader
C4	Try it ... you may feel delight, even reverence
D4	Suited for first-class taste
E3	Lifts you beyond the mass

The total number of people who would say that this idea describes a High End product drops from the very satisfying 70 above to a lower, less satisfying 44 (Figure 4.8). This means that 44 out of 100 participants would perceive this proposition as High End – a sizable increase from the baseline (general predisposition) of 30, although substantially lower than 70 percent in the previous example. Unless we knew ahead of time that these would be the "lower performers", we might have chosen this vignette instead of the best performer. No one really knows the difference ahead of time – meaning that the empirical data are important in the High End as an aid to judgment.

From the practical point of view, you do not want to emphasize those messages, which score poorly. They may sound good – but our respondents did not feel that these were phrases that could describe the High End. The US market pilot study had only one element with a strong negative impact. Most of the elements "drove" the High End. In other RDE projects with the High End and other topics, we often are confronted with many more elements having negative impacts. Choosing these poor performers could actually reduce the perception below baseline! That is, we would mess up even before we began, just by choosing the wrong ideas, the wrong messages.

Summing Up

Five crucial lessons should help you create, advertise, and merchandise a product or a service as being a real High End offering:

1.   Experiment, experiment, experiment. It is fun. Rule Developing Experimentation (RDE) identifies the "algebra of High End", and supports this experiment with actionable statistics.

2.   You *can* know the future, at least a little better, from your experiments. Science, even simple applied science, can help you anticipate tomorrow's High End "types of customers".

3.   Don't be shy about trying things out. Our "out of the box" pilot US experiment showed how RDE works in the concrete practice of everyday business analysis. Our experts whom we interviewed in this book knew the High End quite well, but knew it from the perspective of business, not from the perspective of the buyer. The RDE pilot study taught us a lot about what works and what does not. And most interestingly, and important for business, we learned quite clearly that the world of consumers is not a monolith, but a group of overlapping yet distinct realms governed by different mindsets.

4.   Combine ideas for new products, new services, new propositions. New combinations of ideas could be just the thing you're looking for. The result should be a vignette that drives home the perception of High End for the particular group we want to create for, or sell to.

5. There is nothing opaque behind numbers. Think about them as building blocks in one's perception of the High End. High positive numbers add to the perception. Negative numbers detract from the perception. The starting point is the general predisposition to the idea of high-end proposition (baseline) on top of which you build the total offering.

PART 2

"Practical DNA": The Five Must Haves (Rules) of the High End

High end is about a choice, a choice that is however attainable and ultimately within reach. From this viewpoint in a post-political world ... people want to find ways to differentiate and express their own personalities. High End meets the challenge to support lifestyle choices by enabling diversity in consumption.

Andrea Ragnetti, former CEO,
Philips Consumer Lifestyle, Amsterdam

The High End is all about improving the quality of life. Whether improvement comes from luxury products, wonderful experiences, or uplifting actions, the High End of the twenty-first century is all about something "better" than what has come before.

For business, the question is how to get that "better?" What are the rules of the world of High End? Is it about taking a basic product or service and bumping up its functionality and appearance, so that in the end the buyer is offered a better performing yet "plain vanilla" upgrade? It might work better, but is still starved of emotional bond with customers and fails to excite their aspirations. This aseptic notion of functional High End plainly contradicts the essence of "intangible values" we described earlier. Clearly, this is not what real High End is about. Plain upgrades simply have no magic – nothing to move the heart, nothing to excite the mind.

Moving to today's (and soon tomorrow's) High End demands meaningful improvements, often intangible, but desirable to consumers. In the world where rules constantly change at the speed of Twitter, we must understand the nature of this "intangible value", its essence, and how it works.

The domain of the old luxury defines value with a simple formula, which does not include price, can be represented as in Figure Part 2.1

Figure Part 2.1 Value in the domain of old luxury

In the new world of the High End, the customer target is not the rich but the aspiring. Our customer *is* price sensitive. Price plays a very delicate balancing act between seduction and repulsion. It is a seesaw. Make the price too low and you throw away the charisma and, of course, the margins. Raise the price so the product becomes expensive, and you may well drive your prospect out of your showroom (Figure Part 2.2).

Figure Part 2.2 Value as Price and Intangible Value

So what do you do? What are the rules to this new game? You want the money – but what are the right steps to follow? What is the knowledge you need? In the next five chapters, we investigate dimensions of the intangible world with an eye to using them to create the High End.

Let's start with the less than happy news. The expression for intangible value in the world of the High End is considerably more involved (Figure Part 2.3).

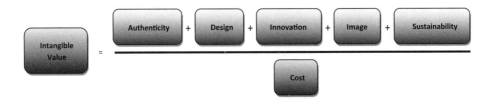

Figure Part 2.3   Value as Price as High End equation

There is a lot to learn here. In the next chapters, we will gradually bring intangible value to life for business, looking at the experience and stories of others, those who succeeded in the High End. In the end we will have captured the essence of the High End in a concise number of simple *must haves*, or rules that could be used, along with RDE, to craft specific propositions. In other words, we'll see how to do it.

Stories from the world of business become more actionable when you can do something in order to make these stories come alive in new applications. And, of course, the premise of this entire book is that knowledge of the mind will help you succeed with customers who will buy into and buy from the High End.

So let's go from theory and demonstration to a new reality provided by knowledge. Harnessing the power of RDE, we conducted a unique worldwide survey involving more than 1,800 qualified High End respondents. Following the notion of mindsets, we divided our respondents into groups, or "types of customers", with different mindset for their *must haves*. RDE looked for general rules about the High End that may work around the world. In a sense, our RDE exercise around the world "sequenced the genome of the High End mind".

Conducted in the USA, the UK, China and Italy, and exploring the five general dimensions of the High End, we uncovered two mindsets of consumers for each dimension. These consumers, as you will see, exist around the world. And the mindsets differ from each other in what turns them on, even though we deal with one dimension at a time.

The bottom line here – the practical importance for business is enormous. RDE's discovery converts the knowledge-base to targeted, highly acceptable offerings to the consumer. Each rule about mindsets in a specific High End dimension gives us a hint about what to do/offer/say for a specific customer, based upon knowing that customer's mind. To cap it off, we created tools using that knowledge, allowing you to create specific offerings for a mindset, and then to discover those mindsets in the customer population.

The Global RDE Survey of High End – Defining Consumer Mindsets

The previous chapter taught us that RDE reveals and measures the dimensions of the High End. That was a preliminary study, just to get an introduction to the High End, to see what might work. For this larger multi-cultural project, we extended our focus to different countries, different values, and different cultures. We selected four different countries to explore – China, Italy, the UK and the USA. We chose a solid, long-term partner for our studies, Survey Sampling, Inc. (SSI). It always helps to work with the best, with people who know the pitfalls, allowing us to spend our time on the knowledge, not on the "hygiene" of the study.

A key issue in research is who does one interview, and why specifically that group and not others. The question sounds simple enough – *who is the target for the High End*? *Who* would be the most likely customer for the High End, and how does the customer's mind work? Should we search for all prospects who were not uber-rich? Was there a lower band, below which one should not interview, even if these people would occasionally buy what we consider to be a High End?

The definitions of middle class were slightly relaxed to ensure that we would obtain opinions from the wide range of High End product buyers, both current and future. We decided not to be overly narrow, but to look at today's High End customer, and the most likely tomorrow High End customer as well. Based on the input from various industry insiders and with the guidance of SSI, we surveyed only the participants in the following income brackets, because they would be our most likely High End customers today and in the near future:

US: $75,000–$200,000

UK: £40,000–£110,000

Italy: €40,000–€100,000

China: RMB 100,000–RMB 400,000

Geography became another issue to deal with. Where should our customer respondents live? We limited the participants to the urban and suburban areas because many of the future directions for the High End are most likely to emerge from the heart of vibrant urban cultures.

Finally, we had to choose whether to particularize the element list to each country. Some of our advisers suggested that Chinese customers would not understand some of the concepts that UK and US customers would understand. The opposite point of view, which we later adopted, was to use precisely the same elements across the countries translated for the local language. This would give us 100 percent comparability.

The foregoing were the hard questions to deal with – not questions of science or knowledge, but issues and opinions about practice. They are always the most difficult, and the heat that they generate often is far greater than the light that is provided.

Rules of Thumb to Interpret High End Impacts

To help making more sense out of the results, we expand the simple guidelines introduced in previous chapters. Here are these rules of thumb of interpretation of the impact values:

Impact > +15 means an exceptionally strong push by the element towards High End. This is a "keeper", for advertising and brand building. The element really works.

Impacts +11 to +15 mean a very strong push by the element towards High End.

Impacts of +6 to +10 mean a significant but not very strong push.

Impacts from –6 to +6 are close to 0 meaning that the element probably doesn't do much.

Negative impacts lower than –6 mean that the element pushes away from the High End. You probably don't want to use the element, unless you must for some legal or strategic reason. It's not buying you anything else.

Although the data might sometimes look intimidating and even boring, do not succumb to these feelings. We show the data in graphical form in the body of the text, and put the numerical data into the appendices. As you become increasingly familiar with the results, we feel that you will probably turn to the appendices more often, because that is where the granular information lives, and where you see precisely what you ought to say, and how the element will perform.

Making the RDE Example Come Alive: Stories and Science

The five rules with the corresponding dimensions of the High End are:

1. It's all about the "beef" (dimension: authenticity and value)

2. It's all about the "experience" (dimension: design and experience)

3. It's all about creating the "new" (dimension: innovation and leadership)

4. It's all about "fame" (dimension: image-making and people-reaching)

5. It's all about higher values (dimension: sustainability and simplicity).

In describing each of the rules with its matching dimension, we follow a simple structure comprising three distinctive parts:

Snapshots: We begin with *snapshots* demonstrating what happens when business uses High End rule, and when business manages to ignore it.

Stories: Then we move to the *stories* that deepen the meaning of the rule. The stories put more flesh on the structure, and add the human element.

Consumer Mind Science: We finish by looking at the science behind the rule, taking our lead from the particular RDE survey devoted to that particular rule. We look at what happens in general, by country, and then by mindset. You can use the information in your business right from the RDE exercise.

Sections: It's hard to work with rules in general. We have to break those rules into simpler components. For each survey, that is, for each rule, we look at four aspects, or factors. In that way, you can better understand how the High End works. So our High End Factors are four questions, capturing the essence of the stories in each chapter. They are the synthesis of what we learnt from the concrete world of business, and they became the starting point of RDE experimentation. In short, the High End Factors of each rule connect the worlds of business stories and consumer preferences.

5

Rule 1: It is All About the "Beef" (Dimension: Authenticity and Value)

The company of the future should guard and nurture the core "idea" that represents its intrinsic value to people, and those "concepts" that translate such idea into concrete propositions. All the rest should be simply outsourced to the best makers and consultants in the world. In India, Bharti, a mobile communication company, outsourced everything, even its core technology, maintaining the control on the customer relationship that represents their real value proposition. We are rapidly moving towards, or better said we already are, in a global economy where the "idea" is all that matters, and all the rest is simply outsourced.

Rattan Chadha, Entrepreneur and Founder of Mexx,
The Netherlands

"Beef ..."

Where would you rather shop for food – supermarket or a farmer's market? Whole Foods has merged the two practices, boosting its own market value by 1,500 percent, clearly proving the value of the authentic experience in the farmer's market. Think about that experience then next time you go into a supermarket with its "packaged feel". Although prices are premium at Whole Foods, price resistance has been low due to the added value that the brand culture extends to its customers. Even in times of economic downturn there are customers who want premium, who want the High End in food.

"... No Beef"

Authenticity in the High End, like authenticity in luxury, is becoming increasingly important, perhaps because our attention is often focused on the contrasting opposite, counterfeiting. Authenticity gives people that extra reinforcement, that additional bit of a true soul. *For that alone it's worth the premium price.*

It is tempting to move beyond authenticity, to increase sales and profits. Kate Spade, a US High End brand which eventually fell into the "replica trap", started out in a very boutique, organic manner. Customers who bought Kate Spade products felt as if they were "let in" on a well-kept secret. Nevertheless, once that secret got out, the company flooded the market trying to meet the demand, over-exposing the brand. Kate Spade was knocked off quickly. As a result, their bags lost appeal. So, counterfeiting is not a plague of luxury industry only – it happens at the High End as well. To stay "authentic", High End brands must watch out for any excess in distribution – and for copycat knock-offs as well.

Authenticity and Value

The notion of "authentic value" in the High End is more complex than it is for luxury, perhaps because of the ambiguity of "authentic value". *Unlike luxury, provenance is simply not a prerequisite for the High End.* With the price that might be high yet within reach, the value equation depends on a mix of emotional and functional benefits. Perceived exclusivity is a definite player, although the democratic High End allows everybody "in" who can pay.

What do you do now, when the old guard, provenance and "real" exclusivity, are NOT any longer the strategic principles that govern tomorrow's High End? There is one common feature for High End propositions – high quality. *Quality – demonstrably superior quality, quality that broadcasts itself, quality associated with emotional authenticity and functional value – that is the soul of High End.* It is all about its authentic nature, and genuine value that people get out of it. Simply called "the beef", that is, the "real thing" in the words of the late and beloved Clara Peller, actress in a Wendy's Restaurant commercial.

Consistency, Location and Origin

Where you came from makes who you are. This is a truism for luxury. For High End, a more relevant definition is: The ones who "designed" you (your "parents") define you more than your actual place of birth. Origin is an important driver to get into the High End. In our increasingly flat world of outsourcing, things are not made any more in the land where the brand association might suggest. Advertisement promotes a product as designed in Italy, engineered in Germany, made with French elegance. Yet, the small-print label brings you to another part of the world – manufactured in Malaysia, assembled in China, woven in Pakistan.

Apple skillfully exploits the "flat world" opportunities. Apple products are *"designed by Apple in California"* and then *"Made in … wherever"*. Extrapolating Apple's successful experience in democratizing luxury, the future region of production for High End is probably China and other emerging economies. Therefore, look to the near future when *designed in* or *design(ed) by* become the key phrase for the High End, overshadowing the possible downside of manufacturing in another country. *Designed in* or *by* will be the key phrase to communicate quality for the High End.

The High End should connect the premium nature of the item with its origin, ideally with a believable story which convinces, if not necessarily one which entrances. The story is not the one that luxury has, where the consumer "knows" the truth, but rather a plausible one that uses some of the accepted strengths of the place of origin. It is even possible to turn outsourcing into a distinguishing asset and value while doing so in a completely ethical way. Lacoste, for example, chose Peru as the place for inexpensive manufacturing. Peru itself sounded more exotic and pristine than did other locations, making the same basic items appear more special. In turn, such creative messaging of the source helped to preserve and raise price points, recapture distribution, and thus rebuild the brand from its slump.

Outsourcing may actually increase the appeal of a High End product, if at the same time the cachet of the country of production is on the rise. For instance, along with other emerging Asian economies, China could find an additional opportunity. China could well become a powerhouse in the outsourcing model. In the near future, *Made in China* could express a special technical competence, or perhaps even a degree of excellence, from a country that is seen to be waking up. Design contributes to such renaissance. We will talk more about Design and the High End later on.

FIAT 500: Italy's Most Beloved Car Returns

Our next story takes us to the heart of automotive design, Italy, and to the outsourcing havens of Eastern Europe. FIAT is the Italian automotive company which recaptured its position and image thanks to the almost-impossible turnaround driven by its CEO, Canadian-born Sergio Marchionne. FIAT is a classic example of moving from bankruptcy to corporate resurrection, capitalizing on its history and authenticity.

A good example of how to reach the High End comes from the FIAT 500. In a sense, this one car did for Italy what Ford T did for the USA. It provided an automotive access for post-World War Two Italians, who purchased it en masse. To most Italians just two generations ago, FIAT represented a move from riding a Vespa scooter to owning a four-wheel family mobility with a roof. It seems to be a long shot for High End aspirations. However, the newly re-launched FIAT 500 demonstrates the fundamentals of the High End:

- it is priced right to gain healthy margins while being within reach, with a feeling of high value, both emotional and functional;

- it builds a very strong emotional connection with people because of its authentic heritage and its meaning in Italian history;

- it is an "authentic" Italian design vision, although the cars are assembled outside Italy. The car's parts are largely shared with other models such as FIAT Panda and the Ford Ka, in order to achieve the necessary savings.

FIAT provides high quality products with an aspirational value to customers. The company has made it a policy to "strut its stuff" in emerging markets with big potential – Brazil (where the portfolio is increasingly expanding to include European models), India, Turkey and Russia. And there is an even stronger game plan. FIAT's strategy goes beyond competing in the low margins "basic car for everybody" category. An example of realization of this strategy is FIAT Linea. While other makers import into Western Europe their low cost basic products, FIAT designed and delivered an Italian high-quality product, successfully sold in Eastern Europe, Turkey, China and beyond.

FIAT has not tried to project the feel of luxury or exclusivity. It positioned itself as accessible rather than exclusive, as historically meaningful and individually touching rather than giving a feel of "class". There is a story behind that. The world of FIAT 500 is not luxury at all. The car is saying "Here I am … you can acquire me". Quite a different feeling from what Rolls Royce, Bentley or Ferrari, communicate to their buyers. FIAT weaves a dream reachable by means of a transaction. Most of all, this is a proposition which feels "authentically Italian" to almost everybody.

At the end of the day, there's a lesson to be learned. People associate a great deal of intangible High End value to such perception. The corporate decision to re-launch the FIAT brand by going back to its core of making beautiful looking small and mid-size Italian cars was supported by the new corporate-wide design center. The aesthetic premium of Italian design was to be "baked in" to the product.

The emotional value of a great story could be a great help. Capitalizing on the lifestyle and the nostalgia of Italians for the age of their *dolce vita*, the brand new leading High End car FIAT 500 is manufactured in Poland, not in Italy. As there is no expectation that the FIAT is hand assembled as a Rolls Royce, there is no need for the demonstrable purity in the product story, which would just cut the margins.

Our lesson from FIAT is that authenticity is one of the key ingredients for the High End, and when properly taken advantage of, can bring a popular, low-cost product into a higher level. Here is the crux of the problem that the High End marketer must face – combining vernacular design with outsourced production, within the reasonable boundaries of perceived authenticity.

Affordable Price, Collector Value

> *Residual value is one option that can enrich the High End artifact or the proposition. Every artifact potentially can become an object with residual value if it survives long enough in time. … … One way to build up residual value is the creation of limited editions. I personally believe that there is a business opportunity here, but only if this dimension is correctly interpreted*

> *Andrea Ragnetti, fr. CEO of Philips Consumer Lifestyle, Amsterdam*

From capitalizing on the memories of great history, now let's move to the task of making High End design into a collectible. It takes some clever thinking and marketing to do so.

In recent years, Swatch raised some of its price points to the High End by incorporating into its portfolio a relatively affordable, yet stylish jewelry collection. But it wasn't only the collection. It was price and scarcity as well. Going beyond well-executed displays and marketing expected for the High End, Swatch discovered the right price point where the customers feels that the item is scarce' (so-called scarcity perception). Swatch realized that good marketing and merchandising could work wonders, so they invited architecture and design masters Robert Venturi or Alessandri Mendini to create those special limited editions. The bottom line and lesson here – Swatch applied the communication codes of fashion to the earlier *uber*-serious category of time-keeping. The combination of these efforts is now part of business history.

Do the mechanisms of residual value apply to the High End the same way as in they do luxury sector, and if so what lessons can business learn? Swatch managed to achieve one of the most desired status levels of the High End, to become a collector's item. You can buy or sell historical collection Swatch pieces on eBay. Swatch pieces occasionally appear in museums and galleries! The brand moved beyond plain commerce, and reached the perception of a cultural item.

Let's go a bit more deeply into the business potential of residual value. Lisa S. Roberts in her elegant book *Antiques of the Future*[1] shows a way to "designed in" residual value to the High End. In her 25-year career as a professional in home furnishing design, she collected more than 300 future "design classics". Roberts' definition of the "antiques of the future" is: "Highly designed contemporary products that will rise in value once they are no longer in production because they represent the best of design in their time".

To be included in Roberts' collection, an object must clearly demonstrate that it possesses one or more of the five critical features:

- Exhibited in museums or included in permanent museum collections

- Designed by a notable architect or designer

---

1   L. Roberts, *Antiques of the Future*, 2006, New York.

- Manufactured by design-oriented companies

- Recipient of major design awards

- Widely published in magazines or books.

Roberts' criteria seem somewhat counter-intuitive because we are not talking about the luxury or art markets, but rather about items that any of us can buy. The High End items are not out of the reach of "everyman", as luxury and art items might be.

The lesson is simple. With the art and science of High End strategy, entrepreneurs and managers can discover the right mix of iconic design and scarcity marketing. Properly executed, in the way that Swatch did but of course appropriate for the product, making an object both an icon and scarce lets the High End business create an impression and extract higher margin. Success means attaining a bit of the magic of residual value, so typical of the worlds of luxury and of art.

If the notion of residual value is attractive, then imagine how to make it even more so by appealing to noble aspirations. Residual value could be an important player in the social and environmental fields although it might sound a bit paradoxical. What if the items that we throw away today are High End, and just might have substantial value in a few years, if only we hang on to them! We probably would see more of these items remaining around our homes, playing longer roles in our lives. Residual value, even the hope of such value, might be just part of the alchemic miracle of High End, from premium margins to reduced ecological impact of consumption over time, all in one proposition!

Outsourcing, Design and Deliberate Scarcity – Tex by Oliver Lapidus

Just above we talked about how to make people perceive a product as High End. The company should limit the production in order to maintain *scarcity*. At the same time, the *price* need not be too high – the product has to be within reach, and should generate reasonable margins. The distribution channels should not be too posh or too limited to support that notion of scarcity. Let's drive this approach even further to produce "authentic value", nonetheless.

Here we look at perceived exclusivity, through scarcity, with class, *but in a mass distribution channel.*

Visionary French couturier Olivier Lapidus created his Tex collection of clothing following the production guidelines of the luxury market – something expected from a French exquisite and refined couture master. However, that is where the "traditional" ended. The line, "Tex Creation de M. Olivier Lapidus", was distributed in the 217 French hypermarkets of Carrefour, a mass-distribution store. There was only one curious thing about Tex, but that was critical. *Tex was produced as a limited edition, available to everyone, but only while the supply lasted.*

The Tex collection was *Made in China* under the supervision of French and Italian production experts. Items in the Tex collection are quite affordable to the middle class, including highly refined suits at 200 or 175 euros, respectively. Tex features excellently cut coats at 150 euros, superb ties at 25 euros, impeccable shirts at 45 euros, and leather shoes at 72 euros per pair. To complete this collection, Tex offers a small collection of home garments and accessories. The quantity of items produced for this collection was as limited and exclusive as the distribution channel is massive. A counterintuitive but highly effective example of High End!

We might expect such High End proposition to be massively advertised, in the best tradition of a large distributor of commodity goods. After all, the common wisdom is that prestige advertising leads to premium margin sales. However, this common wisdom was not correct in the case of Tex, for two reasons.

First, the real novelty, or better, the revolutionary news of Tex, is a combination of the best sartorial quality with the lowest reasonable price point. Raising the price point of Tex by investing relevant cash in advertising destroys this story and would affect, perhaps even endanger, the integrity of the offering. Compressing the margins or raising the price were both options contradicting the High End strategy adopted by Lapidus.

Second, Tex did not need any communication, any advertising beyond word of mouth. The collection rapidly sold out. According to Lapidus, the product itself generated its own best advertising. The buzz created by the Carrefour customers who had been merely exposed to the physical presence of such levels of quality at such low price was more than enough to carry the news from mouth to mouth, all across France.

What lesson, then, do we learn about the High End from the story of Tex by Lapidus? In essence, Tex is a real "degree zero" of the High End, or High End stripped to the essential bone. The High End markers of Tex are: margin generation, outsourcing, design, craftsmanship and authenticity of the overall proposition. Most of all, terrific value delivered at a price point within reach, yet a price point that delivers good margins, and yet is low enough to generate the buzz among customers. Tex makes us reconsider the whole mix of authenticity, location, origin, outsourcing and style leadership.

Understanding and the Algebra of the Customer Mind

HIGH END DIMENSION 1: AUTHENTICITY AND VALUE

Let's move from business stories to systematized knowledge. We begin with this first dimension, Authenticity and Value. Our stories suggest four factors or facets to explore. We now dive a bit deeper into the customer mind by looking at these factors, and then experimenting with them around the world.

We present these factors as questions you might wish to ask yourself. On a practical, individual level, you may wish to think about your current offerings, as we explore these four factors. These four simple factors came from the 75 discussions with top experts and business leaders, and the stories we distilled from them. This is the way the industry sees itself. But what about the High End customers? Do they share the findings and to what extent? What are the "hot buttons" of the customers that trigger their perception of the High End?

1. The *origin factor*: Is the High End proposition grounded in a specific country or area of origin or, just as important, grounded in design?

    Think about FIAT 500. This car which reconnects to the Italian Dream of the 1960s is actually assembled in Poland, and shares the same platform with the anonymous Ford Ka.

Furthermore, properly done, outsourcing becomes an asset for High End brands. The example of Tex shows what can be achieved by transferring competence and professional culture to high-quality outsourcing venues such as some regions and companies in China.

We definitely see the "Designed in ..." side of Origin as a rising wave of relevance for tomorrow's High End.

2.   The *exclusivity factor*: Does the *perceived* scarcity of the item create *concrete* added value in terms of perceived status of the owner? We emphasize the word *perceived* because the High End is not necessarily rare, and the word *concrete* because there has to be something specific to this added value.

The mechanisms of scarcity marketing offer a major opportunity for the High End as a strategy for marketers.

The real High End business finesse lies in the careful and strategic calculation of the best balance among high margins, limited volumes, and the desired perception of exclusivity in people's mind. Limited editions and designer collaborations help a lot here. It is a difficult game – but an exciting one to play, as Swatch and Tex demonstrate.

3.   The *price factor*: Does the item come with an entry price that restricts its accessibility, while at the same time remaining accessible to at least 20 percent of those who aspire to buy it?

The right cost structure combined with the affordable premium price could lead to higher margins.

High End business is driven more by margins than by volumes of sales. It is a different perspective, and a much healthier one.

Considering economic downturns, High End always should be in reach, but always at a premium.

4.   The *residual value*: Can the consumers re-sell the artifacts themselves at the same or even a higher price? Can the company establish a legacy in terms of collections or vintage editions?

Residual Value is a traditional hallmark of luxury. Properly done, High End brands can also elevate themselves to the status of collectibles.

We see cultural marketing, scarcity marketing and design as the main tactics for this strategy – to convert products into collectibles.

CUSTOMER MINDSETS FOR DIMENSION 1: AUTHENTICITY AND VALUE

The pilot RDE test described in the earlier chapter showed us how to discover what specifics drive perception of the High End. RDE also showed us different mindsets which can be found in any population of prospective and current customers. Keep in mind that it will be much easier to work with, message to, and convince a group of people with the same mindset than working with, messaging to, and trying to convince people who differ from each other. Homogeneity of customer mindsets makes the going easier.

Let's use the approach to investigate this first dimension of authenticity and value, in depth, and across countries. What works? We begin with the four factors and with the four elements for each factor. These elements form a good reservoir of starting material: 16 is a nice-sized collection. Now, where's the pay-dirt?

We generated these 16 elements from our interviews with the experts, and from a large collection of High End business stories. There were more elements, but we had to focus, make things simple, clear, and easily doable in the four countries. So we worked with what we perceived to be the most important ideas. Look at Figure 5.1 to get a sense of how authenticity and value might be expanded and dimensionalized.

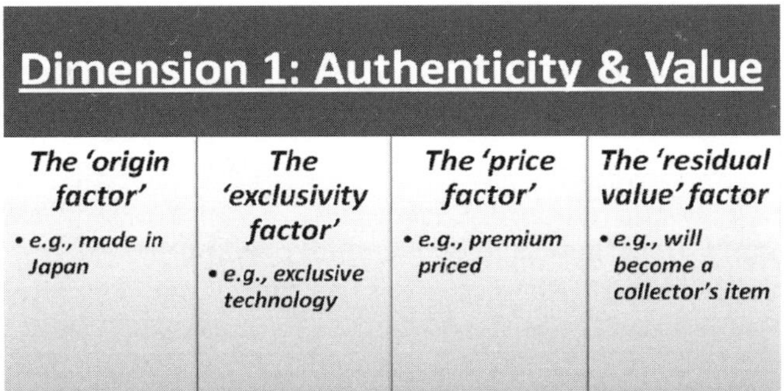

Dimension 1: Authenticity & Value

The 'origin factor'	The 'exclusivity factor'	The 'price factor'	The 'residual value' factor
• e.g., made in Japan	• e.g., exclusive technology	• e.g., premium priced	• e.g., will become a collector's item

Figure 5.1   The four factors for Dimension 1: Authenticity and Value

Now we embark on the deeper understanding of customers. We conducted a large-scale set of RDE studies in four countries – the USA, the UK, Italy and China. We presented our High End customer or prospective "customer respondents" with different vignettes, and instructed them to rate the vignette as a "complete description". The rating scale was how well the vignette fitted the idea of the High End. We followed the same procedure that we used for the pilot study. The only differences are that the combinations comprise 3–4 elements (dictated by the experimental design), and that the elements were identical across the four countries. You can find the numerical results for this first dimension in the Appendix (Table A2).

So, let's start at the bottom, the baseline; the propensity to call a proposition "High End", even without any particular elements. This notion of propensity to call a proposition High End is, in itself ,interesting. Does it vary by country – that is, is an Italian respondent more likely or less likely to call a proposition High End that a corresponding Chinese respondent? We're using experimental science to delve into the mind of the customer and getting to a predisposition, even without the customer actually telling us.

The baseline for the total panel is 26. In simple terms, if an item were to be positioned as generally authentic and delivering premium value, *but with nothing else said*, then approximately *one out of four participants in the project would be likely to say that the item is High End.*

Of course, we do not want to stop here. Let's look at the individual elements. Do individual descriptions drive the perception up or down? We now look at a couple of elements that stand out from the "crowd", specifically the highest and lowest scoring ones, and look for the underlying pattern, the rule that businesses "run with".

When we talk about *Made in … Italy/France/Switzerland/the UK/the USA*, those words substantially increase opinions about a product as High End. The strongest element driving up the perception of High End has an impact of +10. The impact of +10 means that an additional 10 percent of consumers would see the proposition as High End, above and beyond the basic 26 percent (that is, jump from 26 percent to 36 percent, just by talking about the country of origin).

The notion of "exclusivity" is also important – for instance, outstanding service support – and the exclusive mix of product design plus functional features plus service drive High End in.

There are some no-nos. References to the countries of origin outside the traditional sources of High End dramatically drive down the perception of High End. When you talk about *Made in … India/Brazil/China* you actually lose 17 percent of your people (impact = -17), meaning that almost 2 in 10 participants will change their vote. Today, talking about these other origins is not effective, and in fact will be counterproductive. Starting with 26 percent (baseline) but talking about the High End being manufactured in the developing countries causes the impact to drop from 26 percent to 9 percent! The High End is not ready yet to promote the manufacturing countries, but only the "design" countries (that is, "designed in").

MINDSET SEGMENTS FOR AUTHENTICITY AND VALUE

Our pilot study showed the greatest business value when we moved from the general population to specific mindsets. We find the same value here. The most interesting insights into participants' minds emerge when we segment them into groups based on the patterns of the individual impacts. Based on the total number of participants and their patterns, it might be possible to identify two, three or more such segments. Our projects limited the number of segments to just two (due to the number of respondents in each country and to make the results easier to understand). That way, business can target each group efficiently, but need not have more strategies and channels than can be afforded. Two segments are perfectly fine here.

The segmentation suggested two different mindsets. The first group comprised the *Status Seeker Segment* ("it's about me", Figure 5.2). The second group comprised and *Investor/Connoisseur Segment* ("it's about product/service", Figure 5.3). We named these segments by looking at the phrases which had the highest impact for each segment; that is, the phrases that appealed to each segment.

We are going to look at some simple ways to present "what works". Let's look now at Figure 5.2. This figure summarizes what we discovered about the first segment of people for authenticity and value. This segment responds to elements in a way that suggests they are status seekers. But just what works?

In Figure 5.2, the four different factors for Authenticity and Value appear as ovals. The vertical range of the ovals shows the range or spread of impacts of the four elements that belong to the factor. The individual elements themselves are rounded rectangles. The higher the element lies in the picture, the more High End perception it adds to a proposition. (Look at element A2, for example, made in Italy/France/Switzerland/the UK/ the USA). The less the element adds, or even subtracts, the lower it lies in the picture. Look at element D4 (not a purchase, an investment).

Let's go a bit deeper now into the segmentation. First, their baselines are the same. Recall that the baseline shows the likelihood for rating a proposition as High End when the proposition is simply tested as "authenticity and value", but without any messages.

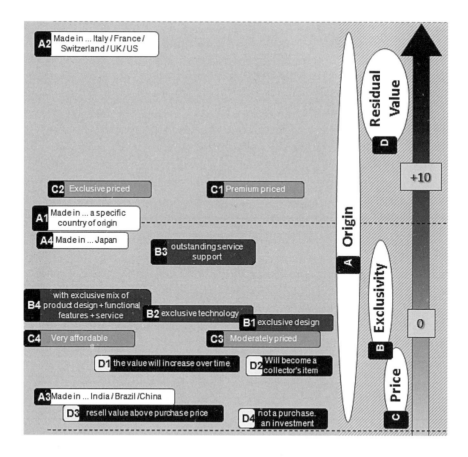

Figure 5.2   "Status seekers" for Dimension 1: Authenticity and Value

Segment 1 (*"Status seekers"*) is quite simple to please – just mention one of the traditional High End producing countries (Italy, France, and so on) and that the proposition is premium or exclusively priced. *Status seekers look for something that is perceived or identified by others as High End.* Status seekers are not concerned with finer characteristics of High End propositions. It is possible that the status seeker segment comprises the less-sophisticated participants who do not have a strong idea of a real premium proposition. When you sell to them, you ought to attach some general identifiers of the High End (*"Made in …"* coupled with a high price tag). When we put in the element *"Made in … Italy/France/Switzerland/the UK/the USA"* we get a very strong positive reaction. The impact value is +18, meaning that an additional 18 percent of the status seekers say that they feel that the product or service is "High End".

The individuals in *Segment 2* (*"Investor/Connoisseur"*, Figure 5.3) are more interested in product quality and future value in the years to come, and not interested simply in the country of origin. This segment reacts positively to phrases such as *The value will increase over time, will become a collector's item, resell value above purchase price,* and *Not a purchase … an investment.* The investor/connoisseur feels that an item will be perceived as "High End" when described by a message communicating *exclusivity* (impacts from +11 to +16) and *residual value* or *collector's quality* of a product (impacts from +14 to +18). The mention of *collector* is the most decisive (+18). Connoisseurs are very skeptical about phrases such as *"Made in … "* everywhere, especially in India, China and Brazil (rock-bottom at –31). They are even neutral to *Made in Italy!* Connoisseurs are not swayed by catchy *premium/exclusive* pricing (neutral), and they clearly resent *moderate* and *affordable* pricing claims as having anything to do with "premium" (impacts of –14 and –15). So, what are we to make of this group? It is likely that this *Investor/Connoisseur* segment includes more sophisticated or perhaps at least more experienced participants in the context of High End and luxury?

Summing Up

The successful High End product or proposition ought to feel authentic to the consumers. The product should offer high value. Price and origin play a role in this dimension of the High End. Furthermore, perceived exclusivity is a plus. If at all possible, think about residual value, but that may be harder to achieve, especially since the item is not luxury.

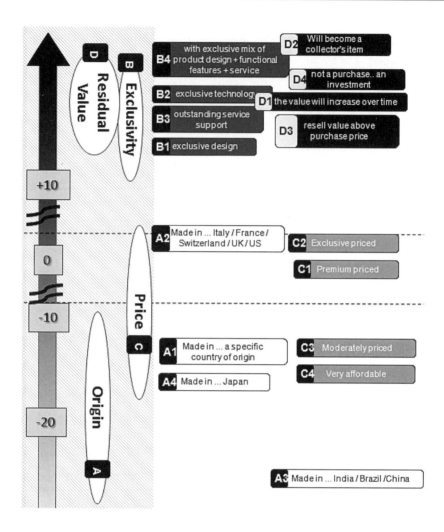

Figure 5.3   Performance of the Segment 2 "Investor/Connoisseur" for Dimension 1: Authenticity and Value

Lessons from Swatch and Tex by Oliver Lapidus show the power of scarcity marketing. Moving beyond scarcity to design, the case history of FIAT 500 combines design and origin. It is no wonder that this car delivers a High End product with a sense of deep authenticity.

Looking to the near future, we may soon expect a switch from "Made in" relevance as quality marker to a "Designed in ... " label as a label denoting quality. Apple and many other companies have done it already. Expect a proliferation of new "quality countries" emerging globally from Latin American textile-makers to Asian manufactures turning their factories into the starting point of powerful brands. In the next chapter, we will see how design is already contributing to this.

Finally, we uncovered two distinct types of customers. These are the status seekers (47 percent) and the investors/connoisseurs (43 percent). The "Status Seekers" are pretty easy to please. All you need to do to hook them is mention one of the traditional premium producing countries (Italy, France, and so on), and that the proposition is premium or exclusively priced. You need more substance with the "Investors/Connoisseurs". They are not interested as much in the country of origin as in the item quality, and what will happen to the item years later. Knowing to which segment a particular customer or prospect belongs will let you "address the right message" to that customer.

6

Rule 2: It is All About Design and Experience

Design is central to the future of brands at various levels. Brands must generate appeal at both functional and emotional levels ... In parallel, design will have to turn to services over artifacts. Because design makes the world better by simplifying and streamlining experiences, applying design to the everyday will be key for a higher level of appeal to people.
Rita Clifton, Chairman, Interbrand, London

Design, Along with the Designer's Name, Brings Success

Think about "degree zero" of design value – when merely the name of the designer propels the product to the High End. Target is one of the companies to profoundly understand the value of that "degree zero". And the consequence – affordable mass market, with design woven into the offerings, and consistently beating its competitors who are just waking up.

It seems almost obvious to state it nowadays: design is everywhere. By creating new ranges in partnership with luxury fashion designers Yoji Yamamoto (Y-3) and Stella McCartney, European sports giant Adidas successfully repositioned itself as High End sportswear, without losing its original customer base. Y-3 brand achieved a status of a cult youth brand, extending Yamamoto's customers into that hard-to-grab world of "cool" youth fashion.

Until the 1980s, Puma was always one step lower than its eternal rival Adidas competing in the same world of mass-market sport shoes, yet without any fashionable image. In the 1990s German designer Jil Sander started discretely putting her name on Puma's shoes, and proceeded to sell them at an exorbitant price in her own flagship stores. Nowadays Puma has positioned itself as a noble sports brand, featuring shoes designed by fashion stars like Alexander McQueen.

Of course, there is more to design than just the designer's name. A good design may lead to the re-invention of entire categories. For example, the introduction of *design hotels* revives a mature (read: boring) category of international hotels. The Delano in Miami, the Mondrian in LA or the St. Martin's Lane in London are the best exemplars in this field.

Representing the "worst-case scenario" in the same industry, the *me-too* presumed-boutique hotels with a poorly executed mediocre, trying-to-look-contemporary design attempt to achieve "bling bling" effect beyond any real substance. Travel suffers from this. High End travel is actually the opposite of this kind of scenario.

Experience Design and Inclusive Design

To get a sense of what experience design is all about, we join Peter Marino, a true style guru and leading architect of contemporary luxury. Marino's customers are a who's who, such as Chanel, Louis Vuitton, Valentino, Dior and Donna Karan. We follow Marino in his conversations with glass artist Jean-Michel Othoniel, written up in the *International Magazine for Swarovski Elements*, published in Spring–Summer 2007. The article traces the experience-design to long bygone royal events.

Royalty of past centuries had access to virtually any comforts and quality of life that were available. In the past, luxury was truly exclusive. Nowadays, comfort and quality of life extend to the much bigger audience, well beyond royalty. Today this extension happens through the mechanism of "trickling down", where High End can also be seen as the luxury comfort made accessible to wider audiences.

Let's paint an experience picture of the past. The seventeenth century party invitations were sent out a year in advance because it took six months to plan the wardrobe –and another six months to get to the party itself, and then return. The events were so complex that some of them, like a king's birthday, required planning for years! Nobody wanted these events to be forgotten. This truly luxury experience was immortalized in marvelously engraved and illustrated books cherished as mementos of the experience.

Now fast forward to the birthday party of the twenty-first century. In the modern experience-design, the sequence of the process goes from impression to memory. The steps begin by triggering people's interest, and end after ensuring a lasting memory of the entire experience. Design intervenes all across the party experience. Digital artifacts, applications and solutions help to create the event as one flow, starting with an idea sketchbook and finishing with long-lasting impressions captured, widely distributed over modern media and stored forever.

All in all, today's design for the High End is about the creation and management of customer experiences, well above and beyond just product styling.

China – Using Design as High End Strategy

In China top brand ends are basically all from foreign countries. There is an attempt to get there by companies that are all in the first stage of this process and also understanding what that luxury means. On the other hand, consider the phrase "Made in Japan". This phrase seems so outdated, yet in some ways, it connects better than ever. It has been quite some time that "Made in Japan" didn't mean world best quality, as it wasn't seeking originality. Only more recently is Japan is reclaiming its distinctiveness though. What has changed that brings Japan to the forefront is the appeal of Japanese aesthetics, which in design we like to call J-factor, combined with the country's now well know craftsmanship and precision engineering. From ceramics to fashion, and increasingly cars, Japan is becoming known for artistic, simple, strong yet subtly complex designs that lead the world.

Karl Schlicht, VP Lexus Europe, Brussels

In the past decade, design moved beyond advanced economies and started to spread outward to the developing economies. The switch from "design of products" to "concept design" and quickly developing creativity promised BRIC economies their chance to move ahead and eventually leapfrog other countries. This process is already underway.

Is it possible in the coming decades for "Made in China" to become a symbol of quality in the same way as the "Made in Japan"? What role will design play in this transformation and extension towards High End?

China recently initiated a program to create 400+ (!) design schools across the country in the next five years. The schools can't help but nurture a powerhouse of design talent. This continuous feed of designers will change the way Chinese companies market themselves. We will see the switch from plain outsourced production factories to "Made in China" quality brands appealing to the rest of the world. If this sounds impossible, let's explore this process which is underway already.

The future of High End in China is based on the country's glorious past. Many venerable luxury companies aim to get back on the map of global High End. One of these companies is Hengyuanxiang of Shanghai. Created in the 1920s as a luxury brand, famous for refined tailoring and excellence in production processes, Hengyuanxiang specializes in branded, wool-based products. When the management of Hengyuanxiang speak of their brand, their vocabulary resonates with terms more suitable to religion.

Hengyuanxiang's business leader, Legend Liu, guided the company to its new brand strategy – *strategic design, that is, design used as major part of one's strategy* to regain its leadership position in the Chinese and international wool markets. Its internationally acclaimed design team produces vital knowledge, the creative fuel for future growth. This knowledge lies at the heart of the creative effort.

The strategy started with a veteran of the Chinese creative scene, Italian-born Davide Quadrio. Quadrio began by involving Droog Design, the world-famed Dutch collective team which rose to glory in the 1990s by establishing excellence in contemporary Dutch design. With Hengyuanxiang's clear goal to become an inspirational brand once again, Droog helped to expand the company's strategic design to public and interior environments. A key strength in the situation was the ability of Liu and Hengyuanxiang's team to expand their design focus beyond products.

As this transformation trend continues, the "Wild, Wild West" economies of emerging countries like China, will once again flourish, but with new talent and with bravery to break rules. And the goal? Quite simply a twenty-first century "New Chinese High End," and a truly world class one at that. The key here is design, properly applied, based on knowledge, able to morph into new areas, to respond to business opportunities.

Yet ... Beware Product and Design Alone: Sony's Qualia

Looking upon the life of the "beautiful ones" as our ideal, the secret dream of many mainstream makers is to reach the prestige of their luxury counterparts.

In the consumer electronics sector, one of the top and most (if not "the" most) prestigious brands is Bang & Olufsen (B&O). An all-time leader in design and quality, this highly regarded company offers a selective portfolio of richly priced, top margins artifacts combining beauty with the most advanced high-tech. It is quite important to note that B&O control all interaction points with the consumers. Other leading consumer electronics brands look upon B&O as the gold standard, sometimes even attempting to play the same game.

With what we know about B&O, let's see what happened to Sony's push to the High End, to compete with B&O.

At the beginning of this first decade of the twenty-first century, Sony attempted to enter High End and luxury fields. In a serious attempt to offer an authentic proposition with a Sony soul, Sony developed a very limited collection of high-tech devices, each representing the absolute best in terms of technology, design and interaction experience. This was not a one-off but the natural application of a superb capability.

Sony Design works at the highest levels of excellence in terms of organizing aesthetic research programs with Italian artisans, masters of crafting the finest materials suitable for luxury products. This craftsmanship touch is part of the Japanese ancient culture. Sony Design's search for purity and excellence shows itself in collections of brilliant research prototypes conceived and crafted with the greatest skills between Tokyo and Lombardy. By itself, however, the Sony brand simply could not make the stretch into the top High End, or near luxury market of B&O. The High End and the luxury markets are simply too far distant for a relatively mainstream maker, even a leading one.

The carrier of Sony's ambition was a new sub-brand Qualia launched in Japan and the USA. Aiming to increase prestige and margin, Qualia had to get a great amount of media exposure to promote the message that the Qualia product experience was to be the best possible encounter between customers and high-tech. Sony truly delivered the best of the best in terms of interaction design, materials and finishing, and more. Expressing true integrity and great commercial bravery, Sony upgraded long-existing technologies like CRT TV to be as good as they could be – at that moment in history, the picture quality of cathode ray tube-based Qualia was better than newer, more fashionable flat screen TVs that had just started appearing on the market.

There was no advertising planned for Qualia – just a superior website experience, and top showrooms in top locations of top cities. For example, the Tokyo Qualia showroom in Ginza offered a genuine brand immersion, with shopping assistants becoming brand ambassadors and playing host for an exquisite experience with the product. Qualia products were instantly admired by the industry players generating a buzz in the industry and causing envy among the competitors. Putting the elements of a High End proposition, Sony had a chance to lead upward authentic substance and superior product experience.

Regardless of superior design, Qualia had a weak point. It had neither critical mass of distribution nor effective, adequate physical retail presence beyond a few selected *salons* where Sony chose to introduce the brand. From the viewpoint of experience design, Sony could not reach High End consumers. Had Qualia been positioned as a luxury product, perhaps it might have succeeded, although the electronics did not warrant the jump to luxury.

There were other problems. One problem was inconsistency, which gives another practical lesson. One of the authors (MB) noticed a superbly designed Qualia flat display positioned in the chaos of Akihabara, Tokyo's "Electric Town", next to Korean price-driven challengers and Japanese mainstream brands. Qualia products started to get into mainstream retail. Whereas the product experience was sublime, the actual purchase experience of those who encountered Qualia in the wrong channels was a killing mismatch. And the invidious price comparison to mainstream makes, especially in the absence of the softly spoken "Qualia evangelists" of the Ginza showroom, dealt a final blow to the experience.

Qualia is a fascinating example; a dream come true just to turn into a nightmare. The lesson for the High End is simple and harsh. Design is not a single product experience. Think of all the experiences, not just the beginning rhapsodical one. Qualia enjoyed the best product design possible, and a spectacular interaction design to go with it. However, one has to think about the experience design in holistic terms to design a brand across *all touch points* so that the breath of High End remains during every moment of intersection with the customer.

The Power of Design: The Stores and Strategy of Anthropologie

Designing High End experiences at all brand touch points is highlighted in the following case of one of the best companies in US retail design, showing the creation of spaces that produce High End experiences by design.

Anthropologie founder Richard Hayne and his team openly dismissed advertising as a marketing tool. Instead, they created a completely new High End approach to retail design. In order to achieve their vision, Anthropologie partnered with the New York hip firm, Pompei AD led by a former artist and a CNN ex-Principal Voice, Ron Pompei. Anthropologie comprises a unique mix of visionary leadership and hands-on talent. With a workforce of more than 50 young creative minds, Pompei AD creates world-class retail design for firms like Urban Outfitters, Kiehl, 66 Degrees North and Anthropologie.

What makes Pompei AD's design for Anthropologie uniquely authentic is the way it transforms each individual Anthropologie *location* into a true local High End brand experience – one rooted in the local cultural and aesthetic milieu. A Chicago Anthropologie store features a vibrant façade capturing the Midwest urban feel. A store located in Los Angeles has a completely different design palette featuring colors that resonate with California sun. For an Anthropologie store in New England, stones, wood and the rich nature of this area constitute the main motif throughout the facade.

Anthropologie's store environment strengthens the corporate brand, and yet maintains the underlying identity of each individual store. This sensitivity stands in stark contrast to most of the competition, whose stores look like clones of each other, no matter where they are located. Anthropologie is worth exploring because its strategy reinforces the High End value of the experience and create rich, sensual and engaging environments. Each store integrates elements of the local architecture, so that no two stores are exactly alike. The decor looks "appropriate" for the location, as well as looking High End.

Anthropologie strategically locates its stores in upscale areas, in specialty retail centers, and in enclosed malls. The market-sensitive location strategy develops a design which echoes the regional climate, architectural context and customer profiles. Each store announces the heritage and personality of the local community through the materials and finishes appropriate to the brand. Anthropologie custom-made storefronts are stunning, breaking the mold of conventional mass-produced storefront systems. Here, design strategy unites the brand, sets it apart from other brands, and fits the local customer.

Anthropologie is not just another example of an anonymously unified American brand. Rather, with its national presence, the stores produce different and appropriate expressions for each locality. There are elements in the store design specifically to maintain a specific visual identity and unity, for otherwise we would have chaos rather than a coherently unified brand. The outcome of this original approach is a shopping experience unlike almost anything else in High End retail today. The bottom line for High End business is to customize, fit the location, and return to a world where the experiences are different, rather than boringly homogenized. There is no need for standardization, if such standardization is negative rather than positive. Henry Ford's adage "you can have any color, as long as it's black" does not play in the High End.

In the end, Anthropologie's approach is not simply a design tactic to distinguish itself from competitors, but rather embodies a completely new High End "ideology of the origin". The Anthropologie brand itself is not afraid to change and adapt its experience to meet the atmosphere of the local context. The results are quite astounding.

Designing the High End Online Experience

> *We are all experiencing "digitalization," which is really only one of many different contemporary currents. In this context, I would again like to stress how important it is for our brand to operate in more than just a product-oriented manner. What matters much more to us is the brand's historical core, its "content-nucleus," which is capable of articulating itself in each and every instance, including digitally.*
>
> Markus Langes-Swarovski, Member of the Board, Swarovski, Austria

Continuing the experience opportunities in the High End, we move from bricks-and-mortar to clicks-and-digits where the shopping experience is taking on a new skin, and business a new opportunity. Digital design creates new levels of experiential engagement. Unlike many aspects of the High End which trickle down from the world of luxury, digital experience may present an exception to this general pattern. Luxury players have been rather slow to embrace the digital world and to create exquisite digital experience. Their reticence should not really surprise, however. The Internet democratized access and expanded it – a route quite contrary to the one pursued by most luxury players. The High End created through Experience Design is the topic of our next story.

Until recently, the combination of High End exclusivity and online shopping was regarded as an oxymoron. Exclusivity was for the few; online shopping, the great equalizer and the gift of the knowledge economy, is for the many. One man and his start-up company changed it all. Probably more than anyone else, Federico Marchetti, founder and CEO of Yoox, Italy's globally successful internet e-retailer of fashion and style, created the notion of exclusive digital shopping. Yoox has a mission – to make the High End accessible to the world through the Web. Marchetti and his team defined the new *Digital High End*.

Here is the essence of Marchetti's recipe – five ingredients of the digital experience that High End business *must* incorporate to create the premium brand in the digital world:

1.   *People on the Internet are real!* You can't see the customer, but they can see you reacting. The brand is important in the digital arena, just as it is for real people in the three-dimensional world. Your customers are forming feelings every time they experience your brand on the Internet, whether you like it or not. So do it right.

2.   *You can interact with customers much better in the digital world than in the physical one.* Recognize this, prepare for it, and treat your customer well. If you forget that, return to item #1 – the customer is a real person, not a cipher, not a number!

3.   *Your customer wants something real, everyday, accessible.* Do not focus on technology, rich content, cutting edge features. These may be fun, they may be challenging, but they are not the only way to build a brand on the Internet. Value creativity and your culture – they are much more important to your customer.

4.   *Don't listen to Internet gurus.* Use your instinct. Your history, your needs, your vision all tell the unique story. Follow that story. Gurus tend to apply the same success story to all. As the adage goes, to a carpenter with a hammer, the whole world is a nail.

5.   *Get real and get serious.* Commit yourself to do something amazing. Oh, and do not be afraid to invest money in the digital world. It is a world of opportunity. Go after it.

So how does Marchetti follow his own advice, make these pieces of advice come alive with Yoox? To attract the mass of fashion-savvy consumers, Yoox develops a portfolio of offerings that we could use as a practical blueprint for the High End.

First, we find the accessible price; the affordable yet perceptibly but not horribly upscale price for end-of-season items. Yoox reaches out to the fashion-aware average consumers by offering the combination of great brands at affordable prices.

Second, to reinforce the feeling of exclusivity, a *must* for fashion shopping, Yoox follows with *limited editions*. These are special projects courtesy of fashion gurus like Malcolm McLaren, Hussein Chalayan, Bernhard Willhelm, Brazilian talent gone global Alexandre Herchovitch and others. Arianne Phillips, famed costume designer and stylist for Madonna and Courtney Love, was also involved in a project, teaming up with Jeremy Scott, and Colette, the Parisian temple of fashion and style. In short, Yoox gathered a true *assemblage of royals* of fashion and style (luxury level) to embody and empower the Yoox proposition (High End level).

So what do we learn from Yoox, master of the online experience, about our High End? Well, the online world *can* have a High End. With its digital retail story; Yoox offers a great mix of authentic brands, genuine limited editions and a pricing policy that translates into real value for wider audiences. This is all part of the experience, a world born out of the design of Yoox founders and leaders.

The "Design and Experience" Dimension

To summarize the lessons from this second High End rule, let's look at the four factors that we believe underlie design:

The *holistic factor*. Does the proposition demonstrate a holistic, coordinated approach to design and experience across all the brand's touch-points?

As Sony's Qualia case demonstrated, excelling in one of the aspects of the mix is just not enough. The High End "devil" is in the detail, and the forefront of people's experience of the brand. Design the retail moment to be compelling, accurate, and pervasive.

The *craftsmanship factor*. Does the proposition provide product quality that a craftsman might deliver with his handmade artifact?

We mentioned how Sony Design promotes the excellence of materials and finishing by involving the very best artisans of Lombardy. This is a great testimony of the commitment by Sony designers to top quality. The challenge for High End brands is to bring the look and feel of craftsmanship beyond just superior prototypes and limited editions into the new world of outsourcing and global production. Here, design works with the different people in the supply chain to identify what is feasible which generate top perception, which limit costs, and which preserve High End margins.

The *design leadership* factor. Do the proposition and/or the designers associated with it possess superior design quality – one that stands out from the average?

This is an aspect of the value of design we mentioned in the introductory snapshots of Adidas and Puma. As designers are today's "gurus" and will likely be the rock stars of tomorrow, will they re-think and lead possible revolutions? Evidences from business success shows that this notion of High End design will probably grow ever more important.

The *inclusion factor*. Does the design approach show sensitivity to the various stakeholders involved in the context, for example business users, end users, families and other social circles around users?

The inclusion factor can become very important in experience, although we do not ordinarily think about it. As people's consciousness evolves, as the role of experience becomes more important, as higher levels of feeling become entwined with the High End, the inclusion factor will begin to play an important role. This factor is worth watching – it may be a sleeper opportunity.

Customer Mindsets for Design and Experience Dimension

How can you discover these rules in a more concrete way? We return now to RDE and explore this second dimension. Let's find out what consumers think about these factors and what types of mindsets exist in the world.

Following the business stories, we looked at the four factors for Design and Experience (see Figure 6.1). Let's review the perceptions of design.

Let's first examine the consumer perceptions from the total panel across all four countries (see Appendix, Table A2). The baseline perception is +30, similar to what we saw for Dimension 1 on authenticity. In fact, as we work our way through the five dimensions, we are going to see the baseline perception, the propensity to label something as marker of "High End", to lie between one-in-four and one-in-three (from +25 to +33), once the participant is primed that the project will deal with premium. This is important because it tells us the basic mindset of the typical participant. We will also see later on that this average propensity does not apply to the four different countries. Each country comes with its own propensity to call something High End. Countries and cultures are not alike, just as minds are not alike.

For the dimension of Design and Experience it clear that the factor we called Craftsmanship is the strongest driver for High End. Elements such as *exceptional hand-made craftsmanship, made with unmatched precision* and *made with the world's finest materials* are the strong performers. Why should we be surprised, here? Hand-made is the hallmark of luxury as well.

On the other hand, our "inclusion factor" clearly does not drive the perception of High End, at least today. Inclusion might play a real role in the future, because "inclusion" is a topic about which thought leaders gave us rather different, far more encouraging feedback. (Perhaps that is one of the reasons they are called "leaders"). Time will tell whether or not qualified public opinion will converge with such visions, as we expect them to do.

Dimension 2: Design & Experience			
The 'holistic' factor	*The 'craftsmanship' factor*	*The 'design leadership' factor*	*The 'inclusion factor'*
• e.g., designed for a holistic experience	• *e.g.,* made with the world's finest materials	• e.g., created by renowned star designers	• e.g., enables minorities to feel more integrated

Figure 6.1   The four factors for Dimension 2: Design and experience

Mindset Segments for Design and Experience

We again divided the participants into two dramatically different, mutually polarizing groups, whose results appear in Figures 6.2 and 6.3 respectively (see also Appendix, Table A3). Keep in mind that these are different people, and not those who had participated in the first study on the dimension of authenticity.

One group responds strongly to the product itself, the quality of the product and the craftsmanship. We call this segment *Focus on the product*. The other group responds to the person and the experience in the wider socio-cultural context. We call this segment *Focus on people*. These two segments begin with a similar baseline. So they begin with the same predisposition to call a product or service High End. But then the similarity ends. Our two design and experience segments are quite opposite to each other in what they respond to.

Segment 1: Focus on the product (Figure 6.2), as the name suggests, responds very strongly to statements about the product. For this segment, elements such as *exceptional hand-made craftsmanship* and *made with unmatched precision* are key for the High End. The segment responds strong to any craftsmanship message. Craftsmanship statements generate extremely high impacts between +18 and +21. These high numbers are very strong drivers, and are a key to getting to Segment 1. An additional one in five participants would consider a proposition High End when you invoke craftsmanship. Segment 1 also responds strongly to the factor of design leadership.

Segment 2: Focus on people (Figure 6.3) responds to the product as a "lifestyle enabler" (that is, *enables people to live according to new lifestyle choices*). These Segment 2 individuals seem oriented to humanistic statements. It's all about people and the product, not about the product itself. Segment 2 comprises people completely indifferent to the statements about craftsmanship and design as well as to the holistic factor, with the exception of "designed for a holistic experience" which is moderately positive. In terms of High End Markers, Segment 2 feels that socially responsible factors like lifestyle choices (+14), diversity (+10), drive the High End.

For the business to satisfy both segments with a single message will be hard. In fact it may well be impossible. Socially responsible claims will attract the people-focused segment while at the same time turning off the product-focused segment. Turning the focus to quality and design leadership ideas will attract the product-focused, but not have much of an effect on the people-focused segment.

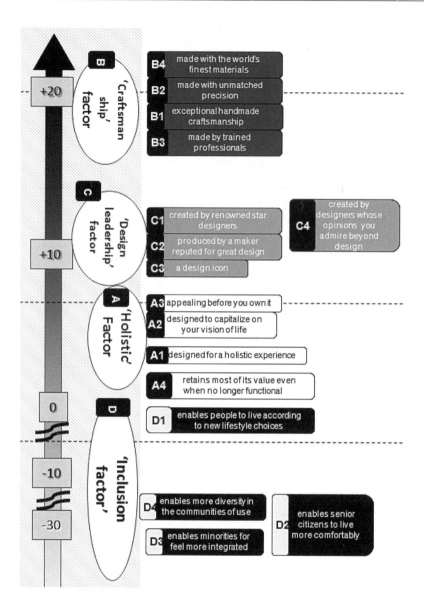

Figure 6.2   Performance of the Segment 1 "Focus on the product" for Dimension 2: Design and Experience

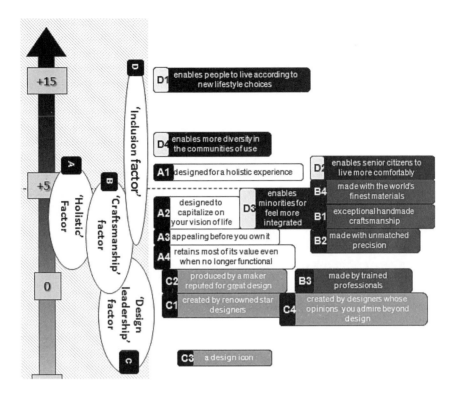

Figure 6.3   Performance of the Segment 2 "Focus on people" for Dimension 2: Design and Experience

In terms of practice, therefore, any strategy to convey High End premium through Design and Experience requires a great deal of "word-smithing", if possible. High levels of acceptance by the two segments at the same time may be impossible. It is clear that we deal here with radically different, virtually opposing mindsets. Competence in strategic design will be required to form the concepts. The worst case scenario in managerial terms is trial and error.

Summing Up

Design differentiates High End from the mass production. It is not "just" the design of products, however. In the world of experience the designer is often becoming a thought leader. More and more, designers become revered celebrities, with the power to change the game by the use of their name, as do Adidas or Puma.

Our stories showed how strategic design for Hengyuanxiang by Dutch Droog Design unleashed the power of design. Droog stretched way beyond plain product design to reach the level of ideas and work on the holistic brand level supporting the comeback of this great Chinese brand of High End from the 1920s.

Distribution is important for design. Sony Qualia, a genuine experiment for a near-luxury brand, explored the criticality of retail and distribution. Yoox showed the alchemy of online retail, design, service, and the artful inclusion of remote customers. In turn, Anthropologie demonstrated the creative opportunities which location-specific design can offer to prospective High End leaders.

The next frontier might be the virtual world. The High End experience will exist far more widely online when the premium brands break out of the store to the browser, migrating the shopping and buying experience to the desktop, handhelds and phones.

When it comes to mindsets, we find very dramatic variation in what is important, and what makes a High End design or High End experience. The consumers divide into two mindset segments: Focus on the Product (45 percent) and Focus on the People (55 percent). People who "focus on the product" respond very strongly to statements about the product. For them, talk about craftsmanship and precision are key. Those who "focus on people" respond to the product as a lifestyle enabler. This second group seems to be thinking more inclusively about others. This second segment might include more progressive-thinking, cultural creatives among its members.

7

Rule 3: It is About Creating the "New" (Dimension: Innovation and Leadership)

Fundamentally, the new middle ground is where people can find affordable solutions to what were once unaffordable luxuries. For example, teeth whitening used to be "for the stars," done at a dentist's office and at great expense. Today, the masses can whiten their teeth for less than $30 with Crest Whitestrips®. The same principle applies to a great many products, from disposable spinning toothbrushes to home espresso makers. This transformation of luxuries into affordable solutions offers an enormous High End innovation opportunity for most companies.

Paul Nunes, Executive Research Fellow, Accenture, Boston,
and Author, Harvard Business School Press

Daedalus Was Right: Innovate to the Right Degree

In recent years, *Business Week Magazine* in the USA featured a cover with words "innovate or die". We can scarcely open a magazine, a newspaper, or browse the Web without seeing something to do with innovation. So innovation is today's mantra as well as being a required second nature to the High End.

The fastest way to fail in innovation is simply by not leading it, sitting comfortably, relaxing in the status quo. "Not enough innovation" is a deadly formula for the High End. Look at Polaroid – once a leading globally respected brand, known for its consumer insights and innovative ideas like instant photos, Polaroid completely missed the changing consumer and market trends, and ended up lagging behind in the age of digital imaging. This lack of vision practically killed the brand. Yet, 40+ years before, one of the authors (HM) was fortunate to have the founder of Polaroid, E.H., sitting in an office next to his in Harvard's Laboratory of Psychophysics, located in William James Hall, on

Kirkland Street in Cambridge. During those heady years Land's Polaroid rode high, the apotheosis of the company that defined innovation. Who could have predicted its demise and terribly sad ending on the auction block for the assets of failed companies?

On the other hand, "too much innovation" is not good to make it in the High End either. Take the Sony PS3. The technological potential of this digital platform was huge, as was its ambition: to become the engine of our future digital living rooms, the heart of our connected homes. Designed with the newest functions and too many efforts to integrate every possible feature, PS3 could not maintain a competitive price, and came too late to market. Due to the imbalance among timing, pricing and people's relative unwillingness or rather tardiness to embrace the valuable PS proposition, PS3 failed to move beyond competing well in its category, ending its life featured at steep discounts. Despite the admirable drive to innovate, PS3 was simply out of balance and out of touch with the quantity and quality of technological innovation that people can manage to absorb as "the new" without experiencing a sense of alienation.

Innovation and Leadership: Crucial Key to the High End

A natural leader in successful innovation, Apple is changing the game, making its products into icons of the time by design-driven innovation. Apple innovates by combining technical innovation with the aesthetics. The result – breakthrough products that incorporate brilliant ideas and ability to break from the traditional ways of thinking.

A business can choose to pursue two different types of innovation: incremental innovation and disruptive innovation. Disruptive innovation involves a complete change of technological paradigm (for example, from horse to cars). The much less dramatic but far more popular approach innovates in increments. Incremental innovation occurs over time within a specific technology paradigm, a kind of evolution. Examples are the move from 1950s sedans to 1990s minivans or SUVs. The various products might look different but technologically they are unchanged; what was a car remains in essence a car.

The stories in this chapter describe how innovation in design revolutionized three categories – home appliances, consumer electronics for fitness, and mainstream jewels – without fundamentally changing the technological paradigms. The innovations occurred through successful partnerships. The results were concrete market successes in the High End.

How Innovation Happens: Technology Partners with a Lifestyle Leader

Innovation for the High End often involves the co-branding between a high-tech leader and a lifestyle leader. The high-tech leader brings its dowry in the form of credible technology breakthroughs. The lifestyle leader ensures access to unique marketing leadership. The assets exchanged in the co-branded venture usually already exist before the marriage, and so the assets are truly dowries, not made-up hopes.

In a story below, Philips was already strong in the technologies embedded in domestic appliances and digital storage, as much as Alessi, Nike and Swarovski already were at the helm of popularity before the partnership began. This is why we cannot really speak of disruptive technological innovation, but rather speak more of an intelligent marketing collaboration – opening new categories and new distribution channels for both brands, or really both corporate partners.

Let's begin at the first "horizon" of innovation, the incremental progress from one product generation to the next one. This is the innovation which keeps the High End brand at the top within its category. We show how different companies join forces to achieve breakthroughs by complementing each other in order to bring the "new" to their respective categories or operations.

Incremental Innovation as a Way of Life: TAG Heuer

> *Over the time, the functional need for watches had become lower and lower. In fact, the time is displayed everywhere around during the day or night. Should you be in your living room, your kitchen, in your car or at work, you actually do not need a watch anymore. Moreover, almost everybody is already wearing the time on their mobile phones. The number of young people wearing watches is constantly decreasing. Yet, several serious market studies clearly show that they still aspire to buy High End or prestigious watches, when they will be able to. "High end and prestigious watch-making are definitely facing a great future*

... It seems that watch-makers are bound to create more and more value to reach or stay in the High End level if they want to take benefits from this huge market opportunity.

Thomas Houlon, Innovation Director, TAG Heuer, Switzerland

Just a couple of hours drive from Geneva, sits the small, sleepy Swiss town in the canton of Neuchatel, Le Chaux-de-Fonds, where nearly 150 years ago Edouard Heuer founded his watch making company. Decades ago, Heuer had established a fine tradition of leadership in terms of timekeeping and time-tracking for sports events. While maintaining the fundamentals of its reputation intact through the decades, during the course of time Heuer somehow slipped into the moving sands of the mid-market, low-entry price, not-so-prestigious world of mundane objects.

TAG Heuer's story presents a realistic blueprint for innovation excellence and leadership. The company got its current name "TAG" in 1985 when "Techniques d'Avant-Gard" absorbed Heuer. In 1999, TAG became a part of the French luxury conglomerate LVMH causing TAG Heuer to *move back into the High End*. Quite likely in the future this move will be seen as the necessary intermediate step towards renewing its luxury status after years of emphasizing the mass-market affordability of its products.

By the early 90s, TAG Heuer was perceived as a "marketing watch-maker", coasting along on an amazing brand heritage, yet surprisingly without any corporate vision to reach higher price segments. The entry price point of the brand was around €90 for a bottom-of-the-brand watch. By the early 2000s, it was obvious to management at TAG Heuer that the brand had to increase its premium positioning and perceived value. Management crafted its own face onto a process used by automobile manufacturers: the Concept Watches. These are "star prototypes" showcasing daring technological innovation in superb design quality. In a symbiosis between R&D and PR, TAG developed artifacts showing the way to higher price segments in all core business product series. This strategy was extremely successful, giving TAG Heuer a huge business potential in higher price segments with the entry price point of the brand jumping to €600.

TAG Heuer's company motto "Swiss Avant-Garde since 1860" reflects its innovative ideas while at the same time respecting the past, underscoring the traditions, leadership and quality heritage – all High End values. Leadership did not limit innovation to R&D alone but extended it into marketing, combining innovation with celebrity marketing. The relation with the golf star then shining (now troubled), Tiger Woods, enabled TAG Heuer to develop the first professional golf watch, a product ergonomically engineered in collaboration with Woods to meet his own personal needs and demands, and therefore by extension the needs of all players. The dialog between Woods and TAG Heuer extended beyond the standard sponsorship, brand-testimonial contract. The collaboration required that the marketers and engineers at TAG Heuer be exposed to the mindset, the ways of working and the discipline of the golf legend. The specific product also fitted the golf needs of TAG Heuer's top potential customers. Press and public opinion ensured the media coverage, boosting the company's image.

The High End lesson from TAG Heuer? Innovation is critical to achieve and to maintain for a High End position. TAG Heuer provides a clear vision for innovation as engine of High End. When the business focuses on products innovation, it encourages functional leadership based on the adaptation of technological features. When the business focuses on brand image and public relations, innovation is turbocharged, producing an impression of a "leading brand". The two dynamics, innovation and leadership, can be synergistic as well, creating an even greater "bang for the buck".

Partnerships: An Emerging Key to Innovation Success

Our approach is a transition model from the "old paradigm world" to a new context. We aimed to achieve the "supremacy of ideas" over any other process or formula, and we therefore integrated in our ways of working the notion that nobody can excel in everything.

Luca De Meo, former CMO, FIAT Group Automobiles, Turin

In the post-industrial economies, joining forces and complementing strengths is increasingly necessary for corporations and their brands. The splendid isolation of becoming the single maverick designer, professional, or even entire company, is giving way to the *realpolitik* in realization that it's tough, perhaps almost impossible, to "do it alone". You might be a style guru – but have very limited access to R&D assets or high-tech. You might be a high-tech giant with thousands of scientists in your labs creating potential future applications – just to miss the last mile that plugs technology into people's lifestyles and customers' dreams.

How do you trigger a true culturally-sound, design-driven innovation for repeatable business success and translate it to the High End? By now, you probably know or can guess the answer: *partnerships, partnerships, partnerships.*

Since his appointment to the post of CEO of a large corporate design department, the author of the foreword to this book, Stefano Marzano, has actively promoted a policy to "grow" innovation by inviting outsiders to collaborate and to partner. Marzano's vision creates a unique path of projects and programs which produce a portfolio of value. Partnership experiences generate at least three major lessons about "how the world works":

1. *We is better than me*: Collaborations stimulate new ways of thinking, raising the bar of organizational ambitions. This is the natural basis to achieve true market leadership.

2. *Two cords are harder to cut than one cord*: In today's competitive, stressed and talent-seeking market, partnerships represent an interesting way to provide ongoing motivation. Partnerships fit people's inner needs for freedom and stimulation. After all, it is logically more stimulating for top talent to encounter the best of the best in international design.

3. *From difference and opposites comes the new*: Collaborations are the best seedbed of profitable innovation. The partnerships demarcate the mutually accepted "true" territory where partners of equal status meet to share diverse solutions to common problems and challenges. Partnerships create a realistic framework for high-speed innovation engines, resulting in true *business* success, ranging from innovative concepts to out-of-the-box marketing and communications strategies, from launch to actual distribution.

Now down to practicalities. Can two or more groups collaborate when it comes to something beyond functional? It's nice to have the vision of a happy future, where the partners respect each other, where all good things are happy. But … the proof of the "pudding is in the eating". Just what kind of pudding does this partnership create, and how does the business person working in the High End get to join the meal? What does this notion of partnership really mean for innovation-led businesses, especially for design-driven innovation?

Successful collaboration and partnership involve two critical factors. One is hard assets, the "something" from which innovation comes. Without that "something", there is really no innovation, just a hope. The second is a bit softer, but no less relevant – a mindset to collaborate, that abiding sense of "we, not just me". What happens when such a mindset comes out in the play between two established players at the top of their respective industries? The outcome may well be synergy between brands, blessed by a design-led integration of competences.

Successful Innovation by Partnerships: Alessi, Nike and Swarovski – with Philips

Inspired by Italian innovators, Philips transformed what in the early 1990s was simply the functional, not particularly aesthetic, category of home appliance into a High End line of products.

By mid 1990s, the domestic appliances market had become exceptionally fragmented. Think commodity, at its peak, with margins at their lowest, competition at its highest, dissatisfaction at its most rampant. Philips was an important player in this arena with the market share roughly equally distributed among Moulinex, Matsushita, Braun and Philips. In turn, the "big guys" were competing with a wide array of local and regional micro-brands, players delivering low-price commodities. Although the rising consumption of the 1950s, which masked mediocrity by simple demographically driven demand, had since long gone, design still did not play a really differentiating role, and innovation was stagnant.

In the early 1990s, Stefano Marzano, who had just been appointed as the head of design for the entire Philips concern, immediately grasped the opportunity to create a partnership for a new High End proposition in the kitchen appliances sector by applying High Design to innovation process. But High Design needed a focus, a structure, and an opportunity. That opportunity was given by the partnership with a premium lifestyle brand, Alessi.

Italy's leading home accessories company, Alessi, was a family enterprise. During the early 1990s, Alessi was going through a generational shift of leadership. Positioned at the top of the High End with its design masters' collections of metal accessories for the contemporary home, Alessi was looking for a way to innovate, and change its very essence to keep pace with the modern world. This search to reinvent was a critical stage for a family company with limited industrial assets, and profoundly deep but narrow experience.

The ground rules for the partnership were simple. Alessi would help the "dull colossus" of kitchen appliances by bringing in the High End Italian mojo. In return, Philips would turbo-charge Alessi's collections, thanks to its massive possibilities as a world-class conglomerate. Philips would help Alessi in the switch to new materials, like plastics and electrically connected devices. Together, Alessi and Philips would add art, style, and verve to a rather dull category.

The business results that emerged comprised a successful family of five products built on basic core functions. This was a new approach focused on the sensory ease of use and interaction with "warm" appliances, better than clinical-looking white plastic boxes.

In the spirit of Alessi's focus on the High End, distribution was innovative as well. To affirm their leadership image, the partners created a joint retail strategy. The offering was to be made selective, encompassing only 15–20 percent of Philip's retail base, with distribution through Alessi's preferred retail channels. Matching this High End vision, the price was set at 3–4 times the standard market prices for functionally equivalent products.

The Philips Alessi line of products was presented to the world in a way to demonstrate true leadership. The International Introduction Event was a multimedia show with an impressive who's who in press, design world and opinion leaders. Staged at the soon-to-be-opened Groninger Museum, the introduction produced impressive media coverage.

Philips-Alessi shows how partnerships in the race to the High End translates into synergy, where 1+1>2. We are dealing here with an evolutionary, rather than a disruptive, innovation. There are a number of lessons, or rather descriptions, of what really happened in the magic interaction of Philips and Alessi. We might speak of the principles of a new anthropologically driven design. Or, just as validly, we might speak of a humanistic approach to the High End opportunity. From the Philips-Alessi partnership, a new design language emerged, which blasted out a new path, a High End opportunity for domestic appliance categories beyond the 1990s. Alessi adopted a new technology of production and entered new categories. Philips changed the name of the game in the market sector, and rose to the High End pinnacle of the categories.

Moving Fitness into the High End "Digital Lifestyle"

Our next story brings us to the early 2000s – a particular moment, squeezed between the hopes of the digital revolution and the numbing aftermath of 9/11. Exercise and fitness had gradually developed into the new hallmarks of High End customers, so it made business sense to penetrate this area. Global industry leaders Nike and Philips had introduced a new line of co-branded portable audio players. These players combined digital technology with new designs, specifically created for the active consumer. Leading to the designs were thinking and concepts of apparel and equipment, combining communications, connectivity and information, in order to motivate athletic activity.

It is worth a short digression to look at the types of product that such efforts produce, and to recognize that with just a bit of design effort one can retool ordinary products for a High End market. The 2002 Philips Nike line of audio products included MP3 players, MP3-CD players, FM radio and active headphones specifically designed for sport. The audio players were designed to be comfortable to wear during sport and fitness activities. Even better, they were innovative solutions designed to be operated by feel rather than sight. They were engineered to deliver a high-quality audio experience motivating for physical activity.

The products included an armband and headphones specifically designed for uninhibited movement. The players themselves were small and lightweight, featuring a sleek and stylish stainless-steel design. The innovative control buttons were fabricated from rubber, easy to grip and protecting against sweat and moisture. The consumer also had the option to use the remote control to operate the products. The CD players sported a stainless-steel casing and provided shock protection to prevent disruption during exercise. The players featured an orange-backlit LCD for easy viewing, and accessories designed for movement including a remote control, hand strap and butterfly apparel-clip for extra convenience.

As we saw with Alessi, we cannot really speak of true "disruptive solutions" for the High End, although in this world of "digital fitness" the specific design solutions generate new opportunities for competitive advantage through ergonomics. The two lessons for the High End are the changed customer focus, and the anticipation of trends. Nike became more tuned to the digital world, whereas Philips became more tuned to lifestyle. A true High End combined proposition was born out of apparently disparate, initially non-overlapping portfolios.

Bringing Jewelry into the Age of High Tech

Active Crystals, a joint proposition of Swarovski and Philips, resulted in a line of captivating accessories, such as USBs in the shape of hearts and locks designed to nurture and preserve our digital memories. Here, function marries form, with the selection of form coming from deep metaphors. Isn't a heart-shaped box the secret depository of a woman's best-kept secret?

Active Crystals positioned ordinary and mainstream commodity electronic accessories such as USB as High End artifacts. With Active Crystals, Philips and Swarovski established a new dialogue between high style on one hand, and high-tech on the other. Supported by a sophisticated imagery art directed by a boutique agency SelectNY, Active Crystals successfully combined the aesthetics of Swarovski's advertising with Philips' general brand identity.

The bottom line here is that technology, even common technology of the digital age, can be brought to the High End through a judicious partnership of technology and style. The partnership between Swarovski and Philips showed a strong proof that partnerships are the path to tomorrow's High End. The nature of these relations? – partnerships between the world of style and the world of technology.

The "Innovation and Leadership" Dimension

Let's look at the four factors in the innovation and leadership dimension, and then subject them to an RDE study to see which ideas work.

1. The *innovation factor*: Does the High End proposition drive the development of its category/industry by introducing superior technological features, yet maintain continuity with earlier product generations?

This factor represents the "degree zero" of the High End. Innovation is "a must" in this domain. TAG Heuer as well as hundreds of other companies, large and small, maintain their edge due only to the constant product innovation and upgrading. The Polaroid example instructs us about the fate of companies that do not maintain their innovation.

2.   The *revolutionary factor*: Does the High End proposition incorporate a paradigm-changing, breakthrough technological or scientific feature?

If innovation is the natural flow of life of High End business success, then paradigm-breaking innovation is a beneficial tornado, which brings the new to change the way we live. Think of Sony Walkman or Apple iPod, and the way they changed how we experience music.

3.   The *partnership factor*: Does the High End proposition create opportunities for a fruitful partnership with non-competing companies, in order to generate and share knowledge, and garner positive attention from the media?

We described the critical importance of previously unseen partnerships. Who would have thought that the design masters of Alessi would go electric? Or that lifestyle leader Swarovski would go digital? And who could imagine that Philips, the name of what once was just a high-tech powerhouse, would turn to new lifestyle dimensions by associating itself with Nike?

4.   The *thought leadership factor*: Does the High End proposition involve the public endorsement and/or direct representation of a leader who stands for the brand in the eye of the public?

We mentioned Apple as one best practice of High End innovation. The real High End mojo of Apple lies in its ability to truly lead, not only by design but also by its CEO. Steve Jobs as the personification of the Apple brand does not require any introduction. This is even explicitly recorded by analysts like Intebrand and their Business Week "Top 100 Brands" editorial team as a potential weak point in terms of Job's personal condition and ultimate succession plan. The essence of this factor is that just bringing a new generation of products is not the best you can do to be at the top of the High End. To be part of the collective imaginary as "the" leader in your category and a leader in contemporary culture is the "real deal".

Customer Mindsets for the Dimension 3 of Future High End: Innovation and Leadership

Let's move to the RDE analysis of this somewhat less tangible dimension. Although innovation and leadership might be less visible to the end consumers, there is nothing here that is superficial for the industry itself. On the contrary, innovation itself is one of the most critical facets of brand image in the High End.

The Innovation and Leadership start from the four factors (Figure 7.1), with the supporting data in Figure 7.2 and 7.3, as well as the numerical data in the Appendix (Table A4).

The baseline value for Innovation and Leadership (+32) is in line with what we have seen before for the first two dimensions. Thus, about one in three participants is ready to call a proposition "High end", when the idea is positioned as a manifestation of Innovation and Leadership. When it comes to the elements, there are no surprises for the total panel. People feel that when the item is "totally revolutionary" (an appeal to the emotions), it will be perceived as a manifestation of High End. Some people expect that a true future High End product will "completely change the way you live", not "just create a new product category". Other drivers of the future High End perceptions include the functionality of the offering.

The participants divide into two approximately equal-sized mindsets, with a similar predisposition to consider a proposition as High End. Let's see the different drivers for each segment.

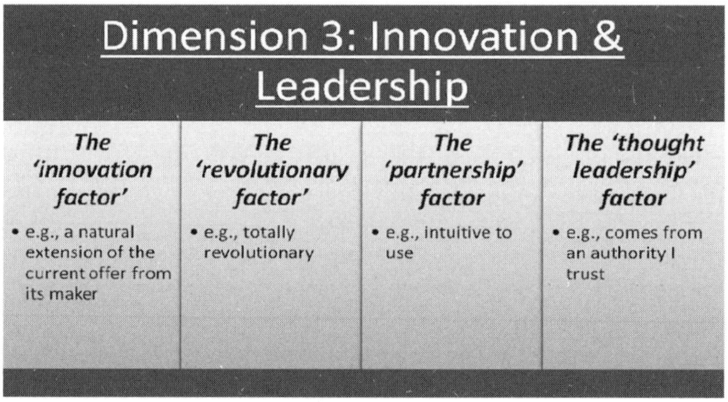

Dimension 3: Innovation & Leadership			
The 'innovation factor'	*The 'revolutionary factor'*	*The 'partnership' factor*	*The 'thought leadership' factor*
• e.g., a natural extension of the current offer from its maker	• e.g., totally revolutionary	• e.g., intuitive to use	• e.g., comes from an authority I trust

Figure 7.1   The four factors for Dimension 3: Innovation and Leadership

Segment 1: "Focus on the leader" (Figure 7.2) considers a proposition as High End when *it does not continue* or extend a former offer. The idea of being "innovative in continuity with the earlier generation of the same product" drives down the perception of High End by 7 points (impact of –7). Segment 1 expects a High End solution to be "totally revolutionary" (+9), something that "completely changes the way you live" (+13). It also should come from a public leader (+6), someone they trust (+7) or "created thanks to a "maverick CEO" (+7). The Focus on the Leader segment responds to the "partnership factor". The offer should be multifunctional and combine advances from multiple industries (both have impacts of +6).

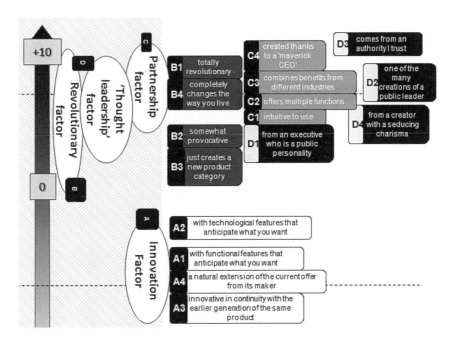

Figure 7.2   Performance of the Segment 1 "Focus on the leader" for Dimension 3: Innovation and Leadership

Segment 2: "Functional innovation" (Figure 7.3) is all about innovation and with a lot of expectations. Segment 2 sees High End products having features which anticipate what you want (+19, an extraordinary impact). At the same time, Segment 2 searches for evolutionary innovation that delivers solutions that are "innovative in continuity with the earlier generation of the same product" (+18) or are "a natural extension of the current offer from its maker" (+13).

Not surprisingly, this functional innovation segment does not want "somewhat provocative" products (–7). The reason could be that these products might not be seen as useful or functional, perhaps resulting from experience with an unwelcome plethora of pseudo-revolutionary products.

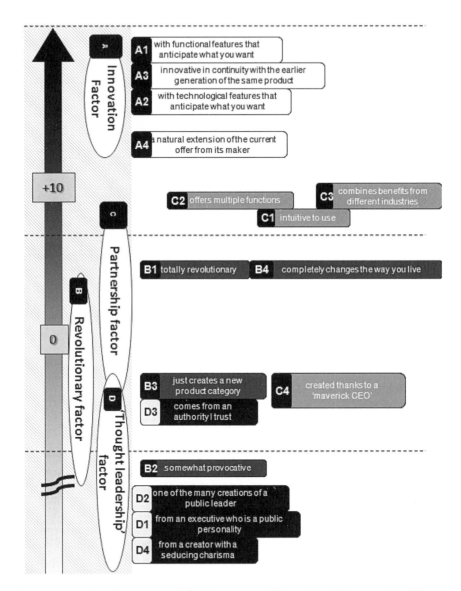

Figure 7.3   Performance of the Segment 2 "Functional Innovation" for Dimension 3: Innovation and Leadership

Segment 2, the functional innovation group, like functionality, but remain very dubious about future flashy personalities who create the products or introduce them. Be simple, straightforward, and not flashy. "From a creator with a seducing charisma" drives down their rating by 18 points; "from an executive who is a public personality" drives it down by 17 points and "one of the many creations of a public leader" drives it down by 15 points. Perhaps people in this Segment 2 do not trust an "abstract", generically described authority, but on the other hand respond positively to the concrete, to a real individual who is well known.

If a single proposition is to be developed for both segments, then avoid focusing on personalities with the exception of "comes from an authority I trust". This particular element is positive for Segment 1 (Disruptive), and neutral, that is, not damaging, for Segment 2 (Functional Innovation).

The two segments agree on statements, which talk about the *partnership*. Finally, claims about future functionality and multi-industrial, multidisciplinary vision and heritage should do well with both segments. Approach the thought leadership factor carefully. The numbers generally do not suggest a positive impact of this factor on the perception of High End. We strongly believe in the potential of leadership messaging for the High End. However, plan this message with the greatest care to turn it into a true "success factor".

Summing Up

You can innovate in the High End by re-inventing products in two ways. For the high-tech companies, expand a person's lifestyle. The second way expands RandD, which is a strategy for fashion and design brands. Leadership is complementary to innovation. However, leadership must be carefully managed in order for the special touch of charisma to be positive rather than negative.

Now, how do you win in this game of constant improvement? Partnerships are the key to the innovation of non-digital brands in the digital age. On the other hand, if you are a high-tech company you increasingly need to part from your "oversupply of redundant features". To get into the High End and succeed, high-tech companies must become more sensitive to lifestyle, and to the soul of their customers. The business process of High Design can create new partnerships, and achieve the combination of High End through high-tech and high-touch.

We learned these lessons for TAG Heuer and from Philips' partnerships with Alessi, Nike and Swarovski. TAG Heuer with a series of basic innovations kept its edge in High End. Its well-managed celebrity marketing became a true creative partnership. The Philips–Alessi partnership showed the value of cooperation among non-competing companies as a way to get into the High End with newly revived, powerful propositions. The Philips–Nike partnership innovated sports and electronics, moving into the High End in lifestyle fitness. Finally, the Philips–Swarovski partnership showed how to bring style and design into traditional, commodity electronics.

Through RDE, we reconfirmed that people differ in the way they think, so that one size does not fit all. There are two different mindsets of consumers in the context of the Innovation and Leadership Dimension: *Focus on the Leader* (52 percent) vs. *Functional Innovation* (48 percent). "Focus on the leader" considers Innovation and Leadership as a High End marker, but the proposition cannot be simply an evolutionary change. It must be more than that. "Functional innovation" is all about new functions and with a lot of expectations from a High End proposition. Functional innovation is more evolutionary, less revolutionary.

8

Rule 4: It's About "Fame" (Dimension: Marketing, Communication and Distribution)

> *Integrity and entertainment are what matters in brand communications.*
> *It's an interaction between the brand and the customers that really*
> *counts. I don't believe that brands can be entirely built neither from the*
> *top nor from the bottom. It's pure alchemy between the two of them.*
> *Federico Marchetti, CEO, Yoox, Italy*

Introduction: When Reality Fails the Image

When it comes to the High End, the devil is not only in the *detail*, but also and especially in the *retail*. To demonstrate this underlying principle, we move to the Far East, where the High End Western brands trade at higher perceived value. Unless, of course, the unexpected intervenes. And when does it ever fail to do so!

Heineken used to be the virtual number one beer brand in Hong Kong because of the premium image. Being an imported brand, Heineken was positioned as the most premium brand, and is expensive, even in supermarkets. However, in order to capture more market share and improve the profitability in Hong Kong, the Heineken brand expanded the distribution to all channels including low-class catering outlets. Drinkers came to realize that the Heineken brand is not that premium, and it does not make sense to pay so much for a beer. The brand nowadays has dropped to fifth position and totally lost its premium perception. The moral of this story is harsh but instructive: reaching people is good – unless it costs you loss of image.

Yet When the Brand Successfully Reaches the People …

Anais Anais, the fragrance by Cacharel, initially was launched by L'OREAL in mass distribution at a near-commodity price. The success of Anais Anais made L'OREAL rethink its strategy, and so marketers removed it from supermarkets, putting it instead in selective distribution venues, such as perfumeries. By the 1990s, Anais Anais rose to the number one worldwide fragrance brand for women.

Anais Anais maintained consistency of the marketing mix (bottle, advertising visual, fragrance and packaging). It reached slightly above the level typical for the mass-market channel and it chose a wide array of distribution standards.

When image-making leads, people-reaching translates into inevitable success, by design, even to the point of jump-starting to the High End from a lower commodity status, as did Anais Anais.

Create Emotional Bonding by Reaching People and Image-Making

By *reaching-people*, we mean the aggregated activities that bring a product or a brand into *physical connection* with the prospective customer, including placing products into distribution, product launch events, service in retail, and so forth.

By *image-making*, we mean the aggregate media-channeled activities which create the perceived High End positioning of a product or a brand. These activities comprise classic advertising, celebrity marketing, viral marketing, and storytelling around the brand.

The High End dimension addressed in this chapter involves marketing communication at the level of both mass media and grassroots buzz. Both types of communications along with distribution move the High End closer people in general, and to the prospective customers in particular.

But (and there's always a "but …"), what else is involved here? Many High End brands in FMCG (fast-moving consumer goods) are distributed in mass retail. The sheer commodity-nature of this distribution channel produces a problem, a contradiction, right off. How does the company discover the right type of distribution in the mass-market channels, in order to reinforce the High End nature of a product? Just think about some of these products, such as the prestigious Moet Hennessy brands and similar groups associated with luxury. Such apparently democratic, widespread distribution challenges the merchandiser and potentially endangers the brand.

The "right" distribution channels allow High End products to shine and manifest themselves. However, it requires some creativity; as the product could simply pop-up unexpectedly in a store, courtesy of the PR planner, although this strategy by itself does not create the High End perception, nor reinforce the fact that the product is High End.

To communicate the High End nature, merchandisers at Peroni Beer cleverly displayed just one bottle in a glass-door refrigerator within the shopping window on a leading London luxury street. This alternative use of physical retail for PR and profiling purposes made Peroni the centre a positive buzz wave, promptly positioning the Italian brand as one alternative High End option in its market. Likewise, Lancia, the Italian fine automotive mass-luxury brand, opened special stores for direct sales in the leading Milanese fashion areas, like Corso Como. Both examples clearly attempt to elevate the status to High End by showing off the best merchandising and interior design in the trendiest part of town.

Distribution and retail are also important as traditional communication engines. We can cite a number of industries, such as clothing, where the store presence is key. Avril Groom's insightful contribution to FT magazine *How to Spend it?* describes a fashion brand for smart ladies called Jaeger. Trying to project an image of the quality, Jaeger changed its retail concept to portray more luxury feel. Here is a very interesting example of a wider High End phenomenon that is on the rise. Although nothing seems to be new in that, the mere locations of the shops are highly strategic, reiterating the old adage: what matters is *location, location, location*. The shops are deliberately located in areas that are perceived to have "affordable shops", and not placed in the too-expensive luxury streets. The Jaeger stores are cleverly connected to business districts where typical customers spends their working time, and discretely enjoy their discerning, intelligent choice of styles by Jaeger with friends, as a shared confidence among friends would be.

Winning distribution strategy and the understated branding generate discrete buzz. Jaeger typifies a specific offering, which probably has existed for quite some time – contemporary trends and optimal quality meeting a reasonable price. This refined "semi-couture" segment demands a very precise approach to location and distribution. Other brands using the same strategy are Dorothee Singhoff's Schumacher of Germany, Andrew Rosen's Theory 10 of New York, By Malene Birger of Denmark, Tara Jarmon of Paris and Patrizia Pepe of Italy.

The Crucial Importance of Service Design for High End Retail

Beyond tangible High End retail features is the "soft" service element aiming to conquer the customer's heart. The notion of exemplary, unique and imaginative service promises to become the hallmark of an entire new approach to customer relationships, which for lack of a better name we call "High End service". In the words of one social observer: "I am not influenced by luxury brands at all, but rather I am influenced by premium services".

Consider quality service enjoyed by those flying in premium classes. Many moderately prosperous and certainly most well-heeled passengers are prepared to pay extra to have better service, especially so when the travel is for professional reasons. Trudging through airports, waiting in long queues, eating food on-the-go, seeking wireless connections and trying to find personal space and time are all important slices of time for contemporary business travelers. The reason is simple. The quality service gives the traveler personal space and time. That quality services is memorable; it allows the traveler to escape, if only momentarily, from the hurried life he or she lives, and all too often endures. This is where the whole notion of "Premium Economy" or "Comfort Zone" class was born. In times of crisis, this seems like a viable alternative at a moderate increase in pricing for a better cabin experience – especially during intercontinental flights.

So, what is the lesson to be learned for the High End business from service in particular and distribution in general? Retail might be clearly perceived as High End's Achille's heel, especially when it comes to distribution through mixed channels where control is not easy to maintain. On the other hand, distribution, retail, and customer service can end up becoming one of the most powerful opportunities for High End marketers, creating buzz, loyalty and finally success. One has to mix retail with other marketing communication activities such as PR to viral marketing and never forget the crucial quality of human interaction in the face-to-face contact between customers and their brands. Do not think that service design and staff training represent merely a hygiene factor. The reality is much bigger; human-to-human interaction offers the business a unique opportunity to reinforce the High End edge.

The Relevance of the Story

Every "big idea" reaches people deeper when told through a great story – the kind of story that builds the brand and makes its image.

Rather than more examples from the business context, let's move to a story from the world of entertainment. It is a story of aspiration and drama, of beauty, and the coming of age of what was supposed to become a new star.

On the 6th of December, 2006, Tyra Banks and the judging panel of *America's Next Top Model* had to decide who would be the winner of the seventh cycle of the contest. *America's Next Top Model* had grown into one of the most popular and successful reality shows in the recent history of TV. The program joins popular culture and glamour, creating a struggle among people to go from rags to the top. What better narrative to appeal people's emotions, and let them connect with characters and story?

The two candidates were CariDee English, from Fargo, North Dakota, and Melrose Bickerstaff, a fashion expert. Melrose was well prepared, determined and driven. CariDee could afford to put herself up to the challenge only because the year before she found the medication that healed her skin. CariDee had suffered from a severe case of psoriasis. Psoriasis had previously prevented her from pursuing her modeling dream.

In the last show, set in Antonio Gaudi's Park Guell, one of the most elegant spots in Barcelona, both candidates, each with a strong personality, performed well. At some point, CariDee made the slight mistake of walking on Melrose's wedding gown, an extremely expensive piece designed for the occasion by Victorio and Luchino. This gave Melrose an apparent technical advantage and CariDee's fans a few minutes of anxiety. Let's go back to the studio, where the final decision was made – who would be *America's Next Top Model* 2006, winning a $100,000 modeling contract?

Melrose had functional skills, passion and determination, CariDee had all of that as well, although a few mistakes along the way of the various episodes made her look more human. More than anything else, CariDee was a great story – a Cinderella-reborn story that made the difference to the judges and to the wider national TV audience. The winner, not surprisingly, was CariDee – ready to enter the world of modeling and intelligently moving on to sign as a spokesperson for the National Psoriasis Foundation, a non-profit organization aimed to raise awareness and offer support to the victims of this disease.

This media entertainment story is a perfect example of the power of the story. It inspires, leaving room for a perhaps short term-lived but nevertheless powerful myth to emerge and sweep the proposition into the High End. The challenge for the marketer of premium brands and products is to discover or create this powerful story, and reach people's hearts at their best and deepest.

Sometimes the story is actually hidden, attracting not so much the wider crowds but the selected connoisseur. The H. Stern story is worth telling for its lessons and its inspiration, how a Jewish refugee from Hitler's Germany turned into a passionate Brazilian entrepreneur. This Brazilian brand of beautiful and rare stones is as a blueprint of High End service that helps to move the company perception upwards.

The story begins with Stern's escape with his parents after Hitler's 1938 Kristallnacht. Many years later, he still steers the company he founded from its original seedbed in Rio de Janeiro, where he settled as a refugee. The company has grown to a major global player in the gem industry. Stern's stores enjoy a strong presence in Israel, including a boutique at Ben Gurion Airport and, remarkably, enjoy a great reach and success in Arab countries, although as a joint venture under a different name. This story is a fascinating and major asset to the mystique H. Stern.

So, what is the lesson for the High End? What do stories tell business, not in content but in terms of the impulse to drive to a higher level? In the High End, like in luxury, a compelling narrative aura stimulates more than just a simple positive response in the audience. A story makes the brand look more real, more connected to the consumer than a faceless value brand. People are, after all, entranced by stories as they have been for many thousands of years. For a moment, take a break, read Homer or Beowulf to see the stories of thousands of years ago which entranced, and in translation still do. And bring the power of the story to the market.

As with many other intangibles, we most clearly realize the importance of storytelling when it is not there. The effect of no story manifests itself by a fatal absence of brand mystique. In that case, although there is an advertisement with words and images, we miss some of the magic, that second glance which makes us turn our head back with interest. Remove a highly consistent narrative soul in the core of a brand and we have potentially a fatal defect, often beyond the ability of any compensating factors to remedy. The magic is the essence in the story, which becomes part of the High End fabric for the particular product or experience.

Fortunately for the High End, and unlike the legend in the case of luxury, storytelling is not inherent and innate. The story can be engineered. The story is democratic, because it is based on the writing talent of High End communicators to create it. Just as the best advertising agencies do.

Swarovski: Advertising Gets the Glitz across the Globe

One must always keep a critical eye on the distinguishing features of one's brand and be able to adapt to the times when necessary. The grammar of our brand will always be marked by "swan-like-femininity," which, by cultivating a sensitive intelligence, we strive to express in a language that will be understood.

Markus Langes-Swarovski, Member of the Board, Swarovski, Austria

If the red carpet is the natural *milieu* of High End perception in the world of movies and art, then glitz is the natural seedbed of perceived exclusivity. Glitz and all that goes with it holds sway as the ultimate image-making to reach customers' hearts and minds. Our next story deals with the most celebrated crystals in the world, and their first brand campaign. Let's follow Swarovski's High End tale in its maiden voyage through the world of advertising and communication.

For more than 110 years, Swarovski has managed to be at the top of its industry without the need of a classic marketing. Therefore it was a signal event when in 2006 the company launched its first "coherent" brand campaign. Swarovski agency of choice, SelectNY, is highly specialized in communication strategies, storytelling and art direction for luxury and High End. SelectNY envisioned, conceived and delivered a campaign with the high aesthetic impact demanded by the Swarovski team. The theme for Swarovski's first umbrella brand campaign was the Greek myth of the Three Graces. World-renowned fashion photographer Craig McDean made a mesmerizing portrait of top models Vivian Solari, Guinevere van Seenusa and Maria Dvirnik. Such theme was then naturally stretched and elegantly adapted to support the aforementioned "Active Crystals" collaboration between Swarovski and Philips. This was feasible because Swarovski's visual storytelling is powerful and flexible, especially when we realize it deals with consistency in fashion branding, a world which routinely changes from season to season. In terms of pure High End storytelling, the campaign combines the glitz of today with the *eternal narrative* of the brand that Markus Langes-Swarovski evoked in his opening quote to this section.

Aurea's Ambilight: A Synthesis of Creating Glitz and Reaching People

Glitz works with any High End product or brand – even if it is a high-tech premium proposition like the Aurea by Philips.

Our story will look at those marketing and advertising elements in the product mix with which one can create the High End, even in a category that inexorably movies to commodity over time. Aurea by Philips teaches us how to reach people, and how to consolidate one's position by means of a premium campaign. We will "mix" the two leading themes of this chapter, namely placement and advertising.

For many years, TV was generally excluded from the world of High End. The exclusion ended on the summer solstice of 2007, when Philips robustly asserted its aspirational position as a High End player by organizing a pre-launch event of its new Aurea Ambilight TV. The event took place in Paris, that European temple-city of luxury, with a stunning show staging fashion models and special lighting effects. The House of Lanvin, the luxury fashion brand, was closely involved in styling the event and the advertising campaign. Emerging designers such as jewel-maker Lorenz Baumer were co-opted in the creation of a superior aesthetic experience.

The placement of Aurea in the very holy ground of luxury represented by the Lanvin boutiques was beneficial for the marketing of both brands. For quite some time after the launch, Lanvin boutiques displayed Aurea products as part of their cutting-edge capability in interior design. Through this display Philips reaffirmed its position as a trendsetter.

By moving back to the spirit of distribution and placement of their top luxury-positioned, first 1937 TV, Philips found in Lanvin a true luxury partner to associate its best High End consumer proposition. Furthermore, the cooperation was not just one-directional. Lanvin associated itself with the best of high-tech, people-focused, experience-driven innovation. From fashion photographers to a relationship with the Lanvin stores, the cooperation moved Philips' Aurea towards the very top of the High End.

Moving to the advertising campaign, Philips went one step further than usual to attract the High End customer by engaging Hong Kong-born director Wong Kar Wai, well known for his spectacular movies as well as for his commercials such as Lacoste. The director's goal was to create a movie of the highest aesthetic impact, which was shown on August 30, 2007. "There is only one sun" debuted at the world wide TV premier of Aurea during the IFA consumer electronics fair in Berlin, creating a new experience for the fair and a new way to promote to the High End customer. The event was capped by a glamorously integrated advertising campaign, featuring Dutch celebrity top model Rianne Ten Haken, elegantly styled in Lanvin clothes and photographed by specialized master of luxury photographer Vincent Peters.

So what are the business lessons that we can learn from Swarovski and from Aurea? When it comes to the High End, glamour in advertising pays off. Launching the product in a High End way provides you a key opportunity that goes beyond standard marketing mechanisms. You can create buzz and make magic happen, and thereby lift your brand above the ordinary. In general, connecting High End marketing communication with the world of luxury (photographers, models, styling brands, communication codes) is always an option you should consider. And, of course, involving appropriate stars and celebrities is always a plus. Just make sure that in the end the efforts pay off.

Celebrities and Fame

Well beyond classic commercial relationships, celebrities can be used as partners to create limited collections or franchised product lines. These celebrities can create a *perceived authority* in the market. The "Berluti and Zidane" case in Chapter 3 ideally shows the way. *You must move* beyond the simple, easy-to-buy relation between the brand and the testimonial, where everyone seems to be "for rent", at least if the price is right. Rather, create a natural-appearing connection between celebrity and High End brand, not a forced connection, not one that seems to have been purchased.

Victoria's Secret is the "affordable luxury" brand which perfected this approach with the mechanics of the fashion system. The system combines the super-model system and the fashion show in order to create the ultimate buzz. For Victoria's Secret it is not an issue of a momentary connection with top models as testimonials, a connection purchased for one season, and one where the fit does not seem to last more than the minute or two before the viewer is shunted to the next testimonial. Rather, Victoria's Secret seems to have institutionalized this "testimonial strategy". The result is that Victoria's Secret is perceived as *the* fashion system. The customer does not feel that the advertisement is just another paid announcement from a sponsor.

Of course, there is the space to do more and better. Systematic innovation works well here. This is the way TAG Heuer worked with Tiger Woods in order to create its innovative concepts. A parallel celebrity approach is also well used by TAG Heuer, this time to establish an emotional connection with a historical legacy of the greatest value for the brand. This celebrity connection is with the legend of Steve McQueen, established through the common ground of the racing world. McQueen's passion for motors was undisputed, resulting in his starring in movies like *Le Mans*, and his direct participation in racing events, sometimes against the will of the managers to whom he committed in his professional contracts. It takes a certain amount of luck for a company like TAG Heuer, or indeed any corporation, to enjoy such a direct and universal connection with a legend. Stars of McQueen's caliber are simply not measurable, not to mention repeatable when it comes to the celebrity aura they project on a brand.

The High End lesson here is that celebrities matter. However, there must be a real connection between the High End brand and the customer's emotions and aspirations. When this connection already exists, celebrities become powerful elements to use in the marketing mix of premium propositions. If possible, High End brands should avoid communicating the sense of mercenary "endorsement for hire" in the celeb testimonials. Rather, the connection must be seen as natural, organic, persisting over time; that is, a meaningful, long-term relation, and not a one-night stand.

Marketing on a Budget: Reaching High End Customers at Low Cost

It is easy to launch a global advertising campaign with the generous budget required for mass media. In times of economic downturn, or when you just can't afford the multi-zero price tag of traditional advertising, you might think it is impossible to reach people and create your High End image at low cost. The good news is that perhaps you can. The trick here is to step out of the constraints of mass media, and focus on the end goal of communication – *truly* reaching people. The question here is what can you do with your High End marketing and communication when you can *barely* afford any?

Our story of low-budget High End begins in an unlikely way in 1906 when Vincenzo Lancia, son of a wealthy family in Turin, Italy, started up a "new economy" company of his times – a car company. Lancia was immediately positioned in the top luxury segment – the same league as Cadillac, Bugatti, Isotta Fraschini, Bentley or Maybach. Lancia sport cars were winning important racing trophies. The brand's technological innovation kept driving success, generation after generation. Until World War Two, the Lancia brand was a true star and a blue chip, equivalent to today's high-tech blue chips.

Lancia's High End existence did not last forever. By the end of the 1960s, Lancia's positioning gradually moved downwards. First, it competed against the likes of BMW, and then it shifted down in the automotive branding "food chain". While still delivering magnificent sedans and coupés such as the Lancia Appia and the Aurelia, Lancia drifted as the memory of Vincenzo faded, and as his dream dissipated. Such drifts in the "second generation" afflict many High End and luxury brands.

Moving closer to mainstream cars, Lancia became simply too small to sustain its position in the High End. After FIAT bought Lancia in 1969, Lancia was slowly reduced to niche, first as "sports luxury" semi-luxury brand, then of preferred city mini-car segment for affluent women. This was the last segment left. Without the segment, there was nothing to stave off financial bankruptcy and brand disappearance.

Changes of design and especially marketing communication were desperately needed. Lancia's last hope was a newly redesigned Ypsilon aimed at the same affluent female target aged 24–35, either independent students, or young professionals, one step beyond the students. The product itself was designed according to a classic High End blueprint, with top quality, sensual aesthetics and, sharing the same platform and engines as the cheaper FIAT Punto, a mainstream European best-seller. The goal was to return to the High End, and to its hallmark, high margins.

Yet, success was not a given, because a good High End product does not necessarily make it per se. It takes image-building and people-reaching to make it. However, by 2002 the cost of mass media was unaffordable with the marketing budget at the bare minimal level. Then Managing Director Luca De Meo, with the resourceful support of creative boutique agency 515 of Turin, took a grassroots approach. This meant bringing the Lancia flavor and essence right to the prospective customer, truly reaching people in their day-life and night-life. The techniques adopted were rather unorthodox, decidedly low-cost, incredibly fresh and creative.

High End propositions and advertisers can use viral marketing as well as anyone else. In one module of the viral campaign, a Lancia Ypsilon car key would be left on a chair of a trendy nightclub: the DJ would call a few times to ask: "Who is the driver of the new Lancia Ypsilon who lost the key?" The product's name was therefore shouted (loud and clear, and by the "ruling DJ"), right where the customer prospects happened to be – right on the dance floor or relaxing in the "chill out" spaces of the discotheque. A second "plot", just as creative a module and a bit more outré, used a love letter printed in pink handwriting, attached by a pink magnet next to the door handles of different competing brand cars (VW Polo, Peugeot 206, Citroen Pluriel, especially Mini) that happen to be parked in front of trendy nightclubs and bars. It was impossible for the potential customer NOT to find it. The letter had a statement of love and an invitation for the reader. It looked naturally written in an elegant copy, sounding like a true love letter and signed "Lancia Ypsilon". This was an invitation both to test the car and to actually fall in love with it at first sight. Of course, people in the selected audience took note of the buzz and remembered the name and the positive feeling that Lancia Ypsilon generated.

So what is the lesson for the High End here? For very low cost, Lancia made the Ypsilon the true "talk of town" among the trendsetters in urban centers in Italy (Milan, Turin, Rome), Lancia reached people, re-established its image of desirable brand, regained its "High Endness" and, most important, sold enough new Ypsilon's at sufficient margin to save the company from bankruptcy. Out of desperate necessity, and without a large budget, Lancia invested a few thousand euros in alternative High End marketing. And the effort reached people, rebuilt the image, and saved Lancia.

Tomorrow's High End Marketing

While marketing communication works today, it is difficult to predict how this will play in the future. The media infrastructure continues to expand and change rapidly, with the traditional running side by side with the novel, and sometimes outré, well outside "the box". In the near future we will see polarization, often extreme, between today's scripted mass media that is indispensable for image building, and the rougher, unscripted, grassroots marketing and viral campaigns. As always, it is not black and white here. People search for those protective ecological niches where they survive and prosper. The media is no different, with its intricate network of "gray zones". The High End attracts talent, and talent will develop methods other than the traditional communications.

There is the other world, the alternative media. Consider community building on the Web. Here is where you will find communities for commonly shared High End products and brands. The natural affinity of buyers of the same High End brand will create these communities. Members in these communities, the owners, will feel at ease with each other, sharing ideas, feelings, and suggestions.

While this is a future in the making, opinions are varied and mixed. Some think that communication is radically changing fast and forever, in a fundamental and paradigm-breaking fashion. Others see an infinite landscape of grey tonalities between the "white" of mass media and the "black" of innovative digital media and viral approaches.

For a few years now, viral communication and grassroots media have become unavoidable, as the content of communication is increasingly being taken over by the consumers of the communication. Just witness the success of Facebook, Twitter and YouTube, as the poster children of the new media. Here, a new game is being played, and in completely new ways.

It is in the virtual world that many High End brands, along with the celebrities, will communicate. "Let's move to SecondLife", a pure "online play", which created new digital notions of digital luxury. There will be ever more new cultural developments in the future of digital branding. For example, sponsoring a regular concert might be a good promotion for a High End brand. In the world of tomorrow's High End, sponsoring such a session in the digital media landscape of virtual worlds will make sense as well. There is already a history of such efforts, as Nokia did in Brazilian SecondLife with Fat Boy Slim. Tomorrow, such efforts might be more powerful, more truly *au courant*. In the virtual world, the customer may be ready to engage in a deeper dialog with a brand, especially a high-tech brand, when the focus is on functionality yet the tonality of communication is one of fashion and lifestyle.

Factors of the Marketing, Communication and Distribution Dimension

As with the previous dimensions, here are the factors we will research with the consumers:

1.   The *grass roots factor*: Does the High End proposition benefit from the buzz generated by culturally-driven, grassroots communication?

As in the Lancia Ypsilon case-history, premium is worth paying for when people speak about it – the more, the better – and preferably in positive terms. Here, methods like the Net Promoter Score are used to gear up brand management to a changing world where customers not only demand to be "kings and queens" for one day, but also act as opinion leaders in their own social circles as well.

2.   The *image factor*: Is the High End proposition associated with a compelling and appealing visual presence, permitting the brand to demonstrate its promise?

Aesthetics are important to build the perception of High End in people's minds. Swarovski is a successful company in various aspects of High End, including cultural marketing and design partnerships for innovation. However, Swarovski moved beyond that heritage, and launched a major classic advertising campaign directed and planned according to the highest standards of marketing and communicating, like efforts more often seen in the world of luxury. In the case of Philips Aurea, a major marketing effort turned the perception of commodity in people's minds, and positioned the product as a high-margin opportunity in the commodity market of TV sets.

3.   The *celebrity factor*: Does the High End proposition benefit
      from believable public endorsement by celebrities, who acts as
      evangelists?

In this chapter, we completed the TAG Heuer story started in Chapter 3 by analyzing the relationship with celebrity testimonial/uber-cultural icon Steve McQueen. Celebrities are key to High End success. They embody people's dreams and aspirations across generations and across income brackets. The celebrity contribution demands, however, the highest degree of strategic thinking, the greatest marketing savvy, to be used to its greatest advantage.

4.   The *placement factor*: Does the proposition take advantage of selective
      distribution, and can the proposition be found in the appropriate,
      image-enhancing channels for the High End?

From Heineken to Moet Chandon, from Jaeger fashionable style to Philips' association with the House of Lanvin and the glitz of fashion models, the *do*s and *don't*s of placement and distribution should be clear as fundamental direction to achieve High End success.

Customer Mindsets for the Dimension 4 of the High End: Marketing Communication and Distribution

Dimension 4 comprises polarizing factors and ideas. In the days gone by, the ideas contained in Dimension 4 are what communication and marketing were all about; reach, surprise, convince, convert, ultimately to sell. The question for the High End is *How*? Compare these two phrases: "I'll give you all the riches in the world' and "Here is the engagement ring, the best I can afford". Which of these two phrases is the more powerful – the bigger but less concrete, or the smaller but more concrete? With this in mind, let's review the data for this dimension that we have divided into four component factors shown in Figure 8.1 with supporting data in the Appendix (Table A5).

The baseline perception of High End for the Total (+28) is in line with that of the other dimensions, meaning that approximately one in four participants would consider a future proposition as High End when the topic deals with marketing, communication and distribution. No elements score particularly well in general. Talking directly about specific aspects of marketing, communication and distribution seem, on the surface, to be modest "drivers" of the High End,

Figure 8.1   The four factors for Dimension 4: Marketing, Communication and Distribution

at least when we average the data for the total population of our RDE study. We will see some segment effects, however, coming up shortly.

In line with our earlier analyses, we identified two equally sized segments with essentially the same additive constant, so both will be equally likely to call a proposition High End when the focus is on marketing, communication and distribution. But they are quite different otherwise. Let's see how the "High End markers" work more in detail.

Segment 1 "Form own opinions" (Figure 8.2) are those who respond strongly when they can see the product in the appropriate context, for example, a soundly designed merchandising area. The impact or probability of a proposition being labeled premium is +15 when people in this segment are told or read the phrase "with a superior point of sale" and +9 for "exclusive on-line offer, not available in stores". If you want to convince Segment 1 that your next proposition is High End, then impress them with exciting points-of-sale and displays in stores. Make your packaging stands out. Keep in mind that Segment 1 customers do not like the typical celebrity endorsements or associations, although that dislike might evaporate with concrete personalities rather than generic idea of endorsement.

Segment 2 may be defined as "Swayed by others and authorities" (Figure 8.3). The name of the segment says it all. Consumers in this segment believe that in order to feel that something is High End they need guidance or reinforcement of their decision in the form of good referrals and reviews. The most impact will come from a friend. This segment may be a good candidate for a viral or social campaign because the participants are easily influenced by "buzz". These individuals in Segment 2 also react positively to the production values of the communication, such as "with top quality communication" and "with the associated colors that are beautiful to you".

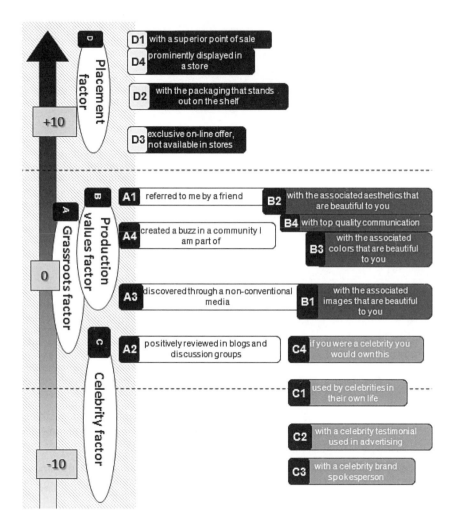

Figure 8.2   Performance of the Segment 1 "Form Own Opinions" for Dimension 4: Communication and Distribution

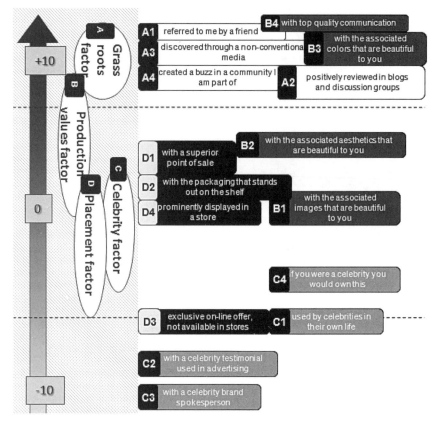

Figure 8.3   Performance of the Segment 2 "Swayed by others and
              authorities" for Dimension 4: Communication and Distribution

Summing Up

Properly positioned association with "right" celebrities and strategically
orchestrated marketing-communication campaigns are crucial to define
the High End image. We explored both approaches to marketing, looking
at competitive and unorthodox grassroots marketing campaigns, as well as
conventional advertising methods.

Swarovski's advertising offered the opportunity to analyze classic, image-
driven, mass-media communication in the High End. In contrast, Philips'
Aurea demonstrated how even groundbreaking innovation requires new
marketing launches to reach the High End status. TAG Heuer demonstrated
a stellar performance in celebrity marketing, specifically one involving the

legend of Steve McQueen as the brand legacy. We closed with Lancia Ypsilon that showed how a great Italian High End brand was reborn, thanks to low-cost highly creative grassroots marketing, coupled with great design.

One message should strongly emerge, especially in these times of economic downturn. *Reaching High End customers at low cost is indeed feasible. It just takes the creative leadership to re-invent the rules of the communication game, as did Lancia.* You only have to do it in different, new ways. This is why we believe that grassroots and viral marketing for the High End will require the best talents in the advertising industry to actively contribute. This need for the best talent will be even more apparent in the emerging virtual worlds and digital branding.

Moving to the Global RDE types of customers, we uncovered two segments: "Forms Own Opinions" (49 percent) vs. "Swayed by Others" (51 percent). The first segment responds strongly and independently when they can see the product in the appropriate context. The second segment, "Swayed by others and authorities", call an offering High End on the basis of guidance or reinforcement of their decision in the form of good referrals and reviews.

9

Rule 5: It is About "Higher Values" (Dimension: Sustainability and Simplicity)

> *I see sustainability as a pyramid ranging from required compliances to potential opportunities for companies and brands. At the bottom level, you have the need to ensure legal compliance to the law in the countries where you operate. This is pure risk management, a basic necessity and a hygiene factor indeed … At a higher level, I see sustainability issues as an opportunity to ensure reputation management … The most appealing level of sustainability is "leadership". Leadership is always excellent to build strong brands, and maintain their equity. I see these three levels of sustainability as a portfolio of options for companies and brands, and I think such portfolio needs to be managed pragmatically and contextually.*
>
> Rita Clifton, Chairman, Interbrand, London

Until a decade ago, sustainability might have seemed to be out of place in a book on luxury and the High End. The winds of economic downturn that started to blow in 2007 will only accelerate the general public demand for more ethics, more balance, more social thinking. The worlds of High End and luxury will not be left unaffected. Nowadays, the focus has already grown to structurally include a new world, best described as "good citizenship", "philanthropy", or "caring for others". Along with plain charity auctions and events, this includes art patronage – in essence, doing well by doing good. Or perhaps, as some define it, *sustainability chic*.

At the simplest level, sustainability is merely one dimension of the High End. We have talked about the authenticity of the High End object, the craftsmanship, the leadership, partnerships, marketing communications, and so on. These all involved adding value, adding cachet, allowing the High End objective or service to be "more". We have reached only part-way into the soul of the customer, which is lifted up by acquiring the artifact, associated with a higher existence. Now for the final dimension, sustainability, where the High End can ennoble the soul of the customer through concern with something "greater". What originally was simply support of a cause, or "doing well by doing good", has been absorbed into the world of luxury and the High End. Moral nobility is now part of this High End experience, rather than just acquisition and mere materialist consumption.

When Things Go Right: Sustainability and the High End

Environmental sustainability can "make a High End brand". Or at least environmental sustainability makes the brand considerably stronger and sharper, as Toyota recently showed with its Lexus brand. By addressing the ecological concern for the environment, one of the immediate demands from worldwide public opinion, Lexus pushed itself into the forefront of public opinion and regard thanks to the quick adoption of hybrid engines.

Look at the simplicity and style of the design of LS600h. The purpose is direct – deliver an understated yet inspiring vision of how the premium segment of contemporary vehicles can look and feel. The important factor, however, is the ecological promise, the true achievement of Lexus in view of the sustainability dimension of High End. A major breakthrough in both innovation and marketing terms, a simple statement to the world – this is the essence of Lexus' eco-success at the highest levels of High End. Sustainability, not traditionally associated with the High End, has just emerged as a concern, positively linked to the High End. The High End is "good" when its artifacts and services can be shown to be sustainable, to be better for humankind. What an enormous marketing opportunity for the High End, which up to now has been associated with the not-very-admirable world of MORE.

And When Things Go Wrong Between Sustainability and Premium Business

Body Shop was created by Anita Roddick in 1976 as a sustainability-driven, premium-priced, accessible brand, with its first shop in Brighton, United Kingdom. The concept was so attuned to the times and people's desires and aspirations that Roddick became a millionaire. The Body Shop turned into one of the most important sustainable business blueprints in this rising tide of cultural change.

Since L'Oreal took over the Body Shop, it seems to have gone all basic – even black plastic (non-recyclable) packaging. Being absorbed within this leading French corporation, the Body Shop apparently did not simply lose its independence: it *lost its soul*. Customers noticed, and reacted with a great degree of disillusionment. After all, it is much worse to break your promise and act below your own ethical standards than to never have committed to making any difference at all. Such changes, breaking promises, has happened to more than one company with inevitably disastrous results. Often, when consumers perceive that the brand broke the originally genuine sustainability position, they move not into indifference, but rather into real anger at being "fooled" and "let down". The sense of loss is personal, just as the notion of sustainability itself has a strong personal component that perhaps no other dimension of the High End and luxury has.

Is Sustainability Really an Opportunity for the High End of the Future?

You might think that the notion of sustainability is just simply irrelevant to your High End business, that these considerations have no place, that money in the pocket of the customer trumps considerations of what is good for the earth, good for people.

Well, in that case, think again. A non-sustainable future, with a plundered earth and a tired mankind, will just not happen at all. So the question is not about *whether* but rather *how*. To understand this, we could just look into today's cultural emergence of sustainable values: *it's ubiquitous!* This is why we depart from the functional and marketing details of High End towards a larger view of sustainability.

By sustainability in the world of the High End we mean the opportunity looms large for the High End brand to contribute to welfare, whether this be society (social sustainability) in general, people's personal well-being (personal sustainability and simplicity), or even the "earth's welfare" (eco-sustainability) in particular.

For some High End business leaders or prospective entrepreneurs the foregoing point might sound counterintuitive, actually irrelevant. It is not obvious that the notion of sustainability, or goodness-to-the-other, whether earth or other people, can really be part of the High End rather than the domain of social consciousness belonging to the few noble souls among the privileged. Simply put, this irrelevance of, and indifference to, sustainability is no longer relevant. Sustainability is becoming a key aspect of the High End, a key aspect indeed. The issue now is how? What should be done? Where are the marching orders?

The opportunity: Allowing Sustainability and the High End to Co-Thrive

Sometimes luxury strategies and techniques trickle down to wider audiences; sometimes High End players manage to leapfrog luxury brands and beat them at their own game. For this fifth High End dimension, we decided to create a landscape of possibilities for future High End success. We did so first by reviewing and presenting both the macro-challenges that will affect our global societies. Then we looked at the issues that affect luxury and High End players when they face the cultural change towards a more sustainable world.

We consider these as *lessons from society*. Some lessons come in the form of simple shortcomings in business strategy, errors made by luxury conglomerates in the process of recognizing the new importance of the noble values for the High End. And the other lessons come from less pleasant, far less amusing sources. They come from a frightening analysis of planetary problems, with the role that the High End business can play.

Luxury industry leaders, for the most part, have up to now failed to achieve real credibility with respect to this crucial theme. In essence, we will look not only at what the High End does well but at what the luxury industry is not doing, how it is missing the opportunities. In addition, sustainability is the most stimulating area where High End business leaders could find opportunities to leapfrog the "luxury establishment" and to beat luxury brands at their own game of sophisticated aspiration.

Tomorrow's Sustainable Luxury: WWF "Deeper Luxury"

When you look in newspapers and magazines, you cannot help being struck by the increasing public interest in sustainability. And so we also see the opportunity for "sustainability-sensitive luxury", as a clear target first for the luxury consumer, and then shortly after for the High End consumer. Of course, this fifth dimension is not yet really here yet in its full manifestation. Rather, it seems to be evolving, as people in today's material economy look for more. The opportunity is even greater when we realize that sustainability is a new "creature" for luxury and for the High End, profoundly unlike anything which has come before. This will be the case even more in times of global economic crisis.

We are not introducing the issue of sustainability either to the High End or to luxury. It has already been recognized as important for the future, and introduced in terms of a proposed program. Our story for sustainability was proven at early stage of our research by the very existence of a WWF[1] initiative. This initiative came from an expected source, the World Wildlife Federation. The origin of the initiative emerged as a response to the rather shocking results of the awareness that sustainability of the planet was on its way to becoming an increasing, soon to be major factor of concern.

What then is the *business* opportunity today for the High End? What should High End business search for in terms of specifics? How should companies, their brands and their managers tackle this multiple sustainability challenge, one of a never-before-seen magnitude?

Ideas to take advantage of the new social sensitivity to this sustainability issue were quick in coming. The initiative, a response by luxury and the High End business world, was publicly launched in November 2007 with the groundbreaking "Deeper Luxury" report, completed within the different yet complementary context of "Authentic Luxury", an online community of top talents who care.[2] Led by Jem Bendell of LifeWorth, the Swiss consulting boutique, this WWF Luxury Initiative pointed to opportunities. Activities that High End and luxury business could take in order to make LifeWorth's findings actionable were then organized in the form of workshops and raising public awareness. These were high profile events, such as the first European

---

1   Internationally, WWF – World Wide Fund For Nature (formerly World Wildlife Fund – except in North America where the old name was retained).
2   http://authenticluxury.ning.com/

version of the thought-leading NetImpact conference, held in Geneva in June 2008, with the involvement of world-leading INSEAD business school.

Now for the "beef". Just what exactly should the High End do to capitalize on this interest in sustainability? The focus of the initiative is how sustainability can be turned into competitive opportunities. The initiative generated innovative ideas for actionable and pragmatic tools, such as the celebrity-focus charter to align celebrity branding with sustainability. Luxury players, and thus the High End players as well, should take the lead in this field. A great leapfrogging opportunity for High End brands will materialize from this, if the High End brands move more quickly than do the luxury brands in the alignment.

We can already see some of the adoption of sustainability as a High End "cause". Although not yet universally perceived as part of the traditional High End, sustainability is now featured by an increasing number of corporate giants engaged with the premium side of business. Sustainability could well define a new world of luxury reference frameworks and key cultural parameters. The High End business leaders should take a note and, where possible, anticipate the trend of involving ethics as a factor in the world of aesthetics and business.

The practical issue is how does the company benefit from today's world-wide focus on sustainability? How does the brand show that it is relevant to this movement? An important point here is that it's a *bad* idea to deploy a few innovative "tricks" to get on the sustainability bandwagon, when those are really tricks, and not genuine. For example, think about the green movement. And then look at a bad business strategy called "greenwashing", where the company does a cosmetic "something" to the product, and by so doing takes advantage of the trend. This can backfire for High End brands, because these brands are often the center of conversation. When the brand comes under scrutiny, especially in grassroots blogs and virtual networks of prospective customers and opinion makers, those false steps and attempts to undeservedly ride the wave will be picked up and amplified. The brand performance has to be consistent, otherwise the company will be "unmasked", quite likely even excoriated by the media for having tried to dupe the consumer by pretending.

To High End business leaders, sustainability is a must because it represents the opportunity to anticipate people's *next* dreams and aspirations for a higher quality of life. Sustainability is the tomorrow that business seeks. There is a cultural revolution going on by which the people of both developed nations and emerging countries will demand cleaner air and water, more balanced societies and a higher degree of personal well-being and peace of mind. It is up to the High End entrepreneurs to grab this massive opportunity to do well while doing good. Sustainable design is a starting point and a systematic means to throughout the process.

Understanding What Makes Sustainability and Then Moving it to Business

Each month we see ever increasing focus on sustainability. Two years before this book was being written, specifically middle 2007, the notion of sustainability was just beginning to penetrate consumer consciousness. It was, at that time, the province of the do-gooder, the social activist, the person perceived as moral, but not particularly business savvy, and having little to do with luxury – think of thought-leaders and academic gurus, and perhaps some whistleblowers in the creative industry.

Fast forward the two years. The sustainability marketplace is becoming more sophisticated and segmented, according to research published by Food Navigator USA. The study identified five distinct consumer groups that food and beverage manufacturers in the USA could specifically target with green or eco-friendly products. More than 75 percent of US adults show some kind of green motivation making sustainability more attractive and imperative for business to engage consumers. *Lifestyles of Health and Sustainability* (LOHAS) consumers, who represent 17 percent of the group, are believed to have the strongest environmental, social, and corporate social responsibility values, whereas the other four groups typically show an increased sensitivity to price when purchasing natural foods, making the sustainability sell a bit harder. The LOHAS segment looks to be the most promising for High End marketers.

If sustainability is so important for present and especially for future High End success, then how can business master it? Certainly there are fans, even disciplines and preachers, so we can tell somewhat by the "heat". But what about the "light"? Usually sustainability and ecology issues are associated with concerns for consumption and the environment. Here is our short-list of "weak signals" appropriate for sustainability for High End. These signals should be built-in to new products and services:

• Acting in a very democratic way

- Social engagement

- Improvement on "ethical" component of product

- Green elements in using nontoxic, natural materials

- Time-saving qualities

- Easy to use

- Easy access

- Health-conscious

- Improves personal space and time

- Provides cultural value.

Looking at the list, we get a sense that sustainability indeed goes far beyond the generalized concern for the environment. Sustainability has business-relevant dimensions, perhaps not dimensions of the original High End, but dimensions nonetheless that will evolve into High End opportunities. The key question is then: *How can High End companies truly understand what is behind this new aspect of people's dreams and aspirations? "Design" with a capital "D" is the answer.*

Across two decades of both primary research and award-winning projects in India, China and Latin America, Philips Design formalized and validated a scheme to define what sustainability is and how it should be managed, thanks to the leadership of their Senior Director Sustainable Design, Simona Rocchi. This was done through both business practice and thought leadership. The outcome revealed three key aspects of sustainability. Each aspect is relevant to the High End, and may well redefine the worlds of both High End and luxury:

1. Environmental sustainability, or the creation and deployment of policies, processes and strategies in order to reduce the short and long term material impact on the planet.

2. Societal sustainability, where the High End corporation and its brands act as a social citizen in every geographical area and activity of involvement.

3.   Personal sustainability or the creation and commercialization of user-friendly, accessible products and solutions, in order to improve the quality of life of the user.

In terms of design, this short list of aspects can become the DNA of a company which wishes to do well by doing good. The Dow Jones has its own Dow Jones Sustainability Index, which applies to corporations as entities. There is no reason why a company need miss the opportunity to be a player in the world of sustainability when desire, resources, and brains are put to the task.

A number of High End brands jump-started themselves into sustainability with good success. We now look at case histories for these three big, promising areas of sustainability – environmental, societal and personal.

Environmental Sustainability: Eco-design

High End lies in the ever-changing middle ground between luxury and mass-production. On the one hand, High End companies bump up against the luxury makers, who have the advantage of just being "who they are". The High End company doesn't have this advantage. It must perform, and be judged on its performance. It must out-perform the luxury makers, and thus create its own world, beyond luxury. Below the High End, we have the everyday, the world of price, where *homo economicus* reigns, and where causes are less important than everyday low prices or everyday good value. So looking at where High End companies operate in the world of business, to have a good cause is to be given an opportunity, an advantage.

Global awakening to the looming environmental disaster caused changes in the values associated with premium consumption. In the current economic downturn, the cultural value of such symbols of achievements and success has suddenly changed. Porsche Cayenne, which used to be a status statement in 2007, two years later became a social embarrassment and a target of public hostilities. Porsche's SUVs are increasingly vandalized in German cities as a token of social disapproval of the perceived values that Porsche was insensitive to the environmental impact of its cars. The challenge for premium brands has thus become ideological. Some understood that environmental sustainability nowadays and in the future "makes a High End brand" or at least makes it stronger, as Toyota recently showed with its Lexus brand. By addressing the global ecological concerns for the environment, Lexus pushed into the forefront of public opinion thanks to the quick adoption of *hybrid*.

In another example, following its corporate promise and utilizing High Design, Philips works on reducing the environmental impact of its products. Technical and design innovations led to optimizing the product weight and packaging, minimizing toxic substances, improving recycling and extending product lifetime. This approach to environmental sustainability results in an ideal mix of Premium Value: "energy saving + green approach + premium price" leading to superior margins. Think of eco-lamps, currently in the process of replacing the traditional bulb.

The question remains, however – how to make these efforts fit the High End? Is there a clear long-term connection of the High End with the environment? Trend research shows that "Eco-luxury" will be very strong in the future. Traditional luxury players might be challenged by new players with more valuable insights in sustainability issues, and the solutions to those issues. This will trickle down to High End inevitably. The result could be a sea of opportunities for those High End brands that can take advantage of the new environmental sensibility. It might be that such High End opportunities exist in many places including business-to-business area.

Social Sustainability: Cause RED – Pop Stars to High End Brand Stars

Cause marketing which proliferated in the past decades is simply marketing by companies as good citizens. Companies adopt causes just as people do. Quite possibly started as an idea for a marketing ploy, it became an increasingly popular way to build corporate image. What better way for the High End company to build a positive image than associating with a cause through sponsorship, and by so doing move the brand into a new dimension. Although cause-related marketing is rightly seen as simply the starting point of corporate social responsibility and overall sustainability, even a small step is better than no step at all.

A widely publicized case of cause-related marketing initiative addresses the huge problem affecting Africa – the AIDS crisis. Under the hyperactive pop culture icon and U2 singer, Bono Vox, non-competing High End brands from Motorola to Emporio Armani and many others publicly support causes associated with Africa. One joint initiative is targeting this pandemic drama by offering concrete cash donations derived from limited editions of (Product)RED™ items, from Motorola phones to Emporio Armani digital watches. Often the limited editions from these companies specify certain amounts to be donated to the causes, with the cause intimately associated with marketing effort. Here we see the principle of scarcity marketing or at least the feeling of somewhat exclusive editions, applied to a very good cause. In a sense, we have here a different thrust of the High End – associating itself with the nobler human virtues, as part of a new notion of status that comes from the last 25 years of engaged pop culture (for example, LiveAid to Live8, the massive pop concerts that since 1986 brought stars closer to charity).

As pointed by John Hooks, Deputy Director of Giorgio Armani SpA in an FT luxury forum, for brands like Armani, RED™ is a best practice of social engagement. RED™ helped other High End efforts as well. Limited RED™ edition of Motorola phones sold out rapidly, at a much higher rate than did regular sets. The Gap products helped lift the corporate brand perception. In general, it looks like societal sustainability may be an attractive opportunity for the High End.

Personal Sustainability: Simplicity

If you feel inspired and stimulated by this chapter so far, then there is even more to be optimistic about. When we move to personal *simplicity*, we discover the art of improving the quality of life by removing the hassle from it. Simplicity is here to stay as a key dimension for the High End of tomorrow. The move towards it has already started today. Paradoxically, simplicity is not simple to pin down. For example, it is not, by default, over-simplification. One of our contributing "gurus", Markus Langes-Swarovski, quoted Einstein: "Everything should be made as simple as it is, but not simpler."

Simplicity fits with the challenge of *personal* sustainability. For the High End, the challenge demands the design and the delivery of artifacts and applications which truly contribute to a person's well-being. Think of sustainability-driven design which goes beyond traditional environmental challenges, incorporating ergonomic and cultural factors to produce individual comfort and peace of mind. Simplicity is the zenith of the High End.

Think of the last time you felt stressed out and unsupported by the artifacts around you, let down by the digital application that should adapt to you, and not the other way around. Most likely it was very recently, maybe even today. This is the best evidence that simplicity is the natural answer to a specific demand for a higher quality in personal life. Hence, we have in personal sustainability a promising field of High End opportunities that should remain with us for at least a decade or longer. Yet, at the same time there is the counter-current. Sustainability fights with the corporate tendency to add features in an attempt to do more, be more, and of course sell more. If one is good, two must be better! The old-fashioned high-tech urges to maximize features and functions often simply overshoots the goal. This is "feature creep", once the hallmark of High End, but today no longer.

The key to High End simplicity is its soul, the essence of a product, which thanks to simplicity manages to retain its integrity. Through design, simplicity can be much more than just the reduction of complexity. It can be a great leap forward towards personal well being. In his tenure as first CMO of the Philips Corporation, Andrea Ragnetti went one step further and put the notion of simplicity in the center of the brand's future. He chose to do so because simplicity is indeed a very strong theme in our societies, in our lives. For this reason, simplicity represents a very important opportunity for the High End categories and markets of the future.

Unlocking High End Opportunities from Sustainability and Simplicity

As a natural next step, we envision that in the not-too-distant future the two universes of sustainability and simplicity will meet. Furthermore, the High End seems to be the natural venue for this convergence to happen. For example, the notion of upgrading long-term durable devices with digital downloads *instead of* replacing high-tech hardware is important from an ecological viewpoint, as well as culturally cool for specific audiences. The notion is particularly relevant for High End makers of digitally based products. Simply put, think of iPod, multiply by thousands of such brilliant solutions, and you have a sneak snapshot of the High End future best scenario. Opportunities are endless.

The ubiquitous emergence of the social conscience towards sustainability presents new opportunities for High End thinking, perhaps going further than the do-gooder mentality that characterizes many traditional efforts. Yet, if we look at the global challenges to sustainability, we can see some major opportunities emerging for companies for cause-marketing or other creative applications. The key question is: *Where will sustainable challenges take us in the future?*

Since 1996, the UN-sponsored Millennium Project has periodically reported on the "State of the Future" in a comprehensive report detailing the key challenges and opportunities ahead of us all. Here are six of the 15 global challenges identified by UN that could be tackled in one way or another by High End companies:

1. How can sustainable development be achieved for all?

2. How can everyone have sufficient clean water without conflict?

3. How can the global convergence of information and communication technologies work for everyone?

4. How can ethical market economies be encouraged to help reduce the gap between rich and poor?

5. How can scientific and technological breakthroughs be accelerated to improve the human condition?

6. How can ethical considerations become more routinely incorporated into global decisions?

(*Source*: "2007 State of the Future", The Millennium Project)

Now let us speculate on the role of the High End in the context of these global challenges. For example, we see an opportunity for an upscale faucet filter-producer to cause-market their product with some portion of the profit going to help developing countries to get drinkable water. But that's only one. There are far more.

We were particularly struck by the positive, occasionally emotional response here, namely the notion of sustainability envisioned as *the opportunity* for future High End. When we tested our ideas with thought-leaders, experts and consumers, we noticed that the connection between the High End and sustainability was not forced, but actually welcomed. Good news even for the realists, as well, of course, for the inveterate optimists.

High End Dimension 5: "Sustainability and Simplicity"

1.   The *green factor*: Does the proposition ensure environmental sustainability?

This factor of the High End is brilliantly demonstrated by Lexus. By making eco-engines of higher range a basic feature of their models, they leapfrogged classic makers like BMW or Mercedes Benz in luxury-related perception. Here, sustainability chic translated into tangible business success.

2.   The *society factor*: Within its span, from concept to factory, from distribution to end user, does the proposition entail policies and strategies to improve the life of all local communities?

Sustainability does not end with a portfolio of cleaner products. It is not only the "what" that matters, but rather and especially the "how". The Millennium Project by the United Nations offers a clear perspective of the magnitude of challenges that true sustainability casts upon the future of humankind. High End finds here the opportunity to redefine its future as the engine of a higher quality of life. In this grand context, cause-related marketing is a very basic approach. For some, however, cause-related marketing is just a good beginning, to jump-start and take action.

3.   The *personal factor*: Does the proposition improve the life of those individuals who adopt it?

High End is ultimately about quality of life. Improvement in their everyday life is the main benefit for customers who adopting and then pay a premium for the High End.

4.   The *simplicity factor*: Does the proposition simplify life for people in a desirable way?

Simplicity is seen here as the next frontier of quality of life. This factor might represent the hardest challenge and the most complicated quality to achieve.

Nevertheless, we are on an aspirational journey towards a simpler world, and we know that it makes great business sense to just join.

Customer Mindsets for the Dimension 5 of the High End: Sustainability and Simplicity

The Sustainability and Simplicity dimension of High End has its four factors (see Figure 9.1), with supporting data in Figures 9.2 and 9.3, and in the Appendix (Table A6).

Our thought-leaders link future High End with sustainability, indeed almost vehemently. We were surprised. But the truth is we should not be surprised at the link, given the vision of our world-class contributors and experts. And our thought leaders were "on the mark." Sustainability and Simplicity turned out to be the one dimension of our five dimensions showing a preponderance of generally strong performing elements driving the perception of High End. All the elements show positive impacts for the total.

To start with, the baseline perception is +30, similar to that of the other four dimensions, meaning that 30 percent of the participants are prepared to perceive a future proposition as High End when the topic is Sustainability and Simplicity. So far, we have seen the baseline hovering pretty much around the same level of (25–33) or so. Our take away here is that it is not sustainability *per se*, but rather the specifics of sustainability that make the difference.

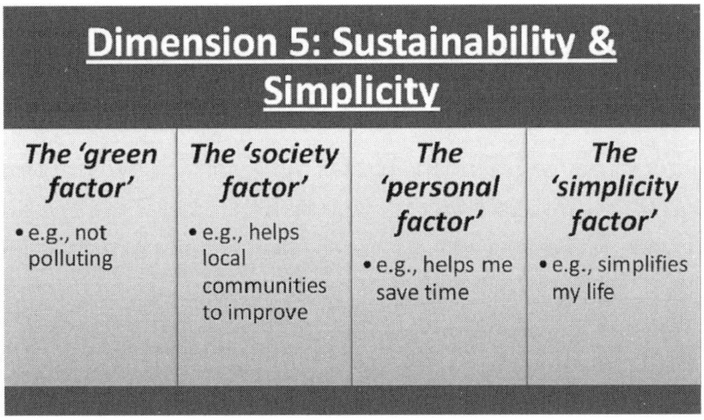

Dimension 5: Sustainability & Simplicity			
The 'green factor'	*The 'society factor'*	*The 'personal factor'*	*The 'simplicity factor'*
• e.g., not polluting	• e.g., helps local communities to improve	• e.g., helps me save time	• e.g., simplifies my life

Figure 9.1   The four factors for Dimension 5: Sustainability and Simplicity

A number of sustainability elements significantly drive up the perception of High End. The phrase *helps to save the environment in the long term* has an impact of +10. A lot of the magic is the language, the word picture that the phrase paints, the hope from the text. Barebones simplicity statements such as *simple to use*, and *makes sense in my life* lack that penetrating immediacy. It should not be surprising. It just might be that these simplicity elements are too "wishy-washy", and nebulous. They do not paint that necessary word picture. Once translated into specific features and applications, their relative impotence might disappear. This is clearly where we see how the distinction between "simplistic" and true, rich "simplicity" will work in the future. It will take genius to be truly simple. People in search for the High End will be demanding judges of how well companies can simplify their propositions, while not reducing the richness, quality and value.

Customer Mindsets for the Dimension 5 of the High End: Sustainability and Simplicity

The participants divide based on the patterns of their responses into two dramatically different segments that we named *Personal and Simple* (54 percent of the total sample) versus *Sensitive* (46 percent).

Segment 1 – "Personal and Simple" (Figure 9.2). Segment 1 is more predisposed to perceive products as High End (baseline perception is (+35) for Personal and Simple versus Segment 2 (Sensitive, additive constant = +25). Segment 1 reacts strongly to each of the four messages about future simplicity (from +10 to +15). Simplicity is definitely a High End Marker for the Personal and Simple Segment. Segment 1 also feels that messages dealing with customization and upgradability drive towards premium.

On the other hand, Segment 1 is not totally insensitive to the outside world. The messages from the society factor also mark the High End, but don't confuse that with environmental and social issues. The latter, environmental and social issues, simply do not resonate well among them. To those focusing on Personal and Simple, notions about plain ecology just don't have the mojo.

Segment 2 – The "Sensitive" Segment (Figure 9.3). This is an important segment comprising people who respond to the needs and condition of the outside world. Anything we tested that related to environmental and social issues was hugely positive with this group (from +16 to an exceptionally strong

+22). And, as we expect, the personal factor will be effective, but less so than the outside world.

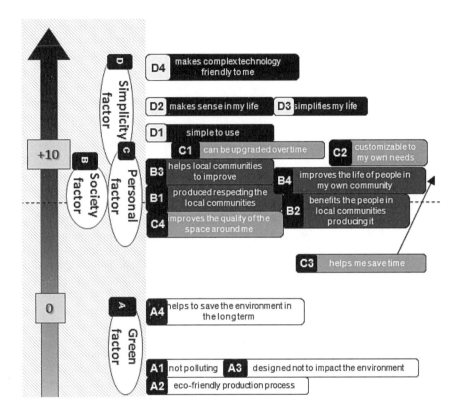

Figure 9.2   Performance of the Segment 1 "Personal and Simple" for Dimension 5: Sustainability and Simplicity

Summing Up

The High End is not about just conspicuous consumption. On the contrary, the High End is about a higher quality of life, anticipating people's dreams and cultural change. By improving the way people live, sustainability is naturally positioned to be a landscape of opportunities for the High End.

We started from a simple fact that keeps becoming more important. Ecologically and socially responsible businesses are perceived as having more of the High End mojo. But the world evolves, and with sustainability the

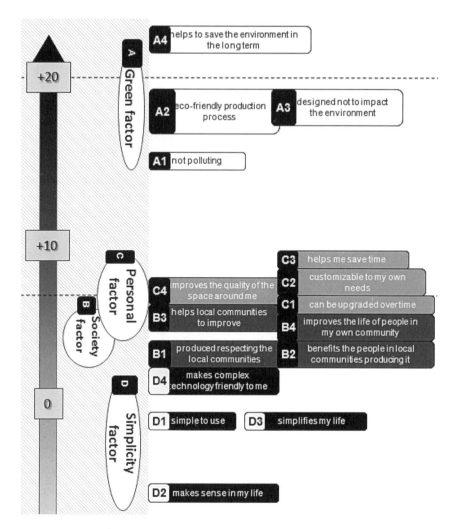

Figure 9.3　**Performance of the Segment 2 "Sensitive" for Dimension 5: Sustainability and Simplicity**

evolution is rapid. We suggest looking at the larger picture of macro-scenarios and global challenges as High End opportunities. We believe that this exercise will turn out to be a way to get continuing inspiration for High End initiatives, as the evolution proceeds ever more quickly.

The Lexus case confirmed that environmental sustainability can be key to product success. In sad contrast, The Body Shop showed the consequence of losing the soul of a sustainability-driven brand. The WWF Deeper Luxury report and the work of the London-based Authentic Luxury Network provided us with food for thought about the challenges ahead of the luxury industry in this field, ranging from passive corporate responsibility to actively changing the world for the better.

High End players have an opportunity to leapfrog luxury companies by innovation and cultural anticipation. There are lots of different ways; lack of imagination and vision don't have to remain obstacles. The Philips Design vision of environmental, social, personal sustainability offers a framework to understand and take advantage of the sustainability challenges. Eco-design allows the company to redefine the rules of the game, by design. Cause-related marketing is, in turn, a way to jump-start using societal issues. With Philips and its Sense and Simplicity positioning we closed the circle of this chapter presenting simplicity itself as a further frontier of quality of life for individuals.

In terms of Types of Customers (Global data), we identified two segments: Personal and Simple (45 percent) vs. Sensitive (55 percent). The "Personal and Simple" customer reacts strongly to messages about simplicity. "The Sensitive" customer reacts strongly to anything related to environmental and social issues.

In an "ideal world", each single High End offering meets and obeys all five general rules, with excellence. That is like Garrison Keilor's Lake Woebegone, where everyone is above average!

Let's "get real". From a pragmatic viewpoint, establish the right mix of rules that apply to your particular business and your country. We based our rules on the solid research. We know that groups think the same, independent of country – that is how we got the segmentation.

We believe from the data and segmentation that the rules with their dimensions and factors are universal. This means that they are scientifically applicable to any region or market you might want to populate with your High End offerings. However, the specific application of each rule is *always* regional or national meaning that you ought to do the RDE study for that particular target region among your specific target customers. For example, assume that your next High End business opportunity is in India. There, you might want to create a customized version of each rule, with India-related case studies and with a segmentation based on respondents in India. In that way you will be well able to make the data actionable for this new market.

PART 3

Vistas and New High End Experiences

In the future, I believe very strongly that anything having to do with health and well being, including biotech industries and solutions for an aging human population will be a pool of opportunities for the High End. On the other hand, explicitly health-wise negative practices like smoking will be increasingly challenged, and here I therefore see a trend over time towards the progressive elimination of opportunities in non-ethic industries, like the tobacco industry might be classified.

Rita Clifton, Chairman, Interbrand, London

As America's famous baseball player and pundit Yogi Berra once proclaimed, *it's tough to make predictions, especially about the future.* Even if you can see the future, the current complexity of the global economy puts enough clouds in your way to make you doubt what you actually see, and understand. For sure, nothing is linear anymore. The simple linear extrapolation, the comforting approach with which experts used to look into the future a few decades ago, is just not valid.

Rather than speculating what the High End future will actually be, in the next two chapters we will share our vision of where it is going to come from. In Chapter 10, we start from scenarios of urban development because cities are where the new High End is being incubated. It is in the cities where you can hear the changes of the near future first announce themselves.

The High End of the future will require ongoing innovation. Positioned below luxury, the High End must anticipate the future in order *to be there* with its offerings. Innovation in the High End demands that a company look into a future beyond its own portfolio. Think society, think sustainability, think cultural marketing, viral marketing, buzz campaigns. The key question then is: how to get there?

We present some key findings about the High End future from Philips Design research programs. But beyond that one-company effort, albeit a very grand one, we complement that information and those insights with an unusual study – sensorial experience preferences and expenditure patterns, gathered by Hakuhodo of Japan in its benchmark Global Habit Survey. We finish with China. We have here a special focus by the experts on China, and what they see happening in the Chinese High End. China is particularly important because the way China evolves will be a blueprint for High End companies. This is our grand tour of the future. Armed with knowledge, stories, and a sense of the possible, we now take our whirlwind trip.

10

Urban Futures: Opportunities for Tomorrow's High End

A high-quality public environment attracts more people to live close to work. Today, more than 90,000 people live in the city center of Philadelphia, the third largest downtown population in the U.S. Forty percent of these residents walk to work. That is the highest percentage of any American city – and the key to our sustainability strategy.

Paul Levy, CEO, Philadelphia City Centre

As the High End spreads everywhere, its future customers also will be everywhere as well – city centers, suburbia, countryside. These new customers will learn and buy through their own channels, conventional and new, in the bricks-and-mortar and in the digital worlds.

The city is, however, historically the cradle of lifestyle and the hotbed of High End developments, not much different from its role as the nurturing womb for so many other trends. The High End inevitably follows emerging lifestyles and new cultural mindsets. The city and the dynamism of the urban environment provide the flow of cultural innovation, the stream behind High End propositions and products. High End products and propositions that meet peoples' dreams, demands and expectations emerge and have the best chances to prosper in the urban scene.

Historically, urban culture has been the most fertile seedbed where new visions, new options, and new styles of living are forged, tested, improved, or all too often discarded. Traditionally, cities were natural driving force of fashion and style, new ways of living in an eternal quest towards a higher quality of life.

Of course, it is not only the cities; it cannot be. No doubt there will be local excellence in certain remote locations, such as Grasse for the fragrance industry or Tuscany for the leather business. These regions will continue to power special sectors of the High End with their superior skills and taste-making technical talent, flavors and sublime ingredients. Yet, the "ingredients" of the High End related to lifestyle aspirations and trendsetting vision will be nurtured and adopted in cities, as always before, in our modernity.

Let us explore what is ahead for our cities, the opportunities to emerge in the near future in the field of High End.

One Vision of Urban Futures: Philips' city.people.light project

"City.people.light" is a major Philips lighting program, focused on innovating for the city. The program looks for the path that cities are taking as they evolve, and with that knowledge offering concrete products for a better future, in the best High End spirit. The program is clearly practical, yet creative; grounded in knowledge yet visionary.

The 2007 edition of Philips "city.people.light" program emerged from business-driven future studies. Designing the program turned into a labor of love, integrating the ideas and vision of a number of world-class opinion leaders. Many urban and architectural masters, true celebrities and design icons, such as Richard Rogers, Richard Meier, Robert Venturi, Denise Scott Brown, and Deyan Sudjic, helped to shape the product with their well-articulated, occasionally counter-intuitive, challenging insights. It was great fun, engaging, but most of all – as a side track – one could feel the High End coming alive in the minds of the experts as they grappled with what would happen, and how business might prosper from it.

Any business exercise of this type must have focus, scope, and openness to be successful, to contribute specifics to its sponsor. "City.people.light" tries to understand the future in order to improve today's life. For Philips, the understanding was channeled to guide corporate innovation towards a high quality of urban life. General trends give direction and become starting points for future "blue sky concepting" and innovation workshops. These sessions took place around the world – in Lyon in France, Philadelphia in the USA, Shanghai in China and Hamburg in Germany. The workshops offered the thought-leading participants a rare opportunity to enjoy an open platform for discussion and networking, while generating their visions of better futures. The output opened opportunities for innovation in the urban High End.

The ideas that undergird these opportunities come from professional leaders in urban planning and lighting design from China, the USS, the UK, Italy, Singapore, Korea, Mexico, Canada, Germany, Scandinavia, and more. The program output was significant, spawning a collective production of nearly 150 concepts captured in a book, and presented at a major industry forum in Rotterdam in May 2007 with nearly 500 urban professionals attending. You may identify here a strategic process that informs many of the approaches in this book, and one that we have found to be uniquely productive.

There was general agreement on many ideas, quite a number of them leading to "designable" High End experiences. For example, city.people.light indicated that the city of the future should aim to be compact, multi-centered, with good public transport, designed to encourage walking and biking as alternative means of mobility with the lowest ecological impact. Its well-designed environment will have socially mixed living/working areas, integrated in its DNA to provide people a safe and productive living. It remains a field of open opportunities for High End propositions to be launched and positioned in tomorrow's urban markets. Let's see how this future urban context looks like, as extrapolated from city.people.light.

The Nature of Future Cities and Their Emerging High End Opportunities

The global directions of tomorrow's cities move in four directions and trends: community, diversity, complexity and density.

Community. The relevance of local communities will increase during the next five years. We can expect a renaissance of the local micro-culture of retail outlets, restaurants and urban icons, locations which then become places to network and to share. High End business leaders should rethink how they would function in cities. They have the opportunity to be where new lifestyles are in the process of being formed, to learn about new trends and to profile and commercialize their propositions. The best specific action tool for business in this context is cultural marketing.

Diversity. The cities of today are engines for individual lifestyles. From buildings to the very bodies and clothing styles of citizens, cities will continue to nurture the difference as a cultural feature. The appreciation of such diversity is part of the natural DNA of a city. The ability of cities to attract unique talent is in part the result of individuals feeling sufficiently anonymous to "do their thing". Within cities that accept and support diversity, cultural creatives lead new economies, and create the "new". High End business leaders need to ride the wave of diversity in order to discover major business opportunities. The specific action tool for business here will be intensive dialog with culturally diverse groups.

Complexity. Complexity is a factor of life in the city, and a mixed blessing. Complexity in its less pleasant moments leads naturally to a search for simplicity. Simplicity, a key direction to create and nurture the High End, is the response to the conditions of life experienced by the majority of urban dwellers. Yet complexity is not all bad. The complexity creates a highly flexible territory where urban space will be adapted to the needs of micro-enterprises. The richness of complex interdependencies resembles a living organism, providing new opportunities for the High End. The opportunities here are to bring simplicity back into the picture, by offering premium services at higher margins. The specific action tool for business here will be an understanding of opportunities from interdependencies in city life, ranging from traffic jams, crime and pollution to positive social change. These insights should provide the seeds of new High End efforts. This urban quality should become the incubator of new, small enterprises, sometimes a galaxy of individual ones.

Density. Densely populated high-rise buildings seem to be in vogue as never before. A dense city is, in principle, a good city that can be managed with less transportation, less pollution, more human scale. This higher quality of life provides a plethora of future opportunities for the High End. Think of Asia Pacific and its megalopolises. Many household appliances are cramped into small common areas enticing the owners to look for better-designed – both aesthetically and functionally – High End products, even at premium prices. The proliferation of luxury in Japan was fueled by the urban condition of Tokyo and Kyoto dwellers. Due to the small size of their apartments, Japanese indulge in the possession of beautiful objects and artifacts, like luxury goods.

How the Growth of Cities Will Drive a Higher Quality of Life

In future, cities will be more and more managed as brands, some possibly positioning themselves as High End, perhaps drawing to them residents in the same way that brands compete to draw customers. These cities will consciously develop their own brand images, emphasizing what to the resident and prospective inhabitant WiiFM ("what's in it for me?"). Dense, diverse, complex and clustered communities will become the norm for the High End lifestyles and trends of the future, ranging from New York to London, from Milan to Tokyo.

City.people.light identified four global urban strategies, which we might call "city brand strategies" that these cities will consciously follow in order to enter the High End.

ACCELERATING CITY

The city will directly aim at the High End of the global urban market. The city will provide the resources and opportunity for its citizens to perform at their highest level. This focus-on-the-citizen is the strategy adopted by metropolises, which aim to become IT and digital leading hubs. Good examples today can be found in Singapore and Dubai. The High End business leader should study the reality of these cities today, looking at their infrastructure and positioning, to get a model of the near future. The cities show-case new and innovative solutions that translate high-tech into concrete quality of life for high-performing professionals.

MEMORY CITY

In an increasingly standardized world, the notion of "architectural memory" becomes the cornerstone of a city, where the past is preserved as one of the major contributions of the city. Memorable locations will be nurtured, creating High End cultural destinations accessible to the tourist industry. Examples of such destinations are European monuments. Just call up on the Web the Harvard Alumni Association to see their many guided tours to these memory cities, with High End amenities at High End prices. The more we leap into our digital futures, the more we want to stay connected to our cultural past providing an enormous opportunity for the High End business leader seeking new ideas. Cultural marketing and patronage of the arts will offer additional options to create destination features to assure this High End profile for the city.

ICONIC CITY

The essence of cities as brands is in their icons: the Olympic Stadium in Beijing, the Guggenheim Museum in Bilbao, Spain, or the Cloud Gate by Anish Kapoor in Chicago. In the last decade or two, an urban "gold rush" to design and build icons unrolled around the world, with a particular focus on public art and museums. The game was well worth it for cities like Bilbao, where Frank Gehry's museum made all the difference between a provincial town and an international cultural destination. For the future, iconic designs in cities will evolve from being just fashionable, towards a more honest integration with the local context. Leading cities will increasingly "adopt" icons that come from the authentic local grass roots.

CONNECTING CITY

As accelerating cities will be increasingly more and more virtual, connecting cities will *physically* reach each other and enable people to connect. The infrastructure of these cities will serve several purposes. An example of this strategy is the rise of provincial airport networks in Europe, based in mid-size towns that managed their provincial nature by becoming low-cost destinations. For the High End business leader, the success of connecting cities offers the opportunity to rethink premium solutions for travelers. In turn, entrepreneurs should find more opportunities to work in these cities because of the lower costs, and the ability to meet other people in social occasions that do not demand travel.

HIGH END LESSONS FROM GLOBAL URBAN TRENDS AND CITY STRATEGIES

Global urban trends show where and how future lifestyles are being incubated. The trends reveal that communities are returning to the cities, increasingly diverse and complex new interdependencies are emerging as cities becomes more alive, and that finally the formerly run-down urban centers are being gentrified as a new world of High End inhabitants realize the value of what can be achieved in the city, rather than fleeing to the suburbs. Philadelphia is a great example of the benefits of such an approach.

To meet their ambitions of future growth for a higher quality of life, world-class cities will adopt a portfolio of strategies for their inhabitants. These strategies include supporting creativity and the digital life, taking advantage of past icons, creating new icons with a genuine connection to history and territory, and reorganizing space for people to connect with each other. In a relatively short period in the very near future, each of these trends should become a new, major opportunity for *previously unexploited* High End propositions. The urban trends are creating truly new opportunities for a High End that might well differ in nature from what has come before. The next question is: where might this "premium revolution" start?

Where Will the High End Hit?

URBAN FUTURES IN EUROPE: SEEDBEDS FOR INNOVATION IN THE OLD CONTINENT

Look to Europe first. The old world cities will be especially interesting to watch as they evolve into High End centers. We expect to see innovation and new aspects of the High End for cities like Essen, European Capital of Culture in the year 2010, which have to convert industrial assets and mindsets into drivers of the service economy and of creative industries. In this game of "cultural re-qualification or death", we expect to see some important non-capital cities of Europe take the lead based on traditional public events and attractions, such as major sports events, museums, historical places and more. As these cities look for ways to gain cachet with their efforts, there will be more culturally focused opportunities for the High End. For example, this cluster of cities includes Barcelona and a number of advanced economy-driven twin cities: Milan–Turin in Italy, Basel– Zurich in Switzerland.

URBAN FUTURES IN ASIA: BRAVE NEW WORLD ASPIRING TO BECOME NEW HIGH END HOTSPOTS

Not surprisingly, Asian cities redefine the way we understand metropolitan futures. Chinese cities represent living laboratories of expansion and growth. It is in China where ancient traditions of urbanism are being updated for the new century, and for a new level of prosperity. One of the city.people.light experts offered a vision of a sustainability-driven Beijing, leapfrogging transportation issues by a new use of the traditional bike and, increasingly, electric bikes. In 2009, China had about 100 million e-bikes – four times more than cars. The Chinese capital might want to consider restricting additional automotive traffic in favor of fashionable biking. *Time* magazine quoted Frank Jamerson, a former GM engineer turned electric-vehicle analyst: "What's happening in China is sort of a clue to what the future will be."

Outside China, the two most relevant cities in Asia command opposite extremes of an imaginary wealth scale. These are Tokyo, representing one of the contemporary luxury capitals in the world, and Mumbai in India. Tokyo's postmodern mosaic of lifestyle and pop-culture imaginary will remain a future manifesto of urban High End. In contrast, Mumbai's internal contradictions will remain powerful, oscillating between spiritual serendipity and atomic weaponry factories, between Bollywood glamour and starving masses, between the Indian economic miracle and the challenges of a complex society. For the foreign visitor each city has its own lively schizophrenia. Perhaps they will meet in a few decades when Mumbai is expected to take over the position of the world's most populous city from today's Tokyo.

URBAN FUTURES IN THE AMERICAS: AREAS OF GROWTH AND AREAS OF HOPE

The Americas will be no less exciting than Asia in their next ten years of metropolitan development. In addition to New York, *the* incubator of art, design, nightlife and lifestyle for the entire planet, even in times of economic downturn, other cities are emerging. We see here an emergence of the great Brazilian cities, from Sao Paulo to the carefully designed Curitiba, a true blueprint of High End urban planning. In an oil crisis that would endanger the sustainability of older, automobile-based megalopolises such as Los Angeles, these new cities will have far more advantages. Designed for human sustainability, they will not be susceptible to the breakdown of affordable transportation.

From the optimal city management of Bogota, representing a true best practice of urban sustainability, to the lively explosion of informal economies and networks in Mexico City, Latin America seems to be the most relevant space for experimentation, for innovation. Latin America may ultimately turn out to be a true engine of future trends. Those trends include new, undefined aspects of the High End, which might end up being unique Latin modifications of European and Asian trends.

Lying at the crossroads of the entire continent, Miami might become the next American frontier as it evolves into the cultural and economic junction of the two Americas, North and South. Las Vegas evolves beyond a pure gambling economy, from entertaining museums to becoming the luxury retail capital of the USA. Or Philadelphia's City Centre enterprise for the re-emergence of downtown might be perfectly described as a case study of High End thinking applied to urban life.

The story of Philadelphia City Centre may be foundational, showing how the emerging High End can appear in the downtown of cities. In Philadelphia, one emphasis to increase the quality of life has been on the new use of lighting in public places. To increase the quality of life for its inhabitants and visitors, Philadelphia City Centre embarked on a strategy of installing pedestrian-scale light fixtures on every street in the commercial downtown. With more than over 2,100 light fixtures installed since 1997, Philadelphia doubled the levels of nighttime illumination. In addition to enhanced safety, it has served as a stimulus for a now thriving evening economy. To highlight cultural institutions on Benjamin Franklin Parkway and to accentuate Avenue of the Arts on South Broad Street, Philadelphia City Centre is lighting the facades of over 20 buildings. The color-changing LED figures on South Broad Street will create the first synchronized color changing illumination scheme in a privately owned, North American building.

The "street" for the High End is also important. Street events and improvements are important because they help create the city experience in tandem with restaurants, retail and arts and cultural institutions. The combination of events and High End amenities creates the environment which stimulates word-of-mouth communication and continually re-attracts people to the city center. The fertile interplay between company programs like city.people.light and the entrepreneurial drive of people like Philadelphia's Paul Levy bring such High End thinking to the city. We think that Philadelphia City Centre is an early signal for such High End urban renaissance.

When it comes to moving beyond simply branded products and brand services, our lesson for the High End is that cities are where the business opportunities may prove greatest. Cities will remain long-term seedbeds of the High End, allowing and promoting new lifestyles, while the suburbs and the countryside may not or cannot accept these lifestyles. The city has the resources, the people, the soul. In turn, these lifestyles will nourish the expression of immaterial and symbolic dreams and desires.

Many more cities will be crucial or relevant for our regeneration, and for the next successes of the High End: think of Hong Kong, Singapore, Sydney, Seoul and even second tier Chinese cities like Chengdu or Dalian. The next question is: how will people experience products and designs in this highly diversified global landscape of local urban seedbed for lifestyle?

Cities and the High End: What People Spend, and What People Savor

Hakuhodo, the leading Japanese advertising giant behind countless winning campaigns, conducts the Global Habit research as part of its ongoing R&D efforts. Hakuhodo periodically compiles a global lifestyle report with trend analysis coupled with their Brand Navigator tool. The survey covers 32 trendsetting cities, from New York to Los Angeles, from Milan to Moscow, with an extensive coverage of Asia Pacific, including, among others, Shanghai, Beijing, Chengdu, Dalian and Guanzhou (in China), Seoul, Bangkok, Ho Chi Minh City, Delhi and Sydney, plus the Japanese leading lifestyle centers. The scope of the survey itself is breathtaking. Over 20,000 participants in a year provide information to create the integrated source which lays out consumption trends, product/ brand perception and media usage. The Global Habit study covers the vast array of product categories such as automotive, consumer electronics, mobile communication, personal care and cosmetics and includes demographics, lifestyle, shopping behavior, category perception and media habits topics.

We asked Rieko Shofu, Executive Manager at Hakuhodo's Corporate Design, how their knowledge basket could help us to identify the cities and the segments of urban populations where High End might emerge with new, strong, business opportunities, and what would be some guidelines for business development.

The worldwide spending patterns were the first crucial test. Hakuhodo looked into people's willingness to spend money for High End propositions, brands or services in search of "what is hot, what is not". The extremely polarized outcomes were stimulating – like the painter who, before mixing an articulated palette of grays, starts from the pure tubes of absolute black and white.

Extreme opposites are the best way to start looking into any issue, to gain some degree of immediate first understanding. The highest score globally for potential success of a premium proposition was recorded in Hong Kong, with young people up to their late 20s willing to pay a premium to possess their luxury "Fata Morgana", that is, the fantasy of what they want. In contrast, Singapore recorded the lowest score.

Let's delve more deeply to understand what makes these two extremes.

According to Radha Chadha and Paul Husband, who covered Singapore in their book *The Cult of the Luxury Brand*, Singapore is at the most mature stage of the evolution of the luxury market. Singapore is approaching what they call the "way of life" stage, where luxury consumption is integrated in everyday life. Despite that evolution to luxury as everyday, the Singaporean shopper still focuses strongly on price. The theme of the Singaporean shopper is "visible status at a reasonable price plus resale value". This is an important equation. Perhaps frugal Singapore is the place to teach us a lesson in value at the High End. Singapore seems to be the market where price only translates into value when there is *real* value to be found in objects and services: this puts Singapore in a strong position on the map of future opportunities for High End success.

Compare Singapore with Hong Kong. The cities lie situated reasonably close together in Asia, the most promising continent of the next decade, but they differ dramatically. Our lesson so far is that cultural and regional understanding is key to business success in the High End. Hong Kong requires a more ostentatious image, whereas in contrast Singapore demands a better image management of function and residual value. Each city is poised for the proliferation of High End, but the business must be aware of the differences in order to succeed. Geography and socio-cultural understanding of differences are the basis of success in the High End.

Now move to Japan and beyond, where the survey shows yet another set of patterns. Spending in Japan peaks among the young consumers, 20–24 years old, providing the first "age-based" opportunity for High End. Moving to Taiwan and Korea, we see High End buyers spread across all the ages. In Taiwan and Korea, the young consumers, aged 15–19, are far more inclined to pay a premium than are the older consumers. The rest of Asia Pacific, including the major Chinese cities, as well as Kuala Lumpur, Ho Chi Minh City, Manila, Bangkok and Jakarta, as suggested by Hakuhodo, are less promising, despite the lure of Asia itself.

So what are the lessons that business can use from this type of information? We see five global trends that may dictate the nature of High End products and services.

First, it is about *the younger consumer who buys publicly visible premium*. All over the world, the *younger generation* seem more likely to invest their money into premium. This trend is good news for the future of High End. We expect an increasing willingness to accept a premium price. What might, perhaps, influence this trend are such dramatic wild cards as the economic impact of higher energy prices or environmental catastrophes, or the global financial crisis which started in 2008.

Second, it is about the *older consumer who buys quality of life* propositions. When the price is high, there is a general decline in willingness to spend among older consumers, that is, those ages 50+. They are conservative. They do not spend their money on "stuff". However, here we might be missing a more sophisticated proposition, such as the Ambient Experience hospitals, which might well attract the aging baby boomers. Although we just do not see it yet, it makes a logical sense to think that luxury and High End categories for *private healthcare* will expand in the future. We do see medical tourism, so why not medical High End?

Third, it is about the *higher hanging fruit*. Marketers ought to rethink their strategies for those countries, cities and demographic segments that show less inclination to spend. An understanding of *cultural fit* of the High End to each city's culture might be relevant here, to better position the product as affordable luxury. Culture mores, norms, expectations are critical. The pricing strategy for less-than-excited customers ought to take into account these cultural mores. This seems even more important during the economic downturns. Perhaps business might consider how to merge High End and the new "non-conspicuous consumption", creating a muted, discrete High End. Luxury has been doing that for years. We strongly advocate this direction, especially in the light of the recent economic downturn.

Fourth, it is about avoiding *false positives*. In the BRIC markets (Brazil, Russia, India, China) and for emerging markets in general, *do not* to position a High End product as an "out of poverty enabler". This strategy might generate good sales at the start, but those good sales are actually false positives. It is probably better to raise the bar by emphasizing quality and offer *affordable premium*. FIAT did that with the Linea model designed for emerging markets (see Chapter 5) – a full featured Italian car that could be priced for the emerging markets. Here price and quality with cultural fit will generate heartfelt brand adoption and long-term success.

Fifth, it is about *experience*. Experience matters everywhere in the world, and it will increasingly do so, but there will be deep cultural and aesthetic differences among the different cultures, countries, regions. Experience is the ultimate connecting link between brands and people. This is why the fine details of how experiences are of uttermost relevance to the High End designer and marketer.

Urban Sensory Experience for the High End

> Scent branding is also an interesting development. The power of scent is its uncanny ability to forge strong emotional connections and identities. Of all our senses, our sense of smell is the only one hard-wired to the emotional center of the brain. Branding agencies are realizing the potential of scent in the development of sensory identity systems, but they need to partner with fragrance houses in order to creative unique emotional signatures. Right now very few branding/ advertising agencies have the necessary knowledge and expertise (art and science) in scents.

> *Alex Moskvin, former VP, IFF, BrandEmotions™ Agency*

In the world of retail, that actual moment of interaction between High End products and customer is the real "proof of the pudding" of the entire premium equation. The world of the senses, the ultimate portal between people's perceptions and High End products and brands, usually means the chemical senses (taste) and smell. These are the key sensory characteristics of High End fragrances (perfumes, cosmetics, soaps) and foods, attributes that can be varied, and the impressions which lead immediately to liking (and disliking).

Yet other major senses (vision, audition, and touch) also present opportunities for the High End business to win by being sensitive to the senses. Hakuhodo made a holistic analysis across its 32 cities of the Global Habit Survey. The objective was, in the end, quite broad; discover how customers respond to the different sensory inputs, what this might mean to them, and how business should capitalize on what people search for in their sensory experience. There abound opportunities for High End in more refined sensory experiences, including visual, auditory, and tactile reinforcements, anticipating breakthroughs in *sensorial experience design*. Culture-to-culture variations in aesthetics and design will affect the nature of this experiential High End. Cultures which value taste and smell will evolve High End experiences in foods and perfumes. Cultures that value appearance will evolve High End experiences based on visual design. What a splendid opportunity for future High End success, geared to the senses and their pleasures.

The infinite variety of experience demands vital information that captures the differences, particularly charting "sensory cartography" around the world. From these patterns, the High End proposition will take on characteristics appropriate for the consumer predilections. Knowledge of sensory predilections, although general, creates a platform by which to understand and guide tomorrow's developments.

Here are some opportunities for future experience design coming from the sensory world:

Sight, which incorporates fundamental design qualities such as aesthetic appearance and colors, is important for customers in the most visually oriented urban cultures. Find these cultural preferences in Delhi and Mumbai, followed by Ho Chi Minh City, Singapore, Jakarta and Bangkok. The least visual urban hubs appear to be, in decreasing order, Seoul, Tokyo and the Kansai area in Japan. In the future, High End could greatly flourish when based on sensorial design; for example, the visual orientation of Chinese wealthy classes.

Hearing, the sense associated with sounds and music, is much more important in London and New York, but far less relevant for the Chinese and Indian major cities, as well as Taiwan. Tokyo is perhaps the lowest ranking when it comes to the importance of sound. Creating a High End sound design experience for Japan entails a completely different sensory profile than does a High End experience focused on New York.

Touch comprises the key High End dimensions of texture and feel. The sense of touch is most relevant for Asian cities in Taiwan, Hong Kong and Thailand, followed by Milan and Seoul. Touch is almost irrelevant in Japan and in Malaysia. This seems yet another important regional implication, especially for product designers, when they select the ultimate solutions in terms of High End materials and finishing.

Smell "paints" a completely different picture, with its strongest appeal in New York and London leading the pack at a great distance, with the Kansai area of Japan in third place, followed by Manila and Seoul. Delhi, Mumbai and Singapore are at the end of the list, with customers feeling that smell is far less relevant. Smell is highly regarded as a sensory input for enchantment and experiential design, especially in cities such as Milan, or by the Chinese wealthy classes in major cities.

Taste (and flavors) strongly resonates with Japanese in Tokyo, with Koreans and Philippines (especially Manila). Taste is far less important, perhaps almost irrelevant for customer from London and Ho Chi Minh City. Turin, the virtual capital of the Slow Food movement, focusing on traditional methods and artisanal production, was not screened by Hakuhodo, but you might expect Turin in northern Italy to be in the leading group.

What, then, are the business lessons here for creating a High End experience or proposition? The connection between sensory experiences and High End emerges from the common aspirations of people, be these aspirations sensory gratification or merely the desire for a better quality of life through improved experiences. Understanding the cultural differences in sensory experience enables and sometimes may drive business success for those who aspire to High End commerce.

To understand China, a nation set to surpass Japan economically quite soon, we need to answer a fundamental question: how to achieve High End success in this specific geographic context?

Spotlight on China: The Awakening Colossus for the High End

China is a fast growing market … China is the world's third largest consumer of luxury goods, accounting for 12 percent of global sales. If this trend continues, then by 2015 China could well surpass the US to become, along with Japan, the world's largest purchaser of luxury items (Time Magazine, Style and Design Fall 2007). *According to the Hunrun Rich List, the wealth of the richest 50 Chinese is almost 6 times higher in 2007 than it was in 2005. Those that have been enjoying High End goods will soon be looking for the luxury market while the newly rich will start to buy higher end products.*

Bessie Lee, CEO, Group M China, Shanghai

China is an inevitable choice for spot-checking our regional understanding of the future High End. We will not dissect the topic by statistics, but instead rely on the sharp vision of the likes of Bessie Lee, CEO, Group M China, and Richard Lee, entrepreneur and successful Hong Kong tycoon, thanks to his business acumen in the luxury markets.

What is the value of innovation in China, and what will be the future of "Made in China" with respect to the 1980s explosion of "Made in Japan" as a quality mark of own homegrown High End? And, of course, what are the business lessons for today?

For the High End to enter China, one key is *respect*. Respect is a deeply embedded value in the Chinese culture, and has been for thousands of years. The drive of the present luxury market in China is to have the brand gain respect from its customers, and have the customers, in turn, gain respect from others around them. Building respect around a brand and its products is crucial.

What does respect mean operationally for the High End business effort? The answer is an amalgam: a respectable shop location, respectable endorsing celebrities, respectable sales consultants, respectable social commitment, and respectable distribution company. All these interact to achieve respectable brand development in China. To repair a brand that has lost its respect would be costly in time and money, and perhaps even impossible.

Compared with the West, media habits of Chinese consumers show about a ten-year lag. From a practical point of view, many of the strategies that succeeded in the West in the 1990s can still be adopted effectively in China as long as the content remains relevant.

Let's look at what High End business ought to do today, in light of the Chinese patterns of media consumption. First, tier 1 cities (like Shanghai or Beijing) have already been overrun by celebrity endorsements, so endorsements probably will cost more and be less effective. However, tier 2 cities in China (like Chengdu or Dalian) may still benefit from a well-chosen endorsement. Second, High End brands must be careful regarding whom they choose to endorse their products. In China, many celebrities have been vastly overexposed. Third, the celebrity must also fit the image of the brand and display integrity in his or her personal life. A way to achieve this integrity identifies an up-and-coming star in a rare but appropriate category such as motor racing or tennis, cultivate the start and build up a meaningful, not just an expedient, financial relationship. When the endorser hits the spotlight, the brand, which backed him from the beginning could reap the benefits. Nike did this successfully with Liu Xiang. The practical advice here is to structure the communication strategically to make sure the brand stays visible.

The High End brand must use other strategies in China to control the distribution and enhance the user experience. The consumers must feel their High End purchase is sufficiently rare and the experience consequently truly elite in order to justify the purchase. If the product spreads itself too widely or the shopping and purchasing experience does not hit the right tone, then the brand may lose its authenticity. Furthermore, distance "enhances". Buying a product in Hong Kong seems more exotic and indulgent than buying the same product in China, even if the Hong Kong price is lower.

What about China as the source of High End? Today the label "Made in China" for High End products may even be negative. So, what to do here? The big challenge for Chinese business leaders aiming to get into the High End is to change "Made in China" from a negative to a positive. Historically, the change had been done at least once before, with "Made in Japan". The question is "how to do it", not "what to aim for." The answer may be to turn the "Made in China" to a meaningful appeal to Chinese heritage.

The goal is to appeal to the Chinese to buy their products with pride, and then to move out from China to the rest of the world, with improved products, and with a different positioning of China, one that deals with history and legend, and not just with innovation. This will require the "story", so important in the High End.

So, what are our lessons for China, and specifically how can the High End penetrate China as customers, as well as use the China-made label as an imprimatur of quality? Here are five ideas for "High End China":

1.   Respect and proper understanding of aspirations are "musts" to engage High End customers

2.   Innovation is crucial to meet expectations on the lifestyle and aspiration

3.   Celebrity marketing requires understanding of national and regional cultural differences to ensure true effectiveness

4.   Distribution requires knowledge about the specific urban realities of Chinese first and second tier cities. The nature of the city in China is critical. Adjust the profile of offerings to be appropriate for each city.

5. "Made in China" will not become a High End marker on the short term. It will take time and some strategic moves. Chinese brands can rely on their powerful historical and cultural heritage as a reference, and on the lessons they can learn from the ascent of "Made in Japan" from commodity to High End marker.

Summing Up

Understanding urban futures is key for High End success. It is really simple. Cities are *the* cultural incubators where lifestyles and trends are continually formed, and reformed. Cities are the real-life cultural R&D organic labs. It is in cities where cultural innovation happens.

Macro-level dynamics of changes in EU, US and Asian cities differ from each other. Urban macro-trends are captured with the keywords community, diversity, complexity, and density. High End solutions will respond where these trends will play a role, and this covers pretty much all of advanced and emerging economies, even through the crisis. A few urban approaches emerge at global level: accelerating city, memory city, iconic city, and connecting city. These will be the frameworks for new lifestyles to which the High End can appeal.

The Hakuhodo Global Habit Survey teaches us about the cities, their expenditure patterns and associated senses. These insights give the High End companies some necessary information to help create better, and most of all, appropriate propositions. The Hakuhodo data show where people will have the propensity to spend for higher quality, and how High End marketers and designers should tailor the specific natures of their Experience Design offerings.

At a more macro-regional level, China presents a special opportunity, both as consumer of High End, and ultimately as producer. It is in China where an entirely new world of High End may emerge, coming from a country that is intensely nationalistic, proud of its heritage, and with a purchasing power that can turn inwards to the "Made in China" as an emerging label of pride. It will take some time, but it is coming.

11

Premium Products and Experiences through High Design

Design will grow more and more towards being a leading organizational factor in corporations and enterprises, as a truly key function of the company. This has always been the case in fashion and luxury companies, where CEO and Creative Director often coincide. This approach will migrate and proliferate to other industries, where the presence of Chief Design Officers will soon become the new standard. Also designers' thought leadership will surely grow into becoming one of the key dynamics of consumers' targeted industries.

Graziano De Boni, former President and CEO,
Valentino US, New York

In the "aristocratic kingdom" of luxury, styling confers competitive advantage in a world where brands joust with each other to conquer and maintain their impression of "premium", and even "sublime". The kingdom is ruthless, its citizens stop at nothing to get to their stations and hold them.

Just a step lower, in the neighboring land of High End, the "substance of style" also acts out its leading role for brands, and even for enterprises. And perhaps in this land of High End one might even say that design plays its greater role. Lacking as they do any real "pedigree" in terms of their actual origin or exclusivity, High End products need the aura of styling to be positioned on the higher rung of the product ladder. But it is a truism that there is way more to "design" than just "styling".

We see a profound manifestation of design in all its power deeply rooted in the organic life of Italian design districts. Some of these districts are truly among the most successful luxury and/or High End creative hubs in post-World War Two economies. There, day in and day out, design goes far beyond pure styling to create premium value. In those districts, design moves up the corporate ladder, where it embeds itself in the mores and rules of corporate governance for repeatable business success.

The High End depends on emotional connections. In fact, we might say that a great deal of what we call the High End is the projection of one's emotions onto products, which, in other circumstances, would be considered "ordinary". Without the provenance as art has, without uniqueness as luxury can boast, the High End needs emotion connections so much that success demands ongoing understanding and the anticipation of people's needs, dreams, aspirations, and emotions. With this in mind, it should come as no surprise that those working with High End brands always think about how to create a harmonious relation between people, objects and the environment, both natural and man-made. We will explore one corporate strategy to discover, formulate, and then achieve this harmonious relation. This is the *High Design* process pioneered by Philips Design, in the Netherlands, but adopted, respected and studied world-wide.

High Design to Create Premium Value

This chapter about process for the High End comes from the thinking and design methods that the author of the foreword to this book, Dr. Stefano Marzano, CEO and Chief Creative Director, Philips Design, created and implemented during a 20-year period from the middle of the 1980s. The notion of design as a humanistic exercise is not new, but it is new within the context of the order to create a fertile, nourishing stream of opportunities for business success based on the systematic creativity of designers. Within High Design, we find the creative smithy who hammers and even welds together the "product designer", the "sociologist", together with the technical and managerial talents of business, science and even poetry. The outcomes address the needs of today and tomorrow in an amalgam combining elegance, art, and an eminent orientation to the business performance. High Design is optimistic, realistic, actionable, repeatable and pragmatic leaving in its wake knowledge, artifacts, and services that populate the world of the High End.

First, a formal definition of High Design:

High Design is the human-focused, research-based, design management process for repeatable business success. High Design integrates the input from socio-cultural disciplines and people research, and then makes that information and insight the starting points of every design project.

High Design is meant to culminate in insights and then in artistic direction for the design of products and services. High Design is inclusive, not exclusive. By delivering cross-cultural, lifestyle-anticipating premium concepts and propositions, the High Design approach produces deep engagement with all stakeholders, both customers and people in general. And, in doing so, High Design becomes an effective business process to create actual products for the High End. The High Design process provides those two starting points, in a repeatable, business process.

The "secret sauce" of High Design comprises three specifics.

Basis: future-oriented human insights achieved by Philips Design through proprietary approaches and programs. These insights generate ongoing knowledge. The skill is to understand, in new and deeper ways, the needs of people and the trends of culture. The knowledge directs the "function" of creative management.

Where: at multiple levels. High Design looks at future trends and people insights, both for immediate application and for long-term direction. It is important to realize that in the fast-paced world of business, the "tomorrow" is inevitably sacrificed to the real, almost unsatisfiable demands of "today". Tomorrow is never as important as today. So, High Design was created for both today, to generate new products, and for tomorrow to guide the company vision, mission and portfolio.

What: it anticipates, sometimes shares, and then guides future technological developments. High Design tools and skills bridge the gap between what people will want in the future and what technological applications can offer. High Design acts as a friendly guide. It understands the people, knows the technology, senses the limitations, and prescribes the near and the far. And, when appropriate, calls in collaborators in and *open innovation.* Indeed, when High Design began this approach, companies did not think about such collaborations as a matter of standard business practice!

Despite the focus on business process, High Design has worked well with the creative community that has to develop for the High End. Knowledge is worth waiting for, worth getting, and can supplant the instinctive but vacuous kneejerk reactions so common to business. Thanks to the High Design Process, Philips Design developed a robust portfolio of projects and business models with Philips and with cooperating third parties, non-competitive leading

Fortune 500 corporations such as Nike and Levis, and design leaders such as Alessi and Cappellini (read more in Chapter 7).

The Roots of High Design: the Lombardy Design Districts

A comprehensive vision of what design is and is not emerges fully formed as the Greek goddess Athena emerged from the head of Zeus. It is time to explore the "ideological blueprint" behind High Design. To do this, we invite you to the starting point, the landscapes and colors of the Po Valley in the north of Italy. It is here that we find the "regional innovation engine" of Italy's design-driven High End, the "cradle of High Design".

Professor Roberto Verganti of Politecnico di Milano, who won the prestigious Compasso d'Oro (Italian design "Oscar") award for his research, believes that fertile networks of creative leaders, business entrepreneurs and R&D experts in a local region provide the context for the sociological equivalent of "basic research". Of course, the research is not "scientific" per se, but rather living research actively involving society, culture and aesthetics,[1] aspects that are important in the High End.

One of the Verganti's approaches we call "humanistic design". Another, perhaps more accurate, name might be the "Lombardy District" approach, giving credit to the place where it occurs. Look at the natural social and human "ecology" of the district. To all appearances it is chaotic, seemingly lacking conscious direction. Listen and you can't help but hear the opinions of the free-spirited minds engaging in professional networks. These informal circles perpetually fluctuate, creating new groupings of people, new ideas, new inspirations.

In Milan, similar to a few other large cities in Italy such as Turin, a big community of designers and entrepreneurs, taste-makers and trendsetters, academics and innovation leaders, mashed with the cultural "humus" – fine arts and advertising, galleries and nightlife, luxury and avant-garde shops – constantly "incubate" innovative design ideas. Naturally occurring, informal networking and dialog among talents and professionals with different backgrounds have one focus – to invent the *new* by anticipating what people dream and desire. In a sense, they resemble high-tech bio-scientists, filled with vision and hope, working in their incubation labs, the refuge and living

---

1   Roberto Verganti. "Innovating Through Design". *Harvard Business Review*, December 2006.

room of their mind. These spontaneous and uncontrolled sparks of diffused creativity result in brilliant High End business success. This process led to the birth of the great Italian lifestyle-defining masterpieces of interior design and home accessories represented by the world-class brands Artemide, Zanotta and Alessi.

The holistic and organic Milanese, design-driven innovation approach comes alive during the progression of three phases:

- The process begins with *Absorb*, where the cultural analysis and social research leads to reflection and inspiration in the process of forming the insights. Whether it is a designer's self-observation or the intuition of an industrial leader, the extreme organic nature of the opinions circulating behind this free flow of potential product ideas resembles the natural Italian lifestyle to sit at a bar, conversing with friends. Somewhat similar "coffee machine" rituals in companies stimulate the design process. Around the coffee machine there spring forth unprompted dialogs and free flow of ideas, often fragmented episodes of yet another and larger dialog shaping within the urban cultural flow of information and discussion. The city where this behavior takes place plays the key role. It is the home, the protective shelter. The city plays a key role in connecting individuals, offering the necessary environment for naturally emerging creative excellence from the collective group. (For discussion of urban communities and their crucial role for future High End, see Chapter 10.)

- The second phase of the Milanese way is *Address*, when the actual delivery of products, services and solutions happens. With the craftsmanship and the professional skills of the fine masters in manufacturing, the greatest technical sensitivity to colors and materials and their best rendition become the principal differentiating enabler of design with the goal to achieve premium value. Here loom some problems, however. Business success, business considerations may do some damage. Outsourcing enabled by globalization and digital technologies over time might affect this capability. It is up to the Italian talent to meet the challenge of keeping up with the new.

- The third phase, *Announce*, delivers innovation beyond conventional marketing and communication. *Announce* comes closer to the techniques of "cultural marketing". We see here a somewhat similar tactic as the one that led Prada to create its art foundation. The difference is that the Milanese design approach works by exhibiting design pieces in museums. Who can resist that? The strategy seduces the market. Thus high art institutions are brought into the process. But it's not just museums; the *Announce* phase is much grander, more extensive. *Announce* moves forward on other fronts, complementing its efforts with books and other publicly present ideas, and the creation of high-profile communications. There are even exhibitions of the highest quality staged in the shops of selected top retailers. All in all, this is a strategy that is at once humanistic, grand, visionary, and groundbreaking.

But what results from the effort? What tangibles remain after the effort has finished, and the shows close down? The foregoing recipe of crafting design collectibles converts everyday superior artifacts into actual collection pieces. To qualify, a prospective item should be seen in a museum. In this emerging connection between potential collectability and museum-quality we see the High End deliberately pushing up towards the world of luxury, rather than being forced down by economics to the world of the everyday, the low price, the common. *Announce* in Italian design incubates a potential "residual value" for High End products.

By now you can well appreciate that the true inner workings of the "Milanese creative district" does not project an image of a formalized, simple process that companies want and consultants offer by the truckload. Far from that. Rather, we see an "implicit" non-linear design process that resembles a tree with branches protruding in directions that we sometimes expect, but just as often comes the unexpected, the new and delightful.

Cooperation within a district embodies very loose, informal and ongoing forms of partnership. It is like a dance with steps that are widely known, yet which has never been formally choreographed. The rules are unwritten, but the process flows almost automatically. Different companies harmoniously work together to satisfy the customer and to be ahead in style and delivery.

We are not just talking about Milan alone, but the whole north of Italy. The cooperation works in Turin in automotive and transportation design; the

Eastern region of Veneto for eyewear ; in Tuscany for leather, and so on. The "Lombardy model" actually works all across Italy, beyond regional borders. In the Milanese design district, or indeed in any of the other creative districts in Italy or across the globe, from Silicon Valley to emerging economies, we find the trend to bring to the table competing and fragmented companies with different specialties, known for different types of excellence. The outcome makes business sense – it creates premium value.

No model is perfect, and the Lombardy model is not perfect either. The model, which works so well for design, has a drawback. While utilized by many design-driven, small family-owned Italian firms, the model cannot easily survive in the large corporate environment with its different ecology and with different stresses. Yet the Lombardy model consistently produces wonderful luxury and High End creations, without any apparent "conscious" corporate control of large business conglomerates. How then can business, so accustomed to structure, hierarchy, reporting, processes, and return on investment, take the soul of the Lombardy model and transform it to something that the corporation can tolerate, perhaps someday even warmly embrace?

The Lombardy Model in the Big Company: Basics of High Design

High Design achieves in a structured manner what the Lombardy model does informally. In contrast to natural scatter that we find in Italy the High Design process comprises a structurally formalized arrangement and flow. In High Design, people with different competencies and from different expert fields gather in carefully facilitated workshops. In these structured environments the people interact, contribute, and create the "new", nourished by an environment where creativity and knowledge are allowed, even encouraged to flourish. The "process" description of High Design best resembles nothing as much as the master artist's studio where many artisans and apprentices work together to create masterpieces, in truly horizontally managed teams, and not just under the guidance of the visionary maestro working in splendid, vision-driven isolation. In a nutshell, High Design translates the culture of Italian design districts and their networking richness into structured, high-tech, corporate-scale processes.

What is the magic that transplants the artist studio to the corporation, the creator or premium to the business world of the regimented and profit driven? Strategically, High Design moves beyond business to the souls of the cooperating experts, whether social scientists, artisans of the mind, or artisans of the material. There is a genuine concern for creating a good human "future", and the group realization that such creation of the future can be accomplished only with a singular focus, with the level of control that comes from a business perspective.

Intellect and knowledge characterize High Design. One might think that with the quarterly need for corporate profits, there is little room for the deliberate, knowledge-building, contemplative activities of High Design. Instead, one might think that as in most corporations, all would be aflutter in creativity, in that excited, business-world pace which values activity as the true heartbeat. That is not the case. In sharp distinction to what one might think, of the unfettered artist, the lone genius, and an army of lesser talents running the actual business, we see a different, more deliberate, and more measured activity in High Design, focused on succeeding through knowledge plus creativity, not just creative talent alone. High Design moves beyond industrial applications, straight into trend analyses, studies of what the future could be and what artifacts and designs could produce premium for that future. In other words, it is an approach to create the High End.

From an operational viewpoint, High Design converts the Lombardy model into a repeatable business process. High Design becomes simple, allowing it to survive the corporation, allowing it to become repeatable, and to give it the promise of prospective scalability; in short, knowledgeable artisanship and creation harnessed to the realities of business, but without losing the soul.

High Design comprises five repeatable phases. Note the discipline, and yet the freedom in that discipline – the *alphas and the omegas* of art and business: initiation; analysis; concept; finalization; evaluation.

Rather than pontificating on steps in a sort of pedantic, prosaic, perhaps mind-deadening manner, let us look at the innards of High Design with something which lives and breathes consumer, and yet produces a High End experience. We chose a very challenging concrete High End project from the Philips portfolio to demonstrate the approach: returning true High End "magic" to the commodity world of TV. The big challenge here is culture and expectation. Philips was not a luxury player and some earlier attempts to move radically upscale through product excellence deployed by major competitors from Japan (for example, Qualia) led to big disappointments. Let's see how

High Design made a difference this time to creating the High End through a deliberate, knowledge-creating/using system.

High Design "Struts Its Stuff": Aurea by Philips

Since its birth in 1891, Philips has always tried to associate itself with light, and the experience of light. Light has a long history here, ranging from bulb to valve, to tube, and to TV. Today TV is a common, with everyone having more TVs than they can really watch. But in 1937 a TV set was as precious and rare as palladium is today, selling in the USA for about 40 percent of an average annual income. TVs were marketed, distributed, and sold in a luxury environment; personal service was a sine qua non. No one would buy a TV without expecting guidance, advice, helpful and courteous sales. With TV came exclusivity, and of course in turn the TV became a true luxury of the time.

Fast forward these 70+ years, past wars, past space travel, past the Internet, and stop at today. Well, we see that now, TV is sold in mass-market environments making it a commodity; its price eroded down to 3 percent of average annual income. The entire experience certainly is not premium, despite the advances in High Definition, and the 500 channels for those daring to subscribe to all of the offered cable channels.

Beyond the ordinary of the TV and its experience is the banal advertising for the product. Marketing messages for TV sets are boring, formulaic, fact-filled, but reasonably useful for comparative shopping: technology plus features plus size plus price, with key focus on price/screen size ratio. The value of the TV brand is virtually irrelevant. The majority of the modern flat-screen TVs build their products around LCDs produced by the same few companies. Makers like Bang and Olufsen were rare exceptions to the rules of what seems an unstoppable drift towards the commoditization of this specific market. Until Philips' Ambilight TV was created by High Design that we briefly reviewed earlier.

Enter Aurea, return of the TV to the High End. After all these years Aurea picks up on the authenticity of what TV originally was, back at its origin. Furthermore, Aurea is business as well, bringing back higher margins, the objective of the High End, and by so doing recreates the economics of TV in a more attractive incarnation. In the TV commodity, Aurea's high-tech heart

"Ambilight' enables the leap back to the High End and the much higher selling price.

With all this trumpeting, just what is Ambilight, this technology which pulls the TV back to High End, out of commodity? And, at the end of the story, what strategies can we learn to apply to other commodity businesses wanting to vault to the High End?

Ambilight TV builds upon the notion of integrating lighting into the frame of the TV. Let's stop here for a second to remark that this merger of lighting with sound and vision is a typical example of a High End innovation. The innovation combines apparently distant technologies from different market sectors. The technologies can be held by the same company or one of the technologies or perhaps even both can be bought or licensed. The goal is simple; anticipate what people will want in a high-quality experience in their living room.

Of course, the specific nature of the technology changes with the times, and Aurea is no different. It's not the material from which the product is made, nor necessarily the external design. Rather, in keeping with today's focus on "knowledge" as a differentiator and competitive advantage, Aurea's "secret ingredient" is proprietary software. That software intelligently manages the delivery of ever-changing lights of different color and intensity in order to complement the images flowing on screen. And the magic – what is it about this simple technology which so lifts Aurea from the world of commodity to the world of High End? It is the High End experience that Ambilight creates. The result is far more than the description might lead one to expect. For the best visual effect, and a memorable visual experience, Amblight immerses the viewer into the cinematic experience with an aura of light complementing the moving pictures. From the viewpoint of the High End customer, we might say that Ambilight is the first TV technology able to enhance the pleasure of viewing in a new, holistic way, in the privacy of one's living room, on demand.

And now for the rest of the story. So, how did Philips Design do it, and what practical lessons does that hold if we want to do the same thing with our commodity product or service? Let's dive into the five phases of the High Design project that led to Aurea's creation. As we dissect Aurea, keep in mind that we are combining trends, knowledge, artistic design and technology. We are striving to create something new, something that is relevant to people, something that is *au courant*, today, in tune with the times and the readiness of the consumer to adopt.

Phase 1: Initiation: Nothing starts from "scratch", emerging right away fully developed. Philips has its stakeholders, each of whom has expertise, and of course some degree of bias. For Aurea to succeed meant bringing together different skills. The assemblage comprised radically different groups of not necessarily compatible mindsets, from the Philips Consumer Lifestyle group, to the Business Unit for TV, to Lighting and so forth. Nonetheless, the cross-functional team worked well, with the expected sensitivities addressed and assuaged. From the start, Design acted as "the" facilitator of dialog, and afterwards integrated the results. Arguably most crucial for success of this phase was the formal *Design Briefing Document* coalescing everything into the vision and the direction:

> *Directly address the emotional interests of consumers and their lifestyles*
> *– design a product which fits with the consumer's interior architecture*
> *and offers a more immersive viewing experience.*

Phase 2: Analysis: "How does soft science anticipate the future?" The team began with a roughed out idea, not knowing exactly what they were looking for. The general outlines were reasonable: a product to be successful on a time line between two and five years. To create knowledge that would give direction, Philips used "long-term social scenarios". The operating principle was "what would the future look like (the more concrete, the better)?" What will people want? Or better, not exactly what they want, but who are these people, what is inside their minds, what will be their aspirations, what ordinary things will they do in their ordinary lives that will allow Philips to create something for that commonplace future reality? With energy and enthusiasm, with give and take, acceptance of alternate views of reality, the Aurea design team created its own synthesis, merging together information, insights, even not necessarily well-founded opinions from the abundance of trends and benchmark activities, consumer insights and visionary design roadmaps. And, in the end, the Aurea team functioned much like the groups of individual artisans and even competitors in the Lombardy model, corporate equivalent of Milanese "organic knowledge" about socio-cultural preferences in the near future.

Phase 3: Concept: Every company demands deliverables. Phase 3 created these deliverables. The High Design team selected a number of design directions addressing people's needs, and some anticipating future dreams. From these directions, they created a number of "concepts" to further refine and test. This concept phase is important. It produced something, which means that the process was productive, and thus measurable. That which gets measured gets done and promoted. During this phase when the specific Aurea concept was generated and nurtured, clients continued to stay involved. Some of the Philips Design "magic" was made real through workshops. These workshops, face-to-face meetings really, ensure that the group became a team, that they discussed the specifics, and when necessary came to a consensus.

Phase 4: Finalization: We now move to the next step, where corporate design acts like the "craftsman" of the Milanese masters. *"The proof of the pudding is in the eating"*. Companies, like chefs, should be judged on what they produce, not what they proclaim. It's ok to talk about the future, but what exactly does "the thing" really look like? The Aurea group translated the concepts into models and into digital applications. The software and hardware created with the artisans, the engineering, and all inspired by knowledge, comprised the second work-product of High Design. The first work-word had been knowledge. Reality has a way of intruding, demanding flesh on the bone, not just ideas. So the designers had to consider the actual product, not just the description. The group designed the specific aesthetic nature (materials and colors), working together with a highly accomplished visual trends team. The "How" of this effort to create the actual "thing" was again data-based, and not just intuitive guesswork. For a decade prior, Philips Design had systematically watched and measured culture, anticipating not only Aurea, but many other opportunities. CultureScan, the name they gave to the process, created the knowledge that would inform what Aurea would look like and feel like. The design team, like any other development group, had to be involved to see what came off the assembly line, what the injection-molded parts looked like. Was the product assembled correctly? … Were there any flaws that didn't show up when the product was designed? … And so on.

Phase 5: Evaluation: And finally, companies simply cannot live without testing, especially where consumers are involved. No one can anticipate customers who inevitably vote with their wallets. And so evaluations occurred, not so much as the report card for the creative group (certainly a no-no), but rather to inform, to carry back the voice of the customer. This type of evaluation, or rather voice of the consumer, is always welcome, when presented in a constructive manner. It informs future efforts.

At the very end of this months-long effort, Aurea by Philips was launched in Paris, then two months later in Berlin. High End products do better when presented and sold in High End venues. Aurea, born out of a rigorously facilitated creative process, delivered higher margins in a market infamous for its price erosion and shrinking profits. High Design created the High End opportunity for Philips, just below luxury, and a world of new opportunities. And the benefits to Philips? The effort established Philips in the High End, crucial in this market primarily driven by cost-efficiency.

Lessons for the High End Lessons from High Design as a Process

High Design is a knowledge-intensive process for repeatable business success. The knowledge-seeking efforts explore people's future needs and aspirations. For more than two decades, Philips Design has used the High Design approach to move forward, and enrich design. The result moves beyond traditional, conventional Industrial Design to incorporate sociology, anthropology and psychology, each of which leaves its own contribution to be felt, touched, seen, and heard. The roots are simple and battle-tested for centuries. We can trace them back to the collaborative vibrancy of Italian design, which wins awards, produces legends, and makes money.

We see three major lessons from High Design that we can apply to the High End. The lessons, by their very nature, tell us about how business can use knowledge to penetrate the High End.

- Make the process transparent, public, and owned by the group, and not by a guru with power. Philips devised High Design to be a clearly structured and transparently manageable process, organized according to the ISO quality standards. That foresight is important. It helps later on when the excitement of creation inevitably gives way to the reality and then to the occasional but inevitable drudgery from implementation.

- Blend inspiration with knowledge and systematics. While capturing the benefits of the "organic way" to cultural innovation of Italian design districts, High Design is rational and repeatable over time.

- Invite the "others" to participate, and give them the opportunity do so. Even people who may be "far away" from the topic can contribute more than we realize. High Design enables multidisciplinary innovation. In the end, High Design offers an ideal venue for facilitated dialog across different professional specializations, from sociologists to engineers to marketers.

Experience Design in Practice: Looking into Tomorrow

We have just seen how High Design underpinned the success of Aurea by merging high-tech applications from lighting and software in a rigid commodity category like TV. We were dealing with a dinosaur waiting to become a gazelle. But there are other vistas, other challenges, especially the *new*. What happens when creative power unleashes disruptive innovation? What should we expect in the uncharted world of tomorrow's High End, where we have no entrenched dinosaurs waiting to become gazelles?

High Design steers innovation across the entire company portfolio. Now it's a matter of divide the horizons and adapt the process to the horizon. We have three different horizons. Let's look at how tomorrow can be designed.

At the very farthest, we "probe" the remote, long-term scenarios (Horizon 3). In the middle we have the moderately near future, where Aurea fits (Horizon 2). We have the immediate tomorrow where the issue is not the long-term opportunity, but rather the need to get a product out tomorrow (Horizon 1). We will elaborate on the theoretical side of this model in Chapter 12, "Design for Tomorrow". Here instead we intend to focus at the practical power and the pragmatic results for business success generated by its application over time.

A Dream is Born: The High End Bedroom, *Nebula*

Sometimes things work out in a way not exactly expected, no matter how much planning has taken place. Our next story is about how you get from Horizon 3 to Horizon 1 through a number of projects, from prototype to applied solutions. The theme is contemporary design, a vision for the High End that was born out and then matured to actual products with High Design process. We deal here with the experience of bedrooms, and how that experience can be pulled into the future.

Providing a higher quality of life is one of the key reasons why multidisciplinary teams congregate all over the world to create and define tomorrow's High End products and applications. After Pine and Gilmour's 1990s book *The Experience Economy* appeared, the term "experience" has been adopted and abused by some experts in just about any business you can name which involves a consumer. It seemed natural that in discussing a sector like the High End nobody missed the opportunity to reference the world of "experience". To properly articulate this theme, however, is a challenge. We decided to tackle it starting from what actually was born as a dream, a designer's dream, precisely.

During the summer of 2001, Philips Design engaged in an exploratory series of long-term innovation programs in partnership with the Royal College of Arts. We spoke earlier about the importance of knowledge for the High End. This "learning partnership" is one of them.

One partnership project at Horizon 3 level, *Nebula*, created an "immersive bedroom environment" for the year 2020, where high-tech and superior interaction design met. The goal was to make a room that would be sensitive to a person, in a new, profound way, what one thinks about as the idea of the future. Nebula's design and its technological underpinnings provide a person with a seamless, anticipatory and pervasive experience. The attraction of high-technology was even more interesting because at all stages the participants were told to think of the people, and not to focus on the technology. According to the principles of High Design, the most important side of the project was its people-centric design.

Nebula's bed was not an ordinary place to sleep. Intelligent fibers transformed this bed into a real-time, real-life, remotely controlled place that would detect the state of mind and the body condition of its occupants. The notion was to adjust the settings of the entire room. The room itself was no longer merely a "blind and deaf environment", but a true high-tech media interface. The ceiling itself was the space where the "room" could project content, such as movies, sports, news, or even atmospheric stimuli, in order to provide welcomed sounds and background images. Thanks to the creative flexibilities within the rigor of High Design, Nebula was born as a designer's "dream of preferable futures". It was time to "announce" it to the world.

Now enter High End to complement High Design. Immediately upon reaching the vision of what Nebula would be, one of the first steps to do so was a partnership with Italian luxury furniture masters Cappellini. Their job was to transfer the principles of Nebula to the everyday home, in simple terms to create top design quality for high-tech interiors, at High End and even luxury prices. Here was a way to activate the *Announce* phase of Italian district design. By the announcement, one could test the reaction of media and opinion leaders to the ideas behind the Nebula concept. Would the idea be greeted warmly, even enthusiastically, or perhaps would it be greeted by a merciful yawn to dash one's excitement? The resulting concept collection of luxury furniture was presented in the Milan yearly furniture fair "Salone del Mobile," universally regarded as the most important event in design worldwide, a sort of "Night of the Oscars" for creative leaders and newcomers. The intention was clear: "announce", test, and generate as much buzz as possible in the world outside.

There is an important High End lesson here: partnerships work. Philips, not a luxury brand itself, joined with Cappellini, a brand famous for luxury interior design, in order to launch the vision of seamless, integrated high-tech behind the Nebula concept. Philips announced its vision by "shooting to the stars" (the world of luxury), in order to gain visibility and profiling "on the ground" (the media and the press of the High End design world).

Philips management recognized and then adopted Nebula as the manifesto of Philips CEO Gerard Kleisterlee for his vision of the world of consumer electronics in 2020. Imagine a designer's dream proving so strong that it becomes the embodied vision of a major corporation. This alone could be considered a major achievement in strategic relevance and acknowledgement, for what had started out simply as a research exercise to probe possible futures.

The Unknown Made Tolerable: Ambient Experience for Hospitals

Nebula had led to a major breakthrough in High End experience, although not yet in the home of the future, as some might have expected. Rather, after the successful "proof of the pudding" and great public interest, the ideas behind Nebula introduced a higher quality of life in a much more delicate and critical aspect of our everyday – the hospital experience.

For most hospitals, technical functionality rather than user experience is the rule. In the world of efficient and central health care, functionality always overshadows comfort and emotions, just as in the case of factories, where cold austerity and efficiency always trump human warmth and caring. An impersonal, cold environment does not help doctors and nurses to reduce a sick child's fear, calm an anxiety attack, or just relax the patients and their families. Enter the humanistic focus of High Design, materialized in the Nebula prototype and its vision of tomorrow's experience. Such happy materialization would lead to something far more important to people, the definition of tomorrow's healthcare experience – *Ambient Experience Design*.

We refer here to Ambient Experience Design (AED), which is the High End approach to the everyday experience of hospitals and institutionalized health care. Ambient Experience Design becomes the High End brought to where it can be most helpful, rethinking the physical environment and digital technologies in the way they interlink. AED is the ultimate convergence of moving image, sound and lighting around the medical suite of high-tech equipment. Within AED, high-tech is flexibly adapted to the ultimate demands and needs of people. Hence we will not speak of an AED environment as an MRI scanner plus a modular lighting solution plus an audio-video dramatic installation. Instead, the AED environment is an experiential milieu, where the various applications of superior TV and displays, sound systems and LED sources converge. Patients receive instructions for their examination in the form of cartoons; stakeholders will work in an appealing environment with a soothing soundtrack to cover the noise of healthcare devices. Light is *managed*, used to relax minds and ease the tension of examination, to make the experience better.

With more than 50 AED applications installed since 2005, from Chicago to Sao Paulo, from the Netherlands to the Middle East, AED solutions for healthcare quickly became a world class, High End success story. The driving principle is simple. Behind the fully immersive, highly responsive examination rooms, the same design dream of Nebula beats like a heart – a uniquely human-focused, highly integrated high-tech marvel.

Peeking at the innards of AED, we see three design breakthroughs, which bring this lighting concept to a new level in sophistication and also in sustainability of the patient, nurse, and doctor souls:

- *Environment, not just the machine, is holistic.* The AED design for medical equipment moves beyond the actual machine unit. The design includes the entire environment creating a markedly better hospital experience for patients, their families and healthcare professionals.

- *People are first.* The AED exercise focuses around people, not technology and not around the corporation. The person himself is the center of the experience.

- *Quality of experience produces better health.* AED improved the medical performance of machines, as well as substantially improving both the comfort and health of the patients. High Design also improved the environment, and so the working conditions improved for the staff and the visiting relatives. We consider this as one of the best practices in terms of "inclusive design".

But was it worth it to the patient? Did the High End experience make a difference? Metrics help here to measure business success. At the Chicago Lutheran General Children's Hospital, one of the first to install ambient experience environments, the sedation rate of its youngest patients dropped by 30–40 percent, a major improvement that delighted the patients, doctors and administration. A better hospital experience generates other business benefits. For example, one of the metrics of hospital popularity, the widely popular Net Promoter Score, indicated that the hospitals adopting AED solutions enjoyed higher ratings. When asked, 30 percent of patients at "Advocate Imaging Specialist" in the Chicago Metro area responded that they chose their hospital based on physician advice, often triggered by AED solutions installed in such hospitals – making AED a marketing asset for hospitals.

There is more to the notion that the High End experience can be designed, just as a product can. Philips designed into these machines substantial *flexibility* and *scalability*. Both factors make AED appeal to the most demanding potential "High End commissioners" in the healthcare world – such as the cosmetic health care industry in the Middle East, catering to high-net-worth customers willing to fund the surgery out of their own pockets. The health care experience can become not only a part of the High End, but *even enable a true luxury experience.*

At the same time, and to bring benefits to the masses, High Design teams *flexibly scaled downward* the reach for AED solution by stripping out some of the "over-the-top" features of this High End medical experience. We are not talking about commoditizing medical care, but rather of keeping the High End notion, while making the experience more accessible to more people. For example, additional AED projects are performed in Rio de Janeiro, for Minas Gerais and Espirito Santo. These are general hospitals. The AED has been *scaled down for wider distribution.* Philips Medical Systems named this scaled-down version "Insight" which provided only wall projections and lighting effects. These scaled-down versions show that parts of the High End can integrate experience with design in a holistic manner, for the less privileged audiences as well.

In terms of the business implications of design and the High End, AED "solutions" for hospitals are prestigious to hospital management and deliver high margins to Philips. This is what the High End is about. AED demands a major investment from healthcare customers. These AED environments adapt to the user almost one-on-one. Thus they work well to soothe the patient in a difficult moment of the examination, whether the patient is a child or a senior citizen. They also appeal to those patients who can easily choose one hospital over the other. AED solutions increase the quality of life for all those involved, and they allow the hospital to "jazz up" its marketing communication – always an asset for a hospital.

What the High End Learns from Ambient Experience Design

Our journey started from designers' dreams and High End interiors and ended up in a new vision of surprisingly friendly and clever hospitals. This jaunt from bedrooms to hospitals shows the vibrant core and soul of High End thinking. High End is not just about fancy stuff, brands that can be bought for just a little extra money. It is not a mere "happiness from a spent wallet". The High End exists and flourishes beyond conventional categories, beyond geographies and economies. The High End, in different manifestations, may live at the same time in "everyday uber-luxury" hubs like Singapore and in the heart of emerging countries where the dreams and aspirations of the High End are a serious matter. And, ultimately, High Design enables these High End dreams to come true.

Here are the *hows* and the business magic:

- High End is about improving the quality of people's life

- High Tech applications and people's "trends" drive the High End

- High Design is a specific process for creating premium value, designed to be repeatable and scalable

- High Design unlocks the full potential of Design by fulfilling people's dreams and aspirations through a systematic approach – even if the journey to the High End takes a few detours

- Ambient Experience Design is an example of innovation of the way hospital suites work – making life for the patients, doctors and nurses better and with top margins.

Summing Up

The natural cycle of Italian design, exemplified by the Milanese district of luxury and High End interior products, demonstrates the principles of a business success process. The Italian process, although no one but an outsider calls it that, organically unfolds. The process begins privately with informal conceptual visioning, and ends publicly with the actual profiling of products in superior venues like museums and other culture-defining settings. The urban nature of cities such as Milan or Turin nourishes the process. Cities provide the necessary "cultural greenhouse nursery" by getting people together, where they can "bounce ideas off each other", and where they can "observe the world, and dream of what could be, of what might be, of what should be".

By its profoundly unorganized, organic, natural structure, the Italian approach to design-driven High End lacks efficiency and effectiveness. Stefano Marzano's High Design brings vibrancy to the world of business. Marzano's industrial vision captures all the fundamentals of the Italian design districts while offering a number of advantages: repeatability, business focus and multidisciplinary integration harnessed for advanced innovation.

High Design works in practice, providing concrete evidence that the approach transcends theory, and like the Milanese district approach, comes up with specifics, things/experiences that one can point to:

1. Aurea by Philips, an innovative TV set integrating "Ambilight" which enhances the immersion in the picture, and brings TV back to a superior luxury-like experience.

2. Ambient Design Experience hospitals, the groundbreaking concept which puts patients and healthcare workers at the very center of a highly integrated digital experience.

And what are the benefits, the fits to the High End? The Aurea and AED offer superior marketing opportunities, and create higher margins. And at the same time the experiences make a difference in people's lives, as diverse as tension-freed home relaxation and entertainment, or tension-filled hospital examinations. Ultimately, they both contribute to a higher quality of life, according to the very nature of the High End.

12

Design for Tomorrow

My belief is that "discontinuous or disruptive innovation," that is, paradigm-changing innovation, is absolutely critical for the reinvention of consumption that will be required if marketers are to capture the opportunity in mass affluence. Luxury offerings must be re-thought and re-engineered to make some version of them affordable to the mass affluent ... So marketers and product developers need to begin with a clean sheet of paper and imagine solutions to problems affecting only the very wealthy today, and then these solutions can trickle down to the mass affluent.

Paul Nunes, Executive Research Fellow, Accenture,
Boston, and Author,

With this chapter, we now move from the world around High End "as is" to the actual creation of premium, where our stories show High End *in the making,* where design plays a key role. We introduce this chapter with a simple question. Exactly *how* can High End companies of the future manage to break stifling corporate silos, to create the new, the unexpected, the future High End? In order to do so, High End brands will have to manage the challenge to pursue the new customers who cannot even articulate what they want. The fundamental challenge to the High End marketer is then: how to mold today's technological opportunities into tomorrow's specific people-focused prototypes, and then ultimately into affordable consumer products. When we talk here of innovation we mean the wide range from the immediate next generation of products in the portfolio to probing the possibilities in the next 20 years. We see High Design, the proprietary Philips approach, as a versatile "growth engine blueprint" which enables long-term success in the High End. The issue and trick is simply "how?" What has to happen to make tomorrow a reality? And, more importantly, how can the business of today create those tomorrows for the High End?

We begin with what might be a platitude, but an important one, an organizing principle. Innovation design can be viewed as a process of translation, from soulless technology to High End benefits, from creative talent to corporate management, from *"what if"* to *"wow"*. Now enter High Design, not as the artist's tool or as the Lombardy story of organic yet informal creative networks, but this time as the strategic approach to manage innovation, from new product generation to long-term company strategy. The historically-rooted, culturally-sensitive thinking behind High Design now becomes the specific approach to manage innovation design.

Make it Appropriate and Applicable: Harnessing High-Tech

Think of a birthday party documented on the Web according to your own personal configuration; an online slideshow streaming to your iBook, with your soundtrack of choice from iTunes, perpetually repeating the moments when you experienced joy, happiness. Repeating, that is, until *you* press stop or delete. Thanks to digital technologies, you and just about anyone with a computer can design the party experience, record it, edit it, and then play it to your heart's content, or invite others, willing or unwilling, to share the moments.

Yet it was not always so. At some time in the past the ability to play with electronics, to create one's own movies, slide shows, and recordings was limited to those who were either "techno-geeks", or well off, or both. But innovations don't stay still. They migrate. Technological innovations typically trickle down from the original exclusive circles of upper class to the middle class of today. Trickle-down unleashes increasingly wider access to the sensations and experiences empowered by the technology resulting in democratized experience, ideas, dreams, and reality.

Democratization is not automatic. High Tech alone disconnected from people's dreams and desires is impotent; it cannot enable higher quality of life. Here is the great opportunity for High End. How many people use all or even a significant number of the overly abundant features in their electronics products? Or even know these features exist? In turn, how many great experiences are missed because the technology is beyond the average customer? This is where the synthesizing power of High Design makes technology opportunities into true High End products, services and experiences.

High Touch, High End: Making High Tech Relevant to People

With retail playing a crucial role in the perception of High End value, let's look at the places where the high-tech applications normally find their ways into our lives. And, in turn, let's see how the future High End might look when some of that high-tech is taken from the world of techies, geeks, and electronic cognoscenti and put into stuff and experiences that people will pay more for.

Visit with us Philips Research's "ShopLab" located at the High Tech Campus in Eindhoven, the Netherlands: this is a simulated retail environment where the applications of tomorrow can be experienced today, providing a sneak preview of the future retail. The motivation to create the lab was the competitive advantage conferred when one can explore the future High End of distribution in an actual physical space, rather than through pictures and sketches.

Leaders of some of the best-known luxury brands visit the lab, eager to see the future and particularly the technology showpiece of ShopLab, Intuitive Interaction for Lighting Atmosphere (ILLA). ILLA emerged out of discussions with clients and customers around the world that revealed the need to "understand" the lighting and "atmosphere" requirements for specific products in the store. To sell High End demands a good presentation.

Professional visitors to ShopLab enjoy a fascinating walk in the future, powered by High Tech with High Touch sensitivity. For many applications ILLA makes a joy of our recurring merchandising problem; how to optimize the lighting for each specific product to make the shopping experience more joyful. Through the skillful and customizable use of light, ILLA adds a new dimension to merchandising the High End. Rather than forcing the merchandiser to "guess" about lighting, ILLA creates the experience right there, so that the merchandiser can get a sense of the customer experience, right up front. The light comes from the optimized color selection of background lighting (done by a device named ColorSensor) and from the ability to "paint the show area with light". ColorSensor works by having the user simply scan and point (done by a device named LightWand). The result – a pure fun experience for the merchandiser (and for the merchandiser's children – not to forget other decision makers). Technologies like these will be there in the near future for High End brand managers, marketers, and merchandisers to make a difference. However, the skeptics might comment: it is easy to build a prototype in a lab; it is a different ball game to make and distribute it commercially. The question then is: how to make such High Tech explorations "repeatable" for business success, by design?

Three Horizons of Innovation to Drive High End Development

Building on an 80-year tradition in innovation, Philips Design adapted the "three innovation horizons" model described by McKinsey's Merhad Baghar, Stephen Coley and David White in their 2003 book *Alchemy of Growth*. Since the 1920's, the creation of theoretical frameworks to analyze human creativity is not new in social sciences and psychology, as addressed by one of the authors (MB) in his book, "*The Golden Crossroads*": among the great variety of equivalent options, what makes this particular model by Baghar, Coley and White very appealing to a corporate design center, is the fact that it divides innovation within companies into three distinct sequential yet connected stages or "horizons". Using this as the organizing principle, Philips Design then plotted the three horizons model onto the Gartner Hype Cycle, a business-consulting tool that lays out the cycle of market impacts made by technological innovation. The Gartner Hype Cycle posits initial inflated expectations through growth, passing through the intermediate phase of disillusionment and ending up with enlightenment.

Here we will focus on the business application of this model. Let's look at each horizon, and see how the High End fits in.[1] Once we understand the dynamics, we will begin to see how to use today to create tomorrow. But first, what are these three horizons? What makes them tick? And does the High End have a chance in any of them?

Horizon One: Nurture and defend the current core business within the traditional category that the business has already defined. Horizon One identifies "value" to a large extent by means of traditional corporate functions which "investigate" the "future". One standard function found in company after company is traditional market research. The innovation in Horizon One is incremental, from one product generation to the next, for example, from one car model to its immediate follow up. Continuity might even be an advantage, considering the need to avoid shocking customers with disruptions. For the High End, Horizon One means more of the same, new line extensions, new products that don't shock, and just "fit in". Thus, the operative phrase for this Horizon One is "don't rock the boat – just go with the flow".

---

1   Source: Paul Gardien et al., *Breathing Life into Delicate Ideas*, (2006), Eindhoven.

Horizon Two: *Create new business opportunities outside the existing core but still within the potential portfolio of technology or marketing.* Horizon Two is the area where an automotive maker might release a dream car or a show concept car. Horizon Two requires a bit more imagination, projection into the future, 2–5 years out. In Horizon Two, a company such as Philips might cooperate with the likes of Alessi, Nike or Swarovski in order to successfully reach the market. Also it might merge applications from different market sectors, like TV and LED lighting, already existing in separate technology portfolios, into the new experiences. The operative phrase for the Horizon Two is "welcome the outside – and look at what could be."

Horizon Three: *Create viable options for future growth completely outside of the current business scope.* Here we voyage into unchartered territories. It takes more guts here. The High End business leader might identify highly disruptive opportunities for a remote future, say 10–20 years out. It is important to think future, think broadly, and without fetters. It is necessary to fund socio-cultural future studies and long-term scenario thinking, despite the overwhelming obsession by business with "today". Horizon Three appeals to aspiration. Horizon Three is typified by major exploration and research programs such as city.people.light or Nebula (introduced in Chapter 11). The operative phrase here is "Approach the future with discipline and optimism – it is where you are going to have to live some day. You ought to try to understand it and anticipate it today."

Making Innovation Happen: *Realpolitk* and Stories

Innovation in science and in the commercial world of the High End lives in the common space joining scientific discovery and works of art. The Three Horizons model proposed by McKinsey was not adapted to corporate design to freeze new thinking. On the contrary, it makes the fine art of long-term innovation digestible for a corporate CFO. The systematic approach gives a structure to long-term visionary work. Structure releases the tensions derived from the immediate constraints and concerns of short-term corporate financial performance. The end goal is a bountiful harvest of new ideas. The Three Horizons model treats long-term innovation as a vital investment, and not a cost to be cut at a moment's notice in times of crisis to shore up the corporate bottom line.

Although the Three Horizon Process has not been designed for the High End specifically, still the High End benefits from the discipline and planning that goes into the model. The High End often requires apparently irrational, creative innovation and design – often, although not always – and especially when we realize that the High End has to be more, better, different, new, value added, sustainable, and a host of other things valued by the consumer, now and in the future. This is where this model works at its best.

Horizon One Innovation: It's Pretty Simple. Read and Deploy

Horizon One deals with today and tomorrow, time scales that any corporate planner understands, and time frames that are sufficiently immediate to be put on the balance sheet. Horizon One is exemplified by TAG Heuer's incremental innovations (see Chapter 7).

Horizon Two Innovation: High End Opportunity in Simplicity

Horizon Two offers a wide and fresh vision of preferable futures ahead of us. To demonstrate, we visit a major Philips program – Next Simplicity.

After introducing its new brand promise *sense and simplicity*, Philips turned to design to explore tangible yet inspirational ways that could communicate the brand promise. The ongoing research program at Horizon Two level was conducted in annual "installments", sufficiently broad yet manageable. These installments explored different relevant themes for the Philips brand. Starting from healthcare, lighting and consumer lifestyle, Next Simplicity progressed into new territories like well-being and hospitality, tapping into the trends of major world lifestyle capitals – from Paris to London, from Sao Paulo to Hong Kong.

Philips publicized these new ideas with a road show, the Simplicity Event. From the previous chapters, you can see that inspiration of the Milan strategy. The Simplicity Event turns out to be the "Announce" phase of the Italian Milan strategy. Each general idea selected for the Simplicity Event was incorporated into a working digital system or artifact. Concrete tangibility did the trick. Seeing is believing. The tangibility proved to be a powerful convincer for the wider audiences, the press and trade specialists who visited the Simplicity Event. The reality of the systems and artifacts announced clearly that Philips was now able to anticipate a tomorrow, and bring to its corporate-produced High End solutions.

During the second year of the Simplicity Event what better "next" than to show the fruits of the labor, the "stuff" of the future. And so a collateral exhibition of actual products designed and marketed based on Next Simplicity concepts demonstrated beyond doubt that Horizon Two innovation by design actually works. Needless to say, most of these products will be aimed at High End markets.

How does Horizon Two work? The propositions do not exist yet, and they certainly are not simply incremental modifications to what is popular today. How did Philips do it?

Philips Design's approach to Next Simplicity comprises three major steps. Knowledge and business meld together in Horizon Two leading to a tangible product.

Step 1: general knowledge – what specific trends are occurring, and do these trends come furnished with "solutions" from which one can create a business? It is important to focus on the business opportunities through one's own corporate lens.

Step 2: envisioning "my" product – finding what the actual product should be, and just as important, what it shouldn't be. This prescription sounds as if it comes from "left field", but keep in mind we are looking at High End design of the future from the point of view of a company which designs for people, and for the pleasure people experience when they touch, see, hear, and use products.

Step 3: "birthing the product" – has the product been made to be simple? Does the product have an "iconic look and feel" that makes the customer enjoy interacting with it?

The Simplicity Event, the "Announce" phase of the Italian model of design-led success, has evolved into an annual forum through which the company can share with prospective consumers its vision for a preferable future. Simplicity Event produces its own inherent large-scale environmental design challenge every year. New ideas, new products, all focusing on the future and the High

End, must also capture the brand promise of "sense and simplicity" while being clearly innovative and additionally customizable to different regions.

Thousands of people have visited the Simplicity events – including media, design experts, customers, marketing gurus and industry thought leaders – and joined Philips in conversation. In addition to the managerial benefits, the Simplicity Events allow employees to connect to the principles of "sense and simplicity" regardless of their background or role. Especially in a time of downturn and crisis, employees now become evangelists, pushing simplicity agenda across the company – from packaging to purchasing – and to demand simplicity and people-centric thinking at all times.

Next Simplicity is not just a preview collection of the future products to be manufactured and sold. The concepts presented are a tangible, inspirational way of communicating the Philips brand promise of "sense and simplicity" for 3–5 years ahead, the specific period encompassed by Horizon Two. Ultimately, Next Simplicity events seem to have evolved into a multi-purpose, strategic tool, designed to be somewhat provocative, forcing the company and visitors to ask the urgent questions that relate to their future and the company's role in the future.

The lessons from Horizon Two apply to High End businesses in general, especially to those businesses which use technology as their competitive advantage. The lesson is about emerging opportunities when those who design the future must break out of the mold of corporate silos and responsibilities. When it comes to design and development, a formalized program such as Horizon Two design offers the opportunity to explore the company's innovative possibilities. The sheer realities of products featured in the Next Simplicity events break down the silos even more.

The "engine" of Horizon Two is High Design, which creates "new" High End offerings. High Design strives to find answers to the questions: *What will people care about in the coming years? What new business opportunities will develop? How should we organize ourselves to respond to these new opportunities?* The Simplicity Events, spurred on by Horizon Two thinking, ignite these debates on a periodic, formal basis. The outcome for a company like Philips is the unique profiling opportunity for the brand to position itself at the High End spectrum of the general debate about the future. The question then is: how do you go from tangible yet visionary concepts to real products performing in the market?

Horizon Two Innovation: Commodity to High End Living Colors

The High End is in the business of creating and selling products and services with top marginal gains. As a High End gold mine, Horizon Two innovation does not stop at ideas. Horizon Two triggers concrete product development. And, in turn, Horizon Two changes otherwise commoditized categories, evolving them into High End ones for specific offerings. This ability to create "High End stuff" is important in a world where commoditization is the inevitable direction for all offerings, simply because of the unchangeable nature of *homo economicus*.

It is not an easy task to innovate in such deeply commoditized category as interior lighting. It is even more difficult to generate stellar margins, especially at a time of crisis. Yet there are opportunities when personalization can be embedded into such an impersonal commodity as lighting. Such is the story that we recount next. The importance of the story for the High End is that High End can be rescued from commoditization by putting the "customer" in the middle of the product as an active participant.

Philips' LivingColors is an LED light source that shines colored light onto a wall or corner of a room. Offering up to 16 million color combinations, LivingColors is a direct and simple way for people to express themselves through personalization of their immediate surroundings, changing as often as they like. It is effectively a new type of proposition – a *luminaire* or the "box" around the light, and light source rolled into one – that has created its own market segment, atmosphere through light.

LivingColors was a direct result of High Design research started in 2003 by Philips to explore the concept of "atmosphere" in home interiors. LivingColors continued the effort to create better lighting atmosphere in luxury retail, an effort that by itself led to only modest acceptance, due to constraints and rigidities in the specific business and retail management models of the sector. Yet, not discouraged by that lukewarm performance and viewing it as just a necessary part of the "innovation design game", Philips Lighting moved to development based on the same vision. This time their efforts were rewarded, thanks to the determination of designers who stuck to their vision of how high-tech applications can improve people's quality of life.

It all started with understanding people's desires related to the type of environment that could be influenced by lighting. It became clear from interviews and from observation that atmosphere enhances a person's mood.

Many prospective customers said that they liked the idea of creating a light-driven atmosphere in personal spaces such as the home or place of work, but were unsure of how best to do this.

The real insight connects what High Tech can offer to what High End prospective customers just dream about. It became clear that the core idea was simple. The capsule phrase is "I like to change things around in my home interior to create the right atmosphere for my family, friends and me". The notion of altering one's direct environment to match feelings and create mood was very interesting, eyebrow raising, intriguing. But how?

The result of the effort is a distinctive LED-based light-source that meets the requirements of "personal sustainability", or best fit between artifacts and people. LivingColors incorporated the very latest LED technology that had not been applied to the consumer market before.

Bringing business-to-business industrial applications to consumers at a premium price might be seen as a classic innovation approach to the High End. By establishing a higher emotional and functional value than a plain commodity lamp, it is likely that customers will preserve their LivingColors longer, and replace them less frequently with other objects – in line with the directions for residual value and ambitions for eco-consumption:

> Fewer objects + more care = less waste: this way innovation meets sustainability, in an aesthetically and emotionally rewarding fashion.

Everything in the aesthetics of LivingColors speaks of design for the High End. From a product-design viewpoint, everything has been done to establish deep relationship between LivingColors and its user. The shape chosen, a graceful tapered stem, gives it the appeal of an exotic orchid. This organic feel is enhanced by the slightly egg-shaped glass in which it is contained. The design philosophy behind the look and feel of the LivingColors is captured by its remote control, which was called a triumph of straightforward and intuitive design. This is due to the large touch-sensitive color wheel that is the remote's focal point. Simply tapping a color on this circle causes the LivingColors to produce that color instantaneously.

The bottom line is that LivingColors is a product that achieved remarkable margins in the otherwise hyper-commoditized context of light bulbs and lighting for home. Even in a world of commoditization, there is room for a product to evolve into the High End when the right "personal" hook to the customer is found. One can reinvent a category, increase margins, and ensure some period of relative competitive "safety". LivingColors achieved what is perhaps *the* major ambition for any High End business leader: a signature and a clear identity in the market for the brand as a High End player. LivingColors reinvented the way customers experience their homes. Priced at premium yet still accessible levels, LivingColors continues to deliver very high margins.

Horizon Three Innovation: The Alchemy of Tomorrow

After discovering actionable innovation of the first two horizons, in this section we focus on High Design applications jumping to a more distant future. Experiments in Horizon Three are truly long-term, mission-critical investments, and not a waste of budget. Philips Design calls these experiments Probes, to give them the gravitas they deserve.

An ongoing revolution will be necessary for those brands and managers who aspire to achieve and maintain the status of High End players. At the same time, revolution or change is unstable, impermanent, and discomforting. Corporations thrive on the mundane, the ordinary, the predicted. Recognizing this dilemma is the first step to figuring out how to make an ongoing revolution palatable to corporate management. This is what Philips Design Probes are all about. The Probes program is the formalized "place" where strategic designers and multidisciplinary teams think "completely out of the box". Probes generate new insights and visions to achieve paradigm-breaking innovation, and attempt to offer radically new portfolio opportunities. An example of the Probe process is the path from Nebula to Ambient Experience hospitals (Chapter 11), which demonstrates how the investment in Design Research pays off, in the relatively short time – just half a decade or so. And to what extent it does indeed!

The future for innovation is not in the "near tomorrow" of Horizon One, but rather the "far tomorrow" of Horizon Three. How can a company prepare for that far tomorrow?

For the management of some High End companies, Horizon Three might seem irrelevant: one would be better off not to be a shareholder of such companies. For others who want to capitalize on trends, technology and customer desires, Horizon Three is very important. "Foresight by design" within Probes is a systematic view on possible longer-term futures, about

15 years ahead, elaborated from a synthesis of social trends. Here foresight starts by observing today's developments in politics, economics, environment, technology and culture. This bed of information is sifted to identify systemic shifts, which might affect the nature of our way of life. Such knowledge allows creation of new IP (intellectual property) and new physical prototypes. Knowing what a consumer just might want in 15 years allows the business to begin gearing up, or at least thinking about it. The ever-increasing competitive world of the High End, mixed together in a witches' brew with commodization and value reduction, should make the corporate mind at least aware, and more focused. It often does. Let's see concrete examples of how Probes actually made the future happen in a process that leads from visionary investment to business application in a short time.

Award Winning Probe Programs: High End Potential

The Philips Design Probes, appropriately titled SKIN, explores how electronics can be integrated within textile and fabrics, embedded in highly fashionable fabrics, and in turn becoming part of the final designs. Named the "best of the best" design concept of 2007 by the Red Dot Design Award, the notion behind SKIN was acknowledged as important by the always critical design community. In keeping with the High Design approach to promote High End thinking for business in the Italian model, SKIN brought Philips Design an opportunity to exhibit in the prestigious Axis Gallery of Tokyo – the trendsetting design "temple" of Asia Pacific. This is a territory bordering the Cultural Marketing techniques of the likes of Prada and her sophisticated collaborations with OMA AMO, or Harley Davidson's museum shows.

In 2007, another Probe concept was selected by MoMA of New York offering visibility for Philips Design in what is universally considered the most relevant design museum in the world.

In at least one case a very good payout emerged, which promises to be even greater. The Probe program New Nomads, dealing with wearable electronics was originally conceived as a pure "Horizon Three Probe" experiment, to be performed in splendid isolation. Its combined outcome became the main trigger and the concrete asset giving birth to a specific industrial collaboration between Philips and Nike (Chapter 7) making it from designer's dreams to business case of profitable success in a mere half decade or so.

Such gratifications are not just sheer luck: they are the destination of a very long corporate journey. Through the three horizons of innovation model, the senior management reviewed and approved each revolutionary concept to be launched within the program of Philips Design investments.

What about the application to the High End? Limited Editions of High Tech-enriched lifestyle objects are one of the possibilities. Although not being the immediate purpose of Probes, which are the visions of the future, this strategy does, in fact, generate the High End product, and can be construed as a positive outcome.

True High End is not just about marketing and branding. The High End can be about a company's fundamental strategy to improve the quality of life, the experience that people go through as they live from one day to the next. "Blue-sky" innovation programs are key to the longer-term High End. As for companies, they will definitely benefit by exploring the future trends ("foresight by design").

As a side-benefit, Horizon Three produces profitable "deliverables" for the company that can see them. The deliverables are appealing opportunities for design and thought leadership in the media and in the cultural institutions, the juice of PR and the seeds of new innovations. Such leadership is vital for those High End brands that aim to increase their perceived status as innovators and masters of what we might define as the "cultural marketing game".

Harvesting Low Hanging Fruits from Blue-Sky Probes: Levi's ICD+ Limited Edition

Digital technologies have dramatically changed the way we live our lives. In less than a generation, we have almost forgotten what it was like to have to look for a phone booth, or to listen to music only at home or in a concert hall. Technological steps towards total mobility and connectivity gave us great deal of comfort. Yet the original question about the future of the digital technologies remains an utterly contemporary. Here is another opportunity to bring in the High End by applying high-tech to people's desires, aspirations and emotions. Horizon Three offers the opportunity of more immediate business spin offs, or "low hanging fruits".

In the late 1990s and into the early 2000s, Philips Design developed working prototypes of Personal Area Network to transport data, power and control signals within the user's personal space. The efforts, begun as Horizon Three efforts in the McKinsey system, produced immediate High End opportunities and deliverables. The group developed design concepts for embedding connectivity, communication, entertainment and geographical localization into clothing. Some of these "far-out" concepts included a Music T-Shirt, featuring in-ear speakers and solar cells to provide energy, and a ski-jacket with integrated entertainment and communication, also allowing for navigation and emergency rescue, through GPS localization of the user. For the road warrior or just the average buyer of High End clothing, there was a solar-energy recharge jacket, including tools for creative playing and communication, such as a camera, a display, and of course a microphone.

Just a decade ago, the idea of embedding technology into clothing was a mere vision. Everybody knew that making this vision a reality meant not only proposing a new life style but also a business revolution – one in which the electronics industry had to be able to think about emotions, and incorporate these emotions into product design in terms of human wants, rather than needs. To facilitate human-focused solutions, the technology industry had to learn how to deal with the emotional business of fashion. Nothing could be more distant from the world of "white aprons in labs" of last century's high-tech science and its corporate labs.

As technology companies go "soft", that bastion of the High End, the fashion industry, has been progressively addressing the issue of functionality in clothing. The work-product includes new types of textiles and styles, which make ease of use and comfort a top priority. Think about the industrial partnership between Philips and Nike.

With this digression into fashion in mind, let's visit the future today, where High End meets High Tech. In the world of High End fashion, the exploding sector of cool jeans is dominated by lifestyle leaders like 7 for All Mankind, Citizens of Humanity, Joe's, A Bathing Ape and Diesel. Consumers happily pay hundreds of dollars for denims sold just a decade ago for under $80. In this $15B+ industry, it is not by chance that the original jeans maker Levi's called one of their premium priced denims *Engineered Jeans*, trying to regain the market share in the lucrative upscale territory.

One of the first pioneering encounters between fashion and technology, the collaboration between Philips and Levi's, created the world's first wearable electronics fashion line, ICD+. The first *i*-wear consumer product was brought to the market in a very limited edition of one thousand pieces, manually assembled in the Philips UK Research labs, with the price of 1,000 euros, befitting a High Tech, High End product. ICD+ was selectively distributed in Levi's flagships, and widely communicated to the press in order to create media exposure by means of both traditional PR and grassroots buzz.

Although some might see ICD+ as principally a PR investment rather than a real High Tech, High End product, the important outcome of this product was confirmation that demand for such a type of product existed among consumers, and that it could make a difference to the Levi's brand. Levi's continued moving in this direction, following the High End path, instead of moving upscale to luxury. RedWire DLX Jeans co-developed with Apple and, released in 2006, were positioned as iPod-compatible or iPod-ready. The jeans featured a side pocket embellished with conspicuous white control pad that proclaimed the hidden premium item, while containing additional functional conveniences such as pausing, skipping tracks, and raising or lowering the volume on your iPod.

ICD+ signals to us how the world is moving towards total convergence, and how new technologies are progressively erasing the borders between industries, areas of expertise, and the values upon which the brand stands. For the High End, we see how new premium value can be created by High Technology coupled with High Design as its connection to people's future dreams and aspirations. We also see an additional opportunity. The High End, porous as it is, continues to absorb from the world around it, adding value, and evolving to where it can still command a premium. The ICD+ fits this pattern perfectly.

Our story has a very simple lesson for the High End. Disruptive technologies, such as wearable electronics, satisfy not only the primary functional needs but also the more abstract, intangible and perhaps not yet expressed emotional desires. ICD+ was one of the first experiments to respond to such dynamics by actually creating digital fashion. Most of all, ICD+ introduced perhaps the first highly disruptive, paradigm-breaking "intelligent fiber" technology directly to prospective customers in selected retails. A proofpoint of the high value of innovation programs in the Horizon Three level.

Designers in Tomorrow's High End

THE QUICK AND EASY ANSWER

You might have noticed how deeply the role of High Design goes, well beyond the notion of "design" during the styling years of the industrial age. The question then arises: What will happen to design and designers in the High End of tomorrow? A hard question to answer … or is it? Let's look at the role of design and designers, given all that we have said about the nature of the High End, that reaching for "more", for "better", for "style".

The nature of the profession places design leaders squarely in the middle of many crossroads. Designers live in the worlds of aesthetics and philosophy, of the spiritual pursuit of beauty and the material dimensions of resources, of ancient archetypes and the digital age. Designers are exposed to culture and consumers, to economics and marketing. Designers must respond with ideas, creations, and foresights about what should come next. And of course designers have to feed themselves and their families, as well as keep a reasonable roof over their heads.

So with all this, again what will happen to design and to designers? Designers will be "keepers of the flame" for the vision and soul of High End brands. Even today, we see designers turning into storytellers, who combine art with the tale that the High End needs. The designer might well be the rock star of tomorrow's High End.

THE BUSINESS ANSWER

Where should design be housed? We see the rush to outsource, as one company after another sheds its expenses. Everything is outsourced – why not design as well? If you can outsource innovation, or buy innovation from others, then why not just buy design as well?

What a politically sensitive and emotionally charged question! We believe that outsourcing design development works on certain projects works only for a limited time. Only internal designers really understand the brand roots, cultural habitat and character nuances of the brand. It takes years to learn and express them. Outsourcing design does not help to grow a brand's design personality. Rather, design has to be retained within the company, to give the company a continuing true sense of the product or service. "Being premium requires being authentic as one key factor of a brand's credibility", stresses Karl Schlicht, VP Lexus Europe. Lexus' Chief Designer Wahei Hirai brought the turnaround in design, and did so not from scratch, but rather because he knew the inner values of Lexus better than anybody else did. Only true evangelists can spread the gospel successfully.

AND SO THE ROLE OF THE DESIGNER IN THE HIGH END IS ...

The designer is a social antenna, capturing the essence of the times, and then recasting that essence into practical, profit-making applications that speak to people's senses and minds. But designers are more. Designers are the "raconteurs" of the stories and ideas behind the brands they shape. Designers are business people, artists, alchemists – most of all, they are the "shamans" of people-centered consumption, capable to channel "what people will want" into contemporary business processes.

Designers are social creatures as well, working in the studio of the master, albeit the business rather than the noble or church patron. We see that social structure more clearly in High Design, which finds its intellectual origins in the undisciplined yet productive heritage of the Italian district-driven approach to design innovation. In return, the Italian way to design finds in High Design a corporate process, an organizing principle and philosophical vision that can move the specialness of small family companies and networks to flourish in Fortune 500 corporations. The bottom line: a continuing stream of High End creations, responding to the times, conjured idea by designers, offered by companies, consumed by customers.

Summing Up

High End enterprises will have to stretch their innovation portfolios to stay ahead of competition by adopting the latest high-tech applications by anticipating people's dreams and desires. One winning strategy uses the practice of High Design in order to organize a winning innovation portfolio, ranging from blue-sky concepts to actual next generations of products that go to market.

In line with earlier business management theory, there are three distinct levels of innovation for the designer, all of which apply to the High End.

HORIZON ONE

This Horizon of incremental innovation pertains to the next generations of products, and their innovation roadmaps. This is not a "dull" domain; it is actually a very important investment area for the High End. Horizon One is where partnerships unlock the best opportunities for High End business leaders.

HORIZON TWO

Innovation design stretches the boundaries of the company within the range of ongoing program. An example here is Philips' annual "Next Simplicity" program. Horizon Two invokes for an intermediate level of innovation design. Here emerge the opportunities to spin off new products. The products respond to people's dreams and aspirations. In the short term, these products break the ground and achieve outstanding market performance in margins. The opportunity for the High End business leader in Horizon Two is to gain media exposure by means of brilliant concepts and ideas, and translate these into the next generation of innovations.

HORIZON THREE

Here we find Blue-sky explorations, such as city.people.light 2007. The vision is to "guess" more than to understand how the world might develop in the next two decades or so. These guesses inform the High End, at least in general, and allow for the creative development of ideas of what "might be". Yet Horizon Three produces practical, money-making outcomes for the High End, such as the Levi's ICD+ exclusive limited edition wearable electronics. The opportunity for the High End business leader in Horizon Three is to envision the long term future, and then possibly harvest with exclusive editions.

At the end of the day, design rises to become a systematic process through which to identify and manage future opportunities across different horizons. We have concentrated on High Design as a viable, battle-tested business process of how to do design. High Design structures the way one thinks, prepares one for new insights, and guides the way the designer should interact and work with the High End business. And so, a new tool and a new promise emerges for the High End business, a tool which teaches and truly improves the players as they struggle in the hypercompetitive game.

PART 4

Business Tools That Jump-Start Your High End

Plain premium products have the plus of "added value". ... Often these products offer an extra plus in their positioning by capitalizing on "experience". Here extra value is constantly created by product and technological innovation. Next to the standard product, you will find some extra tailored options or a variety of choices. Then, there is the High End. Quality, whose benefits are the same as the plain premium product. However, an extra plus is given by positioning that is emotional and storytelling. It is feelings here. Additionally, cool design is more and more seen as a decisive extra ... It's all is based upon that little special thing that the consumer allows her/himself to indulge in once in a while. One can't afford it everyday, but once in a while one indulges oneself.

Steven van den Kruit, Creative Director,
Firmenich Perfumery Division, Geneva

An old Indian joke asks the question: How do you kill a blue elephant? The answer is quite simple: shoot it with a blue elephant gun. Aside from politically incorrect and morally repugnant idea of senselessly harming animals, the moral of the story is quite simple: for any task, there should be a right tool.

This brings us to the topic of this chapter – tools that business can use to create, measure, and then profit from the High End. Throughout the book we have mentioned that systematics, RDE, disciplined approaches can become a "secret weapon", or better the "secret sauce" to help create. When RDE mixes with creatives, when the science mixes with the art, we move forward.

Now we move forward, more deeply into the consumer mind. We use the combined power of all our quali-quantitative research findings to generate an ad hoc "High End Toolbox". Here, the intuition of 75 thought-leaders and business experts meets the rigor of experimentation-based consumer research to enable you to create the premium proposition and then communicate it in the best way possible. In these applications, we move from stories to tools and from tool to action. And in doing so we mix creativity, science, art, and business into a user-friendly combination, one that nonetheless will translate into repeatable business success with premium margins.

Introducing the High End Toolbox

The High End Toolbox enables you and just about anyone else to assess where you stand, generate new strategies and create concept ideas for new products. The Tool Box uses our five dimensions of the High End. But it moves beyond stories, and beyond data that we collected, into action. By following what we have done, and then applying it to your opportunity, you "measure" and decode the mind of your prospective customer in a rather pleasant, constructive, and insightful way When you know your customer's mind, you can reach out with what the customer wants. And, when you add your own creativity, you can end up by creating a tomorrow for yourself and your business.

So, without more ado, let's jump into this knowledge-based process. The Toolbox comprises:

- Strategy/Knowledge – The High End Charter, either to assess your current offering and/or to structure your new High End vision.

- Machinery – Rule Developing Experimentation (RDE) – to create the new High End offering in concrete terms.

- Measuring – The High End Typing Tool (HETT) – to identify the nature of the customer mindset, and then customize your communication.

- Although we developed the Toolbox with a systematic process in mind, do not feel constrained by the process. On the other hand, it does not hurt to have some structure as well.

The Strategy/Knowledge Tool: The High End Charter

This tool captures the five pillars, or dimensions, of High End. Think of these five dimensions as organizing principles for your knowledge about the High End. You might want to just guess, but why not use the knowledge as the basic skeleton on which you will create your offering? These are your parameters, to help you understand and develop. They were distilled from our research and described in five universal rules, or DNA, of the High End (Part 2). We summarize them again in Figure Part 4.1. Selected top experts who validated the Charter confirmed that it is exhaustive when it comes to future High End directions. Best of all, you're not likely to go wrong by following the Charter. Think of it as your map, your GPS, to the new world.

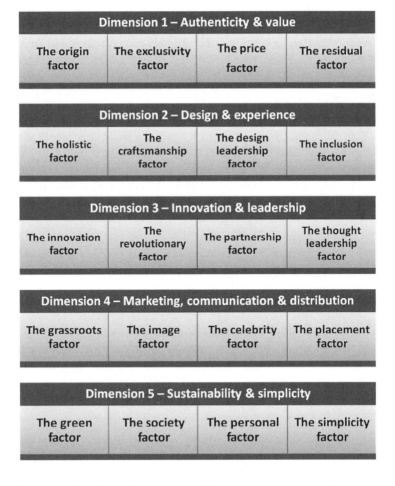

Dimension 1 – Authenticity & value			
The origin factor	The exclusivity factor	The price factor	The residual factor

Dimension 2 – Design & experience			
The holistic factor	The craftsmanship factor	The design leadership factor	The inclusion factor

Dimension 3 – Innovation & leadership			
The innovation factor	The revolutionary factor	The partnership factor	The thought leadership factor

Dimension 4 – Marketing, communication & distribution			
The grassroots factor	The image factor	The celebrity factor	The placement factor

Dimension 5 – Sustainability & simplicity			
The green factor	The society factor	The personal factor	The simplicity factor

Figure Part 4.1 The five dimensions with four factors in each

You can apply the High End Charter to your business in two ways, depending on where you stand at the moment of its adoption. If your management responsibilities are related to an existing offering such as a brand or product already in the market, you will leverage the High End Charter to perform an "Analysis Review". If you work with a whole new proposition such as a start-up brand or a "never-seen-before" product, you will benefit from its adoption as "Vision Generation".

ANALYSIS REVIEW

You already have a product or a brand or a proposition on the market. Your concern is how to decompress its margins by pricing it at a more premium level (re-positioning). In more generic terms, your ambition is to raise its profile and prestige. The most efficient option is to relaunch it with some degree of upgrade, at a higher point of perception in its market. By adopting the High End Charter at the level of strategic review, you can match your proposition or brand or product "as existing" against the state-of-the-art of those trends that "make" the premium as such. This way you can identify the specific performance of your current portfolio with respect to each High End Dimension (that is, Design and Experience). Even better, you then have the possibility to dig deeper into the granularity of Factors (that is, Holistic, Craftsmanship, Leadership, Inclusion). This systematic "gap analysis" through the lens of the High End Charter is "the" step that will enable you to identify areas of weakness in your current offering and –most of all- those "opportunity gaps" where you want to take action, in order to pursue your re-positioning towards the High End.

VISION GENERATION

You are in the process of starting your business from scratch; you might be either an entrepreneur who is starting up your new venture or a corporate manager in charge of a whole new portfolio, perhaps even one to be invented. In that case, you will adopt the High End Charter as the "cartography tool" that guides you through strategic synthesis. Simply put, if you generate your own business pillars for each Dimension (Authenticity and Value, Design and Experience, Innovation and Leadership, Marketing Communication and Distribution, Sustainability and Simplicity), you will have a proposition, based on the trends, that will "make" it belong to the High End. This way, the alchemy of your vision will be based on future-proof directions, with the automatic opportunity to perform in your markets with higher margins and prestige. This is where you definitely want to be these days.

Of course, these two steps can also be performed in a sequence: first analysis of a current offering, then vision generation of a new (re-positioned) proposition. The High End Charter captures the power of trends and offers its actionable synthesis as a coin with these two sides. Because we regard both constant analysis and a powerful vision as crucial to perform in the High End, we strongly believe that this tool should be deployed on regular basis, that is in annual reviews, to keep track of how the proposition or brand or products perform in maintaining their alignment to your High End strategy.

As the value of use of the High End Charter became clear by now, we then need to ask ourselves: how will the knowledge-based strategic insights of the High End Charter connect to the more operational and practical level of our business? This is where the same approach as the quali-quantitative mix of the five "Rules of the High End" (Part 2) comes in handy. There, the qualitative insights of the thought leaders and experts were the basis for RDE segmentation exercises performed with 1,800 qualified respondents in the USA, UK, China and Italy.

Make and Measures: Two Numerical Tools – RDE and HETT

Numbers can frighten people. But if you just stop for a second, relax, take a few deep breaths, and read on, you're going to discover that numbers will be your best friend. Here are four simple steps. Follow them, and you'll know your customers, customize and create for them, and best of all, find customers where you don't expect them. Bottom line – here are four steps. Take each one slowly.

> *Step 1: KNOW: Customize, customize, customize – what you say IS your world*. When you customize, follow the structure that we laid out – five dimensions with four factors each. They should stay the same. The specifics, the individual elements, will change to fit your specific interest – industry type and regional relevance. High End rules and tools are universal; however, they do always require regional focus and cultural adaptation to really work – as all rules and tools do.

Step 2: MAKE: Create the stimuli – what you say IS what you learn. The RDE tools work on ideas. These ideas are simple, concise statements that describe the features, the perceptions, and so forth. They are the key highlights of the proposition from cultural research, from idea generation. But to be usable, you have to put these ideas into simple, easy-to-understand statements, that is, paint clear word pictures. Follow this advice, and your will have the indispensable bridge which crosses the gap between opinions (for example, the stories and snapshots in the book) and statistics (for example, Types of Customers and RDE tools).

Step 3: TEST and MEASURE: Try it, you'll like it – what you test IS what you learn. We encourage you to try the RDE tools. RDE will help you design the High End offering, to determine what it should feature, and reveal mindset segments to help you sharpen the offering.

Step 4: UNCOVER and DISCOVER: Find your prospects everywhere, through knowledge of how the customer mind "works". The High End Typing Tool (HETT), built on the foundation of RDE, enables you to talk to your customer appropriately about your proposition, because you will learn what is important to tell your customer, and what you should avoid.

Discipline Works

Tools are not a magic. *On the other hand* … tools make you do things in the right way. Follow the disciplined approach, and it is likely you will be successful, even in times of economic downturn. Do the right things the right way, use knowledge in place of guesswork, science in place of what seems best for the moment, and you will find something interesting. To a great degree you will succeed. The world is more or less rational. Just deploy your knowledge from the High End Charter alone (which will/ought to be valid for about three to five more years). It's quite likely that this knowledge alone will keep you ahead of your competition. And the discipline from RDE should turn that knowledge into your High End offerings, and move your way up the ladder. It helps to "know" instead of "guess".

13

Creating New High End Propositions

The High End space [in China] is the business class between economy and first. Pricing, exclusivity and style are all part of this … The evolution of a new group of wealthy middle class has created a strong audience for High End brands. This group is keen to show off their achievements in the lifestyle they lead. The High End market is, however, a no man's land waiting to be grabbed … Pricing is important to create the perception of being High End but it is not everything … Brands must educate consumers on what is High End and why …

Bessie Lee, CEO, GroupM China, Shanghai

Perception is everything, at least for luxury and the High End. From the perspective of technology and value, iPhone is certainly not the best product on the market. Ask anyone, especially an iPhone aficionado, about the "Antennagate" situation and you will hear something to that effect. Yet, despite that, Apple has managed to create a perception of a premium product. An excellent design is not enough to achieve that. iPhone was not the first and arguably not the best phone of this type on the market, yet people still lined up overnight to buy it – antenna or not, rubber case or "naked design". *That's High End success.*

In most cases, the mysterious domains of haute designers, ad executives and extremely highly compensated marketing gurus are off limits to the "mortals" such as the majority of business people. Even when not pushed away, we usually and instinctively shy away from them. But why? Especially if that's where tomorrow's profits are going to be. We may be intimidated, but we don't have to be dumb.

We know there is something special about the High End products, about those who know them and create them, and so we are in awe. Yet, it does not have to be exclusive and complicated. Yet we are not talking about a computer replacing a talent. No algorithm can replace a genius who has "right" feelings, vision and experience. But even these geniuses make mistakes and sometimes very expensive ones. For them, the public is frequently quite forgiving. We usually remember the successes but not the failures.

Assaulting the Fortress

So what can be done to help marketers and designers to be correct more frequently and fail less? Could we offer a path for smaller companies in building successful High End experiences, even when they cannot or will not afford a bloated budget? How do we open a window to consumers' minds, particularly related to perceptions of High End Experiences?

All too often people do not know (or cannot articulate) what they want but they are very good in choosing between several options. It is always easy to choose, to critique, far easier than to create. The practical lesson – when testing a sufficient number of wide ranging ideas, there is a good chance we will discover just what the consumers like. This underlying foundation of Rule Developing Experimentation (RDE) guides us, becomes our light of knowledge. Even better, RDE directs us as to *what* to create. Here are three worked examples. They are just that, examples. You can do the same quickly, with the same, and even more precision. You'll have to think a bit, of course; brainpower is necessary. But then it can be your game.

Green Tourism in Denmark

In the nineteenth and early twentieth centuries, healthy food was not always tasty (if ever). People cognizant of their health (although a negligibly minor proportion of the population) forced themselves and their children to consume this "healthy" food almost like a medicine. Nowadays, healthy food is quite tasty. Health-conscious people in the majority do not even crave fat-rich dishes. And certainly people don't crave cholesterol, although they might like meat. Consumers accustomed to skimmed milk no longer appreciate the taste of whole milk; it is just too rich.

The same change is happening in the public's gradual adjustment to the new world realities related to ecology. Sustainability and environmental responsibilities are no longer annoying, *must dos*, but rather crucial items on the plates of the future High End consumers. And wonder of wonders, today *green* has become an ultimate cool idea. It's again sustainability chic.

Environmental sustainability has gone mainstream. People feel that they must go beyond the pleasures of pure consumption to give back, to nourish the environment, to help their fellow people, and honor the non-material part of themselves. High End is not conspicuous consumption, but *the right* consumption. What makes it right? There must a fit between the values in culture and the business proposition. This right consumption goes well beyond the "stuff" of the world into leisure time and recreation. It is all about experiences. The High End experiences will have to be eco-compatible and sustainability driven.

Let's see how the advanced northern Europeans tried to get it right with environmental sustainability. The project we present was funded by the Danish government to promote green/ecological tourism in Denmark. The specific task was direct; uncover the mindsets of the German tourists. German tourists, you see, comprise a significant proportion of ecology-conscious travelers to Denmark. Germany is next door, and why not capitalize on this soul-enhancing opportunity? The Danish government wanted to create a High End experience for the prospective German tourist, focusing on Denmark as an eco-sensitive country – a fantastic High End branding opportunity.

The question is no longer what is eco-tourism, but rather the very practical business problem of *how best to promote it?* What exactly should the Danish government stress in its advertising? What are the hot buttons of the consumer mind and how are they detected?

The project shows how to understand the consumer and how to build the High End proposition using this understanding and the customer's aspirations.

No business will commission knowledge-development and research just to spend money answering one question. With this wonderful opportunity, the Danish Government wanted it all. The questions that this RDE project was expected to answer ranged from identifying target groups/segments for green/ecological tourism in Denmark, to the most attractive green concept elements, to the proclivity of the tourists to pay more for green activities, transport and accommodation: quite a range of information with which to develop a High End proposition!

What happened at the end of the day? Denmark used the RDE exercise to construct "optimal" concepts. These concepts began with advertising to attract German "green tourists". But it wasn't only advertising. The RDE data specified the nature of the appropriate High End experiences. Denmark selected Germany as its main target because Germany had/has lots of people, the notion of "green" is well established, and Germany has advanced national green regulations.

We leave out the details of the project. The interesting part of the project was the insightful results and the way the Danish tourism board built engaging premium offerings.

Three mindset segments emerged from the Danish RDE exercise. These segments were: "The outdoor active" (29 percent), "The green idealists" (38 percent) and "The nature freaks" (33 percent). You get a sense of these German segments by looking at Figure 13.1. *It is quite possible that tourists might not even realize that there are these types of segments, unless the fact is pointed out to them.* Yet it's here, in knowing the tourist mind, knowing the experience to create, that the High End comes alive. The disciplined RDE exercise breathes life into the data.

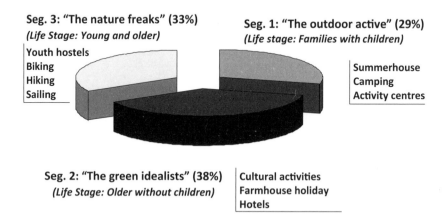

Figure 13.1   German mindset segments for Danish "Eco-tourism", what the advertising should stress, and what Denmark should offer

Segment 1 ("The Outdoor Active") sees nature as a platform for small field trips to beaches, parks, forests and the countryside. This segment of German tourists responds to ecologically healthy food, clean beaches, and so on. The keywords for Denmark to use that will trigger Segment 1 are play, entertainment, coziness and ecology. Segment 1 tourists will pay extra for eco-clean food but not necessarily for the green accommodation and entertainment, although it is not clear how much more.

Segment 2 ("The Green Idealists") stick to green principles on ordinary days and on holidays. They are interested in nature and environmental legislation, food control, free access to nature, alternative energy sources, engaging local population and local businesses and green accommodation. Key words for them are "Green soul"/green attitude to life, ethics and morality. However, the Danish Government quickly discovered that the Green Idealists are not willing to pay extra for most green products and services. To them, "green" should be universal and all-encompassing; there is just no need (in their mind at least!) to pay extra for it as for an exclusive proposition. This could be compared to a hypothetical restaurant's menu with options for "food" and "fresh food". The food has to be fresh. Always. Period. There should not be an alternative to fresh food. Green Idealists think that ecology is a "given", will not make compromises, will not consider alternatives, and just will not pay for the "green" that they so earnestly desire. It is better to know who won't pay more for the High End but want it, than to assume that all customers who want the High End will pull out their wallets to pay extra.

Segment 3 ("The Nature Freaks") see their whole life as a part of nature. They are interested in the North Sea, caves and cliffs, the moors, the woods, lakes, rivers, streams, and so on. This segment is deeply involved in all kind of outdoor activities such as walking and hiking, cycling tours, kayaking/ canoeing, jogging, and so on. They respond very intensely to pictures that create a feeling of being alone with nature, the premises of nature, which are authentic and spontaneous and not hurried. "Nature Freaks" will not even consider non-green products and services, just like the "Green Idealists". And, just like the "Green Idealists", these majority of "Nature Freaks" will not pay the extra money for them.

So now, what is to be done? There is a world out there. The question is – how to tap into it, and make money. The Danish government wanted to understand the economics of green, eco-tourism. Who in Germany *is* willing to pay extra for green products and experiences? We did not see these paying customers in the mindset segmentation, but we knew they were there. Slicing the data a little differently showed a group of 5 million German customers who would pay extra. The group was ready to pay the extra fees, indeed a lot extra, for products and experiences that are labeled green, and positioned as ecologically friendly. We called them "Golden Greens" (Figure 13.2). And cross the "Golden Greens" with the three mindset segments, and you have those who will pay more ... and what you should say to each group.

To sum up, this RDE development exercise shows that prospective tourists from Germany want to see Denmark more and more as a nature destination rather than just a historical or cultural hub. They are quite attuned to eco issues. There is a great potential to build High End experiences in tourism, not only in the Danish countryside and Scandinavia, but all over the world. The opportunity ranges from Japan where the love for nature is a key cultural feature of the society, to the BRIC countries, where urban stress will soon translate in a flourishing middle class demanding opportunities to reconnect to a simpler life, closer to nature.

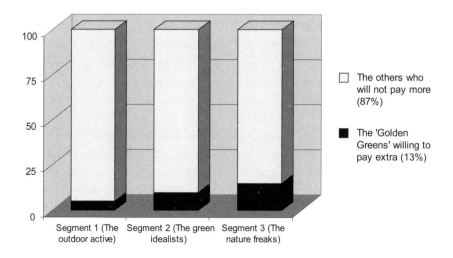

Figure 13.2   Segments willing/not willing to pay extra for green products

From Selling Jewelry to Selling a Banking Experience

Tomorrow's High End is all about emotions and experiences. Although it seems that the banking experience is cut and dried, devoid of emotion, the following case history from a major European bank was inspired by an RDE project related to … a Mother's Day Jewelry mailing campaign. This improbable association will make more sense when you read the following stories.

If it were true that we always think about our parents, then Mother's Day would not be so adored by retailers. Once a year, millions of Americans and people all over the world rush to flower shops, department stores or online sellers to give their mothers something special for that day. Some believe the more "guilty" we feel about neglecting our parents for the rest of the year, the more likely we are to buy something expensive. Hence, a great opportunity for the retailers.

Although celebrated on different days in different countries, the idea is universal. We all want to remember our mothers and try to make, at least for this day, somewhat special for them. When in 1914 Anna Jarvis finally managed to make Mother's Day a national Holiday for the Americans, there was no sense of the immense commercialization it would spawn. But the realities of a society based on consumption could not be ignored. For retailers, Mother's Day was yet another gift, an opportunity to sell their products and services. The uniting theme behind the day is creating special experiences for mother – to compensate for the lack of time spent with her and to make us feel better by doing something good for Mom. This might result is a simple bouquet of flowers, or some bric-a-brac to make Mom smile. Frequently, it is a special event that people plan – a dinner, a theater performance, an outdoor picnic together with grandchildren, or it might be a piece of jewelry that Mom always wanted (or at least, we thought she did) …

Sterling Jewelry wanted to create a mailing piece before Mother's Day in order to trigger emotions and encourage customers to buy from their stores or catalogs. With more than 1,100 mall-centered stores nationwide, Sterling Jewelers is a premier player in the field. In addition to marketing superior quality products, Sterling strives to create a pleasant buying experience for its customers. The company realized that the buying decision process starts long before a customer steps into the store, orders through a catalog or online. Thus was born the notion of identifying the mindset of the jewelry shopper, embedding that mindset in a targeted mailing piece, and then making Mother's Day shopping pleasing and memorable for the customer, and hopefully more profitable for the store.

It should be no surprise that mindset segmentation proved to be a much more efficient approach to marketing than just targeting an average person. The challenge was to use data mining to "score" the customers in a database in terms of the specific mindset segment to which each customer belongs. The rest is easy – once a customer is typed (the mindset type is found), the company sends that customer a targeted, relevant mailing which appeals to the heart of that person, or realistically, which appeals to the heart of that mindset segment.

To make the story short, the results of this controlled experiment dramatically validated the RDE as a platform to optimize market messaging for a High End purchase. Historically, the typical Sterling mailing generated about a 1 percent response rate with an average purchase of $1,339. Sending the right brochure (the right creative) to the right segment dramatically increased the number of people buying (42 percent improvement for the segment called "Optimists" and 27 percent improvement for the segment called "Pessimists"). Just as important, the actual size of purchases increased, measured in dollars, over 30 percent.

That is jewelry – clearly a High End purchase. But what about personal banking, and the High End bank experience?

And now, for the rest of the story. There is hardly any other industry, at the moment of writing this book, so unpopular as banking. The 2008–2009 events in the financial world left an undeniable sense of stigma on financial alchemists and economic gurus. We do not deny this plain evidence. Nevertheless, we want to look at the economic tumble as the opportunity to bring a higher quality of life into the picture – in a true High End way. After all, banks desperately need to re-establish an effective dialog with their own customer base. Even more so for High End banking staff due to the naturally personal relationships there.

Remember that the High End is not about cosmetics or marketing "bling bling". It is all about substance – the real "beef". We do not have the solutions to macro-economic problems affecting global capitalism. Thanks to RDE, we do, however, have an honest proposal to improve the lines of dialog between High End bank staff and their selected, high net-worth customers.

Our previous story about enabling a High End shopping experience for jewelry fascinated some visionary executives in a major European Bank. They faced a similar task in the bank's high-net-worth division. High- net-worth customers have quite specific needs and expectations from a bank. One can easily envision a High End shopping experience for jewelry. How one can build a High End banking experience for these special customers? The *"how"* is important – we are talking about customers with a variety of needs, different mindsets, who value experience perhaps even more than specific bank offers.

The vision for enabling a High End experience was simple. The "mind picture" was a high-net-worth customer coming in the door, being greeted by a bank representative, going through a short "typing exercise", and then identified as belonging to specific mind-segment, all to be accomplished within a few minutes. At the end of the exercise, the bank representative was to "know" the mindset segments to which the high-net-worth customer belongs, along with a recommendation of the type of "language", the words, the tonality, to which this particular customer might respond. The ultimate goal – the customer should come away from the experience sayings "this bank really knows *me*".

Correctly "typing" bank customers was crucial. If RDE could type a customer on arrival at the bank, then the bank could create the best experience for the particular customer, or prospect. Such individualized banking experiences confer a strategic advantage. And why not? Salespeople with years of experience do this … after talking for a few moments with the prospective customer. Why not use RDE to transform everyone in the local bank branch into a far more savvy sales person to generate a High End experience?

Identifying mindset-segments and creating targeted, optimized messages for them is increasingly easy these days. How to match a person to a segment and how to find the "type" of a person (hence the word "typing") are more difficult questions, but very rewarding, especially when the customer is a high-net-worth client. RDE revealed four distinct mindset-segments in this case. Each segment reacted differently to messages about banking experiences. The differences meant an opportunity to improve a customer's experience by understanding a customer's mind.

We will look into the details of this approach in the next chapter. For now, let's imagine a customer or prospective customer, entering a suburban branch of the bank (possibly by an appointment). Our customer is greeted by an adviser who invites him (or, of course, her) to answer a few non-threatening, non-personal questions (also known as RDE "typing"). When RDE correctly "types" a bank customer as a member of one of the four segments, the bank now will make this person much happier. RDE provides the customer representative with a database of features for the experience that have reduced chance to irritate any customer but attract a few strongly. Now the bank is in even better shape because it can use the RDE framework to select these better experience features. In RDE, data and the typing provide the bank with a competitive advantage – better customer experience through knowledge.

Figure 13.3 shows the rules for such interaction giving the adviser a guidebook of communication with a prospective customer (see also Appendix, Table A8).

When our prospective customer "types out" as Segment 1, then the customer representative adviser should talk about how easy and simple it is to access his assistance, stressing that the bank is equally good for personal needs and for business operations. At the same time, the representative should not push the ideas of making the decisions for the customer ("We select the appropriate investment … "). Obviously, this segment prefers to have more control of investments, rather than less control. Knowing what not to say is as important as knowing what to say.

For Segment 2, the positive messages should include one stop for the wealth-management needs, easy accessibility, and so on, and avoid concentrating on fee structure as much as possible.

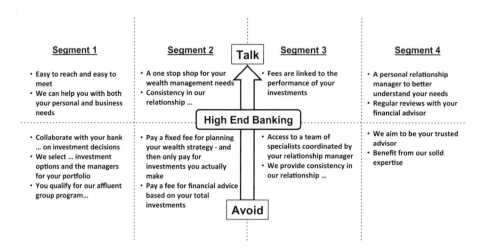

Figure 13.3   RDE-generated "experience" rules for what to talk about and what to avoid when talking to a high-net-worth customer. Typing the customer tells the representative "what to say", and how to engineer the experience

For Segment 3, the messages should be "pay for performance". For this group, the important thing for the customer representative to stress is accountability.

For Segment 4, the messages should be about personalization. Segment 4 want to feel that they are special as individuals, that the bank is doing specific things for *them* as people.

The only "tough" job is, of course, to type each new person who walks into the bank and identifies himself as a high-net-worth individual. Indeed, in this case, RDE was able to correctly type consumers to corresponding segments with probability of more than 55 percent on average. This 55 percent is more than double the odds by randomly guessing chances (given the case of four segments). This 100 percent-plus improvement is not something that any businessman, in any sector, would ignore. This was a major milestone for the industry.

So what actually happened here? RDE enabled the bank to understand the soft aspect of customer needs. In turn, the customer representative made a better, or perhaps a more educated guess, about the customer, creating a more personalized High End experience. The result – better person-to-person experiences leading to more sales. Just as important, the bank employees are happier because they have a tool to create a happy, satisfied customer. This virtuous circle creates an improved customer experiences with potentially even more sales.

So let's contrast the jewelry and bank case histories. In the case of Sterling Jewelers, the better experience came in the form of mass communication, but created a more resonant message. The success came from merging the efficiencies of mass mailing with the knowledge of how to make a more targeted selling message through RDE segmentation.

In the case of the bank the better experience came in the form of in-the-bank interaction between the customer and the bank rep. The approach used RDE to do a short "scratch test" of a high-net-worth customer immediately identified the segment to which the customer belonged, and created a High End experience then and there, through knowledge of what appeals to the particular customer, based upon knowing the segment to which the customer belonged.

In the near future, we see a merge of these two approaches, as companies, banks, and public institutions of all kinds create personalized High End experiences for their clientele. We see a possible future here – "rule books" or guides for creating High End experiences. The next step is to elevate the mass mailing to yet another High End experience, by personalizing the specific offering to the proclivity of the segment to which the prospective customer belongs. In this way, mass customization of communications and experiences will achieve some of the characteristics of today's luxury and High End. The "magic sauce" – knowledge of the customer – identifies the ingredients for the person's own High End.

Beyond the Pocket to the Soul: Promoting Passion for the Arts

The previous examples focused on the commercial side of the business of making money. In our earlier chapters, we saw the crucial relevance of cultural marketing, supporting the fine arts in luxury, and their applications to the High End. Cultural marketing is rapidly evolving into a large world of opportunities for High End business leaders willing to make a difference for their brands. Hence, we conclude our RDE explorations exactly from where we started – the aspiration of High End, namely luxury, this time with a focus on luxury marketing through cultural marketing. Let's see RDE in action in a non-for-profit field, where people are expected to give rather than get.

Today's luxury and High End circles are "gaga" about anything that is fine arts and culture-related. Charity, art and performances are aspirational, traditionally associated with the middle and upper strata of societies. Engaging wider masses in appreciating and supporting art through volunteering, donations and patronizing is important for society. This engagement with a nobler cause is a crucial dimension for contemporary luxury and for tomorrow's High End: one of the authors (MB), in research collaboration with AG, addressed more trends in this domain in his book "*The Golden Crossroads*". The question we addressed here is very pragmatic: How does RDE find right wording, encouraging people to be involved even more deeply?

Recently, two authors (HM, AG) were involved in a massive project to map consumer minds on different topics dealing with sustainability and the world of not-for-profits (Give It!). One of the studies in the project dealt with promoting passion for arts. The Give It! data were intended as guidelines for museums, charities and various foundations to help with support, promotion and fund raising.

In Figure 13.4 we see the RDE-derived rules (see also Appendix, Table A9), showing how the High End promotes the Arts. It's important to realize that there are two segments, and even more important to know what to say to each. The segmentation shows "what is"; the words show what to say. The bottom line is that by knowing the mindset of the prospective donor, one can increase the amount to be donated simply by saying the right thing, or, just as important, not saying the wrong thing.

RDE uncovers two clearly different mindset segments, to be approached with different messaging. These segments are "Personal Improvement" (Segment 1) and "Art for Everybody" (Segment 2).

Segment 1 ("Personal Improvement", 66 percent of the sample) is the bigger segment. We found these people more attuned to "giving" as it related to art, because they show a high additive constant: 42 versus 29 for Segment 2. Recall that the constant tells us the predisposition of a person to do the specific task. Here that predisposition is to donate to the arts.

Segment 1 is primarily concerned with personal sustainability and well-being – specifically improvement for themselves and their families ("Art enhances our children and gives them the ability to become what is inside them" (+9)). They like to be associated with a good cause and feel appreciated for that association ("Be associated with an organization you believe in" (+8)).

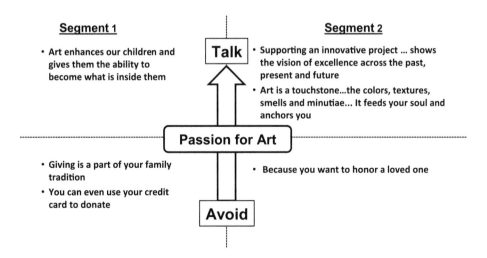

Figure 13.4   "Rules" for talking to potential donors about supporting the arts

At the same time, this personal improvement segment does not want to be "bugged" with financial issues related to donations, tax-deductibility, and so on. The only positive donation-related idea is about having a gift donation matched by the employer. A reference to religion makes them wince ("Fulfilling a religious obligation to help others" (–17)). The bottom line is that it's "about ME and mine".

Segment 2 ("Art for Everybody", 34 percent) is about a stronger orientation towards societal sustainability – specifically doing something for a good cause and involving others ("Encouraging yourself and others to participate in a worthwhile project" (+16)). Working for charities, donating for the causes, involving others is in their souls. It is less about them and more about the cause. This second segment gives because of the cause, not only because it makes them feel good.

So now what are the arts to do? Or specifically, how can the experience of support for the arts be elevated to a more enjoyable, High End, and, of course, more productive experience?

When RDE identifies a person as belonging to Segment 1 (personal sustainability), the organization should engage this prospect by messages about how the children will benefit. Don't talk about the "mechanics" of donation process (for example, credit cards, and so on.), and certainly don't bring in religion.

When RDE identifies a person as belonging to Segment 2 (societal sustainability) expect the person to be more receptive. Talk about innovation, enhancement for the children, participating in a worthwhile project. Do not, however, talk about the memorials for a loved one, or something "corny".

Summing up

When we began this book, we wanted to survey the world of "what is" in order to understand "what will be". We selected the qualitative research interviewees because each of them was involved in the "world that could and would be". But we also wanted to move on from talking to science and from science to "engineering" consumer perceptions.

In this chapter, we demonstrated the concrete possibilities of RDE to unlock the power of High End markets by segmenting their customer base. We used the High End Toolbox for these efforts. With the Toolbox, comprising a powerful combination of qualitative and quantitative insights, you and other readers, business professionals as well as dedicated amateurs, can move from knowledge to creation, from creation to convincing, and from convincing to sustaining.

14

Know Thy Customer: Sequencing the Genome of the High End Mind

The High End is real, and it is where a lot of money can be made. So why present a chapter on "knowing thy customer?" Don't we all know the customer? When customers seek out High End propositions, isn't the best response just a simple matter of sitting and listening, like any good salesperson, and then adjusting the offer to the customer?

The answer to this question is *no*. Resoundingly *No*. Customers for the High End, just as any other customers, whether luxury or bargain basement, do not walk around with their minds imprinted on their foreheads. Unless the customer is clear about what he wants, or unless you have known the customer for a long time, or you're a very savvy sales person, it's likely that you won't hear that with the so-called "third ear".

We are talking here about using the RDE tool. RDE helped us to understand the mind of the High End customer, and how customers differ from each other. We also used RDE to help us to create High End propositions. Now we are going to finish up by making RDE help us selling our High End propositions.

Selling High End Today

It is impossible to escape the blizzard of sales materials that inundate us day after day. The catalogs for products sprout everywhere, with daily mail, devoid now of personal letters, instead bringing us one catalog after another, our name printed on the cover, or better still "resident at". A year's worth of catalogs can become a deadly weapon if they fall on you; the mass and the weight, of course. And the offerings are so varied. In the same day we might receive a sprightly decorated catalog from one of the world's top clothiers, offering us exquisite-looking but really in the end affordable, stylish clothing for business or leisure, for the male, the female, and for the children. Right below, the next catalog would present exotic food such as aged steaks or macadamia nuts. And finally, not to forget culture, we might have yet a third catalog, tempting the wanderer in us with invitations to travel in style to new destinations fully accompanied by an renowned onboard lecturer from Harvard or from the Metropolitan Museum of Art. The bottom line is that stuff that we would buy gets buried. A lot of irrelevant offerings, unless of course we're junk hounds, or rich as J.P. Morgan on a "buying" spree to somewhere.

For most of us, what we get in the mail is just plain irrelevant. When possible, we quickly toss it into the recycled bin, or for some of the more obsessive, we first rip off the mailing label, and then toss. We are still getting these catalogs, of course. More of them are "on target", and most of them are not of sufficient weight to be injurious when thrown across the room.

What is happening here, and why is this relevant to the High End? What can we do better in terms of sales? How can the catalog mailer know the customer's mind better, to send targeted, relevant offers? If we can get to know the mind of the customer, then it is likely we can find what tickles the fancy of the customer. Then it is a matter of offering the High End in the language appropriate for our customer.

A Bit of History: Enter the World of Number-Crunchers in Marketing

One of today's most popular methods, called *datamining*, refers to a statistical approach, the specifics of which are not necessary here. However, the bottom line is that if a company knows that you buy High End products, and it knows something about you – something that can be legally bought from data warehouses (for example, age, gender, residence, income, transaction history with stores and with credit-card companies), then data miners in the company try their hardest to discover patterns. Just think of the jewelry example in the previous chapter. How can the company mail to the "right customer"? Of course, the company can mail to everyone, but that costs money. There must be a pattern that one can discover, so that people who buy High End jewelry can be discovered.

The problem is that these patterns, when they actually exist, are very hard to find. And just because the company finds a pattern for jewelry doesn't mean that the next company, trying to sell High End tours for example, will have the same kind of luck.

So, the question is: "Now that you have the High End product, how are you going to find the customer, to *sell* to your customer, and how will you talk to the customer?" People are different; one size does not fit all, and our work on mindsets suggests different "hot buttons" for segments. Get the hot buttons right, and you may have a sale. Get the hot buttons wrong, and you irritate your prospect. Use irrelevant messages and you may have to rescue your mailing from the garbage can.

Typing the Customer Mind

Our foundational study on the High End revealed that people do not look at the High End in a single way. The High End Charter comprises five dimensions with two uncovered mindset segments in each dimension. There are probably more than two segments, but two segments are easy to work with. What one segment finds to be the High End, the other may or may not. It is not that these segments in any one dimension are polar opposites as much as they differ by what's important to them.

Going one step further, how then do we discover the segments in the customer population? We know that people do not walk around with the segments printed on their foreheads. And to make things even harder, there may be little or no correlation between a person's segment membership and age, income, gender, country of origin, and so on. Those latter factoids about a person can be purchased readily from companies that specialize in "profiling people", but the reality is that these factoids probably have little to do with a person's mind. We would be pretty hard-pressed to predict the segment membership from knowing the purchasable information about a customer. We might know the price range of items purchased if we were we to know income, but we would not know what types of items the person preferred.

Fortunately, in recent years other methods have emerged to understand the customer mind. One method is the approach used by Amazon.com, which looks at the patterns of what a person buys, or the Amazon pages a person views, and then searches for other individuals who exhibited the same behavior.

Although Amazon does not really "know" the algebra of the customer's mind, it guesses that the people who look at the same Amazon pages will be similar to each other. And thus, it recommends by saying "Other people who looked at this page also looked at …".

Going Beyond "Lookalikes" to the "Scratch Test"

What if we could encounter a prospective customer, ask him or her a few questions for about a minute, and from then on know the mind-segment(s) to which the customer belongs? Sounds like science fiction? Not really. Just think about what happens in your doctor's office. Today's primary care physician (called PCP) begins the relation with a patient (for example, you) by taking a blood sample, sending the sample to a testing laboratory, and getting back an automatic report on your blood from the perspective of standardized tests. It is at that point that the doctor better understands you, the patient. Certainly you may fill out a medical history which is dutifully entered into your medical records, but somehow there's a feeling that the real medicine starts with the *blood test*. That is modern medicine.

Let's move this metaphor to our High End customer. We know that the customers differ from each. We have just seen two parallel segments emerge in each of five basic dimensions (See Figure 14.1).

Now that we discovered these segments, we know what to say to each segment. The real question is "who is this particular customer in front of us?" What is the pattern of this person's mind? Into which segment does this person fall, on each of the five dimensions? That information tells us the type of message to give to this prospective customer. That is, knowing the customer's mind tells us what to say and how to say it.

Mind-Typing

The notion of "typing" people is not new. Bankers use typing every day, as do sales people. The real skill is what to ask and how to analyze the typing question. Fortunately, we do not have to invent anything here. Statisticians dealing with the very practical problems of assigning people to "risk pools" (for example, mortgage, insurance) have developed powerful methods that take responses to a few questions, and in turn assign a person to a specific group. Our efforts

Dimension 1 – Authenticity & value	
Status seekers	*Investor / connoisseur*
(it's about me)	*(it's about product/service)*

Dimension 2 – Design & experience	
Focus on the product	**Focus on people**

Dimension 3 – Innovation & leadership	
Disruptive, focus on the leader	**Functional innovation**

Dimension 4 – Marketing, communication & distribution	
Form own opinions	**Swayed by others & authorities**

Dimension 5 – Sustainability & simplicity	
Personal & simple	**Sensitive segment.**

Figure 14.1   The five dimensions and the two mindset segments for each
dimension

here, to uncover the mind of the High End customer, is simpler in some ways than what happens when the insurance company assigns a person to a high or low risk for driver insurance, the bank for a mortgage, or the doctor for medical risks.

Now that we have a basic structure to our prospective customers, how can we use the methods of today's medicine to help us offer these customers High End propositions, and communicate the true value of the proposition? We do not mean anything nefarious at all, in the spirit of Vance Packard's "Hidden Persuaders', the 1950s book that exposed some of the practices of advertising. Not at all. We mean simply "in the spirit of different mind segments, how then do we present our messages in a way that appeals to the particular mind type to which the customer belong".

The obvious answer is to *learn* about the prospective customer. We do not mean learning all about income, credit scores, and the like. Nor do we mean learning about the customer's likes and dislikes by analyzing the trail of web searches, in order to create a composite picture of what interests the customer. Those might have privacy issues. Rather, we propose a different, simpler, more direct approach based on science. Let's engage our prospective customer in a dialog. We may invite the customer to complete a short set of five forms, each having four simple questions. From that exercise, we should be able to type our prospective customer rather quickly, and then present our propositions in a language that is appropriate, that's absolutely "spot on".

There are similarities between the problem that lawyers face when they type the jury and what marketers face when they want to define the nature of a High End proposition. The lawyer may have the rock-solid facts in the case, but in order to win the case, it is critical for the lawyer to convince the jurors. And the jurors have their own mindsets, so the lawyers should be prepared to deal with them. It behooves the well-prepared lawyer to use the proper phrases, language, and tone to address the jurors in the way they will most likely respond to. Fail to understand the individual differences among the jurors and what that means in arguing one's case, and you have the recipe for disaster in court. Marketers have the same problem – talk the right talk to the customer, or perhaps the advertising and sales efforts may be for naught.

Adroit marketers can spot an opportunity in the market, either by looking at trends or by commissioning primary research from experts. Yet, time after time, the marketer makes mistakes. The mistakes are subtle, but rarely made out of poor judgment. Rather, the marketer works in a world where the average does not represent anyone. There may be segments in the population with diametrically opposing tastes and sensitivities to messaging. Marketers who are not prepared to work with these different groups, and instead market to the global opportunity, may find themselves with an insipid offering, or just as bad, an insipid message.

People feel differently about the same ideas: what may be High End to one mindset does not seem so to another. Sometimes, the differences in the perceptions are directly opposite. For many marketers these differences, this person-to-person variability is frustrating, difficult to deal with. But, if truth be known, the variability drives scientists crazy as well. Segmentation helps a little by putting a bit of structure into the mix. Structure informs strategy, and certainly helps tactics.

Armed with the knowledge that there exist different mindsets in the population, and given a way to find which mindset a person belongs for each dimension, we now create a system to help the developer, the designer, the marketer, and ultimately the High End business to achieve success. That is, we use our RDE knowledge to "type" a prospect, so we can design a proposition and/or a message for the particular prospect. We want to remove the worry that we are driving design/development efforts to a bland, artless, rather irrelevant average that pleases no one.

When we "type" a customer to discover which mindset fits this person, we both tailor the message, but being even more bold, tailor that actual offering for the individual. "Typing" actually reveals what particular aspects of the High End offering appeal to this particular individual.

Let's take a look at the dimensions of High End with identified mindset segments (Figure 14.1). We set up the five dimensions to be statistically independent of each other. That means that if a person belongs, say, to Segment 1 for dimension 1 (status seeker for the dimension of Authenticity and Value), the person might just easily be in either Segment 1 for Dimension 2 (Focus on the product, for the dimension of Design and Experience) or Segment 2 for the same dimension (Focus on the person).

In fact, there are 32 unique combinations of the segments, given that there are five dimensions and two segments for each dimension. Any customer should thus match to one of the 32 different profiles, based upon the pattern of mindsets.

Now let's think about using the typing tool. The simplest case is sales. If a person wants to buy a High End product, how do you know what to say to the customer, what to emphasize, what phrases will resonate (and of course be true as well)? A good sales person can probably ferret out that information. *However, just how many good salesmen or saleswomen are there? And are those salespeople "scalable" … can you make more of them, or do you have to rely on previous experience so you then must bid up the price of each proven salesperson?* Furthermore, what do you do with each new customer? For example, suppose you have a new salesperson and a new customer. When the customer walks in, what should any salesperson be ready to discuss and show? And, how do you get salespeople up to speed?

It is important to keep in mind that the participant in our RDE projects was *never* asked about the segment to which he or she belongs, just as in genetic testing no one asks the participant to describe his own DNA. More than likely a person probably never even thought about segmentation, much less thought about the segment to which he belongs. Yet we can discover the person's type from the pattern of responses.

Let's construct a vignette which occurs thousands or even tens of thousands times each day around the world. When the salesperson interacts with a prospective customer, it is important to identify the mindset profile of this person in order to offer the appropriate High End product or service. When the salesperson succeeds, then the customer may well go away happy with a purchase, having enjoyed the pleasant experience that met or exceeded expectations. However, to achieve that success, the salesperson needs to know what to say to this particular customer. How can this particular customer be profiled with respect to the High End so that the salesperson can be prepared to produce a High End experience?

As we saw in the real life High End banking case history, one strategy does this typing with a prospect using a fast (60-second or so) "scratch test". The customer has to rate a set of statements, that is all. Fast typing is practical, feasible and ultimately simple. Once the customer assigns his ratings, the information goes to a computer, which calculates the segment to which the person belongs, along with a recommended script for people in that segment. This procedure is also called "scoring" the prospect, and should come as no surprise for anyone who ever applied for a mortgage.

Armed with this understanding of typing, let's now look at the five dimensions. Our goal is to type or score a prospect. That is, we want to discover to which segment a prospect belongs, for each of the five dimensions. That knowledge will help us, or really the salesperson, craft the right experience for the prospective customer.

HETT for Dimension 1 (Authenticity and Value)

Our statistical analysis showed four key differentiating phrases for this dimension (Figure 14.2). These four phrases most strongly differentiate the two segments that emerged for Authenticity and Value (status seekers versus investor/connoisseur). Essentially, these four elements spread the segments apart. If one segment scores an element high, then the other segment would score the same element low. This means that status seekers (Segment 1) perceive each of the four ideas very differently from the way investors/connoisseurs

(Segment 2) do, thus helping us to type the person as belonging to one of the segments. It does not do any good in a typing exercise to pick elements which perform similarly for both segments. That would be like cutting with a blunt knife, which probably would never cut at all.

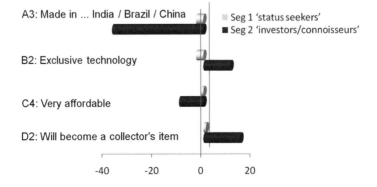

Figure 14.2   **The four differentiating phrases from Dimension 1 (Authenticity and Value) and how the two segments react to these four elements (from the US portion of the 4-country database). These are the four elements that most strongly separate the two segments**

Now we apply this piece of learning to a practical situation. Imagine a prospective customer sitting in front of you. To which segment does this person belong – status seeker or investor/connoisseur? If you guess correctly, then you can adjust the way you describe the piece of furniture you are about to see the person. That is, more simply, you can say the right things, and sell your item!! As you can see from Figure 14.3, it is quite an easy process. The order of the same four elements is changed for each new customer.

The pattern of the ratings on the 9-point scale matches one of the two segments more closely than it matches the other. Depending on the match, we define the prospect in front of us as belonging to Segment 1 (Group A, the Status Seeker) or to Segment 2 (Group B, the Investor/Connoisseur) respectively.

Figure 14.3   **Example of the HETT screen that the customer sees in the typing exercise. The customer simply fills in the four randomized questions, rating a specific proposition in terms of how well does each phrase fit what interests YOU**

Since we know how strongly the customer's rating matches each pattern, the HETT determines whether the customer match to the segment is weak (no stars), modest (1–2 stars) or strong (3–4 stars). Figure 14.3 shows a screen-capture of HETT with the four elements, the ratings assigned by the customer, and the typing result at the lower-left side. In this case, the type of the person closely resembled the profile of Segment 1, the Status Seeker (Group A). The resemblance to a died-in-the-wool Status Seeker was strong (three stars), but not overwhelming (four stars).

Figure 14.4 shows the screens for the rest of the dimensions.

What Do You Say to the Customer?

Now that we know how to type a customer, what should we say? One simple strategy looks at what elements do well for each segment versus which do poorly. We know that from the RDE study. So, in that spirit, let's look at the salesperson's "cheat sheet" in Figures 4.5–4.9. These figures show what elements do well, and what elements do poorly, for each segment in each dimension.

Figure 14.4   Examples of screens of the HETT for Dimensions 2, 3, 4 and 5

All the salesperson need know about the customer is the segment to which the customer belongs, for each of the five dimensions of the High End. That knowledge coupled with the rules in Figure 14.5 should help the salesperson immensely.

We begin with Dimension 1, Authenticity and Value. If HETT identifies a prospect as belonging to Segment 1, then emphasize exclusive and premium pricing to reinforce perception of the High End. Building on top of that, this person most likely would react positively to products produced in the traditional countries of premium goods like Italy, France, and so on. It would not do any good if you talk to this person about resale values and calling this purchase an investment – it will drive his perception down.

On the other hand, if a prospect belongs to Segment 2, then change the pitch to exclusive technology, exclusive mix of design and functional features, suggesting that this item might become a collector's item. Do not try to convert the prospect by nattering on about affordability or offering products from India, Brazil, China or even Japan. That message will simple reduce any possibility of perceive the offering as High End.

In medicine today is common to "sequence the genes" on a chromosome. That is what we are about to do with the High End "genome". At least metaphorically. Let's look at the typing test as a variant of sequencing. There are five dimensions of the High End, which can even assume two (or more) alternatives. So our "chromosome" of the High End mind has its five genes (our dimensions), each of which can take on one of two alternatives. In order to sequence an individual's High End mind, we simply have the individual do five typing exercises, one after another. Each typing exercise determines whether our person is in Segment 1 for that specific dimension, or in Segment 2. Look now at Figures 14.6–14.9 for what to say versus what to avoid, for the remaining dimensions and their segments.

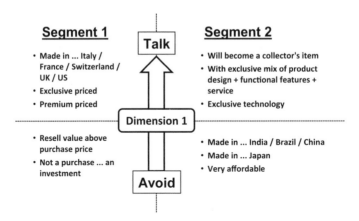

Figure 14.5   **Rules emerging from the HETT's "scratch test" for Dimension 1 (Authenticity and Value). Segment 1 = status seeker; Segment 2 = investor/connoisseur**

Dimension 3 is especially curious. For the people belonging to Segment 1 (disruptive, focus on the leader) in this dimension, there is nothing that dramatically increases perception of High End but there is a lot that drives it down (such as product defined as totally revolutionary or provocative). Segment 2 for Dimension 3 (functional innovation) is quite opposite – nothing drives down substantially the perception of High End whereas many ideas could increase the perception dramatically (for example, intuitive, multifunctional, provocative, and so on.)

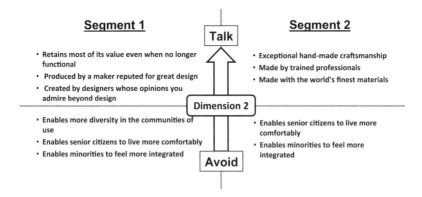

Figure 14.6   Rules emerging from the HETT's "scratch test" for Dimension 2 (Design and Experience). Segment 1 = focus on the product, Segment 2 = focus on the people

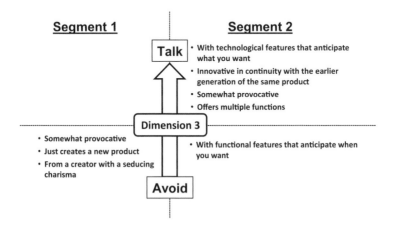

Figure 14.7   Rules emerging from the HETT's "scratch test" for Dimension 3 (Innovation and Leadership). Segment 1 = disruptive, focus on the leader; Segment 2 = functional innovation

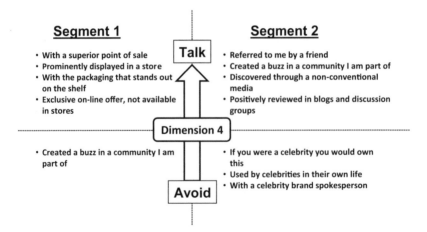

Segment 1   **Segment 2**

Figure 14.8   Rules emerging from the HETT's "scratch test" for Dimension 4 (Marketing, Communication and Distribution). Segment 1 = forms own opinion; Segment 2 = swayed by others and by authority

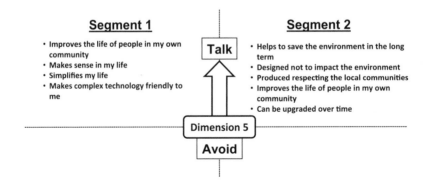

Figure 14.9   Rules emerging from the HETT's "scratch test" for Dimension 5 (Sustainability and Simplicity). Segment 1 = personal and simple; Segment 2 = sensitive

This five-dimension scratch test produces a rich set of rules. Indeed, it is more like a guidebook of communications to this person, a window to his mind. At the end of the profiling, HETT generates a report showing the signature of the profiled prospect customer which graphically could be depicted as on Figure 14.10. Just by answering a few questions a prospect customer gives us an ability to understand in depth her mind and preferences. Now we know how to talk to this person, what would increase her perception of High End and what would drive it down and thus should be avoided.

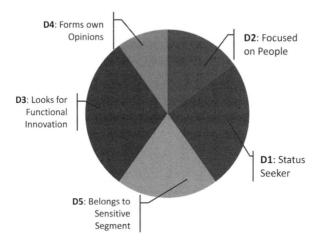

Figure 4.10   **Example "signature" for a particular person at the end of the typing exercise. HETT identifies which segment pattern best fits the profile of ratings by this person for each of the dimensions (D1–D5)**

Summing Up

Simply sequencing the "genome" of the High End mind is an interesting exercise by itself. It tells us the nature of people. Do we discover recurring patterns? Are some segments always correlated with each other (for example, the Segment 1 status occurring unduly often with Segment 1 on innovation (focus on the leader))? That is an empirical question, one good for science.

But what about using these data? We might imagine a scenario where stores type their customers in a short exercise. A customer could be asked at the start of the relation with the store to type himself, in order for the store to provide a customized, more pleasing, more appropriate service. The more the store "knows" about an individual's preferences, the more likely the store can craft this customized experience. And what better way than having the person "mind-type" himself?

But let's go a bit further. The High End is about customization in many ways. What about customizing the communication with the customer, say by mail, and offering the customer private sales "events" tailored to his individual tastes? Individuals who segment on sustainability as "personal and simple" could be invited to special events customized with content that focuses on "the individual". Their opposite number, those High End customers who segment as "sensitive" would be invited to more social-responsibility events, where the focus and content is on the High End shopping, with charitable donations being made on behalf of shoppers who buy at certain levels.

Finally, we might envision a time where the typing or sequencing of the High End mind could be embedded in an RFID tag, for example on a loyalty card. As the shopper moves through the store, the RFID tag interacts with digital signs. The information on the signs changes to appeal to the shopper's mindset segment. *That is, the digital signage would then be programmed to present messaging appropriate for the mindset segment to which the shopper belongs, such information being fed to the sign by the shopper's RFID tag embedded in a loyalty card.* What a wonderful way to personalize the shopping experience, not by greeting the shopper by a countless greeters, hello dear so-and-so, but rather by providing messaging appealing to the mindset of this individual person

The idea here is that it is this level of personalization, not based on previous behavior, but rather on deep interests, which can become a hallmark of the new High End. High End companies could use the technology to leapfrog luxury, to provide new experiences that cater to the individual's soul – a hallmark of High End thinking.

Conclusions

As always, it is necessary to win over not just the minds, but above all, the hearts of one's audience. The successful products will be those which represent a particular mindset, a moral value. I am speaking here of the connection between the world of the products and the people. This animistic bond is invaluable. As mentioned previously, holistic intelligence will most definitely grow in importance. Products that enhance quality of life will presumably always number among the successful – whether in the form of an environmentally friendly automobile or a wellness-focused product that promotes human vitality.

Markus Langes Swarovski, Member of the Board, Swarovski

We began to research and write this book at a time of relative optimism, and we conclude it during the somewhat grayish, darkening days of the 2009 financial crisis and global recession. For the first time since 1987, or even since 1929, the ghosts of a depression appear everywhere in the media, with the global public opinion rapidly shifting from hope to fear, sometimes to panic. We are not economists, nor do not offer any solutions for global economic problems. However, crisis or not, we believe that creating genuine value will always be rewarded. There will be re-alignments of categories and brands, of wealth and welfare. These dramatic circumstances will sharpen the public opinion's appraisal of products, services and brands.

This book does not support the promiscuity of conspicuous consumption and the vanities of marketing "bling bling". On the contrary, we wanted to write about the different ways that scientific research and strategic design increase the quality of life, both materially and emotionally. In both the hard times of an economic downturn and in the possible recovery to follow, this book shows how to spot higher margin opportunities, with actionable tools and a clear vision of how to do well by doing good.

The High End *is* this Promised Land, that golden world of higher margins and greater business opportunities. It works by reaching people and inspiring them to dream first and then enjoy a higher quality of life, at a price within reach. You can apply High End thinking to almost any product or category, from toothpaste to urban planning. In a perfect world, there is an almost "animistic" bond between people and their objects. This bond is neither fetish nor idolatry. It represents instead an excellent description of an optimal future, less driven by technology push but rather increasingly defined by the pull of people's dreams and desires. The High End lives in this bond; business can profit from knowledge of how the bond works.

In order to achieve this superior quality of life, High End brands and business leaders will have to *understand* people, and *anticipate* their dreams and needs for tomorrow and beyond. Such understanding will not come about through bland, 20,000-foot, business-speak, generic global formulas. The bond requires the local wisdom, the *genius loci,* and the regional touch of optimization. It will be that regionalization and customization which makes High End propositions truly unique to customers.

At the moment of closing this book, a worldwide recession reminds us about the times when people spend for something they only absolutely need. Actually, this is *the* reason *why* premium value creation is more crucial than ever before. As Luca De Meo, former CEO, Alfa Romeo and former CMO of FIAT Group Automobiles, pointed out in a recent interview, in Greek the word *crisis* means *divide. Crisis produces the responsibility to make choices.* The choices for entrepreneurs are to downsize and manage by cost cutting, or to liberate the creativity and the leadership of one's company, to survive by generating true High End value. Which path is better? We believe liberation, of course, else we would not write this book. It's something to ponder: merely survive by slowly eroding yourself to death or win and grow by truly embracing the future.

Craving for the best, consumers will still search actively for the quality they learned to appreciate in the last decade, despite economic reversals. It is embedded in the human DNA. Consumers will live in a world where real value will win more and more. It will be a global economy of regional choices, where our roots, the solidity of where we come from, will increasingly make the difference. This is why *understanding* people is ever more crucial. It is the research challenge to combine vision with efficiency in a world where sociology meets the Internet. It will be a new game of innovation, a next wave of solutions, applications and systems that will address the new needs for well-being and peace of mind for of all of us. The next level of High End, and the next wave of business opportunities, might well start from the challenges of wider sustainability, from societies to the planet. These are the opportunities to restructure, revamp, and revitalize consumption, through new values. *Green* is already the new black; sustainability will trigger a new thrust to re-engineer the High End beyond what we know it today, and provide promising opportunities. From here, sky is the limit.

Innovation and sustainability will intertwine in new concepts and ideas. The five High End *must have*s we explored will become the core of a potential renaissance, not only of the world of High End but of our economies in general. It will be in the world of High End where authentic luxury and premium value meet and delight tomorrow's dreams and desires. If this is the ambition, the next question then is: how to get there?

- • We offer pragmatic tools, from the High End Toolbox to High Design in its general principles, from the Innovation Model originally devised by McKinsey to Rule Developing Experimentation. These tools should jump-start and steadily grow your next High End business. The tools and processes create an intellectual infrastructure to effectively and profitably run your next High End projects. Be it a major corporate re-launch program or a new venture, start-up enterprise, you are now fully empowered and ready to set for next challenges, and success. We see three different domains across industries and categories, where High End principles and processes will make a difference:

  - commodities
  - lifestyle-driven brands
  - new territories beyond traditional "old luxury".

These domains are expanding rapidly. Firstly, you desperately need to escape the *commodity* trap. Whether in the automotive industry or with mundane and highly commoditized products such as a light bulb, the direct and immediate application of the High End approaches could salvage business, stretch margins, and re-launch brands. Applying creativity to commodities will help you to redefine the rules of the game in entire categories, and will translate into the new best practices of design and marketing of the next decade.

From fashion to watches, the last decade witnessed many industries giving birth to *lifestyle-driven icons* which populate the world of glamour. Because these are the brands most vulnerable to crisis, there is a push for a reform.

That reform may be soul-searching or re-invention of the business model. Mexx, the European brand of Liz Claiborne, recently announced massive changes in order to return to the original vision, where everything should be XX. According to industry experts, this process actually liberates energy and enthusiasm, indeed far more than expected or even hoped. As more and more brands realize their need to re-invent themselves, our framework for the High End offers a powerful platform for renewal to these very successful but rather fragile mid-size brands. The High End will help them weather the storm and come out with renewed vigor.

As today's luxury is tomorrow's High End, it is wise to monitor what is going on a notch above High End. In the next few years, real *luxury* might even enjoy an increase in sales. Not a paradox, it is a simple effect of a new world where people look for the solidity of roots, of established traditions, and of undisputed value. The solidity of a brand name that has "made it" through decades and crises before, through wars and revolutions, will maintain and increase its appeal. Strong attracts; survivors attract; value protects. At the same time, luxury brands, like their High End colleagues, are not immune to the economic crisis facing possibly the toughest challenges in two generations. Aspiring to *better*, to High End and to luxury are a part of culture and largely determined by the context and time. When glitter and glitz are replaced by a new sense of austerity and moderation, when new religious drives determine a recrudescence of spirituality, the *better* brands will need to seek their soul yet again.

In a world where more experts see Apple as an example of new luxury, or where movements like Slow Food rediscovered the appeal of "the original and genuine", High End brands will need to learn to listen to avoid the risk of being leapfrogged by emerging players in the new territories of innovation, or coming from new economies – BRIC and beyond. We do not have the arrogance to claim an immediate connection between our systematic methods and the artistic world of Gucci and Prada. On the other hand, this aspirational world of *better* will have to change as well – *better* is just a tiny part of the much larger planet, society and culture. It is conceivable that our thoughts just might inspire the luxury and High End leaders to look at themselves from another angle. For them, the book might not be so much a guide, but rather a source of free inspiration and new motivation.

It took hundreds of millions years for the Earth as we know it now to emerge from a huge mass of land known as Pangea. The allegorical land of

High End, explosively growing between the distinct "continents" of mass-produced products and luxury, has been just formed in the recent decades and grows with an astonishing speed. Arguably, the next few years could bring more changes and expansion to this land than all previous history. We are not shy to recognize that the High End is exposed to the risks of the current economic climate, and its aftermath. However, paradoxically research evidence shows that this approach is one of the most powerful solutions to lead us into a new era of more balanced prosperity, more human focused consumption and lifestyle-based sustainability. We do believe that this is a unique opportunity to do well by doing the right thing, and we do trust that its business process translation, the High End Toolbox, will prove a crucial asset in the management portfolio of future-proof companies worldwide.

Whether you are new to this land of High End looking to stake your field of opportunities, or you are trying to defend the hard fought for a place under the sun, if you are in the midst of preparing an aggressive expansion of your existing domain, then it is ultimately up to you to make it all happen. The way that High End will evolve to beat the downturn will greatly depend on the ideas, the drive, the passion of High End entrepreneurs and business leaders. With assets like High Design, RDE and High End Toolbox, you could reach the shores of High End business success faster and easier. We hope that this book gives you a beacon to this land and better equips you to participate in and benefit from the next wave of High End business opportunities. We are confident that the book and the tools will help you make it happen.

We wish you a great start for your next High End journey, to realize what matters the most – your own vision. We wish you to reach gold, and then higher and beyond – to repeatedly, mindfully create premium value. And to do so not just by chance, but by science and by design.

Appendix

The Appendix contains the numerical results of High End RDE studies. The tables show the additive constant (baseline) and the individual impact values for the elements. The data table for each RDE study shows the results for total panel, the two segments for the dimension, and the four countries. In the interests of space we do not present the segments by country, or by gender, and so on. One could certainly create those detailed tables, but it awaits larger studies to develop this granularity.

Working with the Data

Look at one of the tables for a few moments. At first the table will look a bit formidable, like a wall of numbers. However, after a few moments you will see the pattern, the organization of the data, and you will then find the data very logical and very powerful as an aid to understand the consumer mind.

To make sense of the numerical data, follow these four steps:

Step 1: Look at the left side of the table to see the silo or factor. Remember there are four factors for each dimension. Each factor or silo explores a different aspect of a dimension. For further richness we have chosen four elements for each silo. When you read the elements keep in mind that we tried to be specific in the elements, rather than being general.

Step 2: The first column of numbers shows the impact value from the *total panel, independent of country or segment*. The elements are ranked in descending order within a silo, based on the impact values of the total panel. This way of ranking by performance shows you the departures from the general pattern, by country or segment.

Step 3: We chose to create two larger *global segments* for each dimension, instead of four, as it is easier to understand and interpret them, especially for world-studies. The second and third columns of numbers show the impact value from the two segments that we created for each individual dimension.

Step 4: The fourth through the seventh columns of numbers show the impact values from each of the *four countries*. At the top rows we show both additive constant, and the base size (number of participants) for the total panel or for the specific subgroup, respectively.

Keep in mind the following rules of thumb when you interpret the impact values:

1. Impact > +15 means an exceptionally strong push by the element towards High End. This is a keeper element, for advertising and brand building.

2. Impacts +11 to +15 mean a very strong push by the element towards High End.

3. Impacts of +6 to +10 mean a significant but weaker push.

4. Impacts from -6 to +6 are close to 0 meaning that the element probably doesn't do much.

5. Negative impacts lower than –6 mean that the element pushes away from the High End.

Table A1   Performance of 20 elements tabulated for the total panel, both genders, and four mindset segments. The elements within each silo are sorted from high to low, based on the impact value from the total panel

Silo		Element	T	M	F	S1	S2	S3	S4
		Sample size	373	71	302	52	91	94	135
		Baseline (additive constant)	30	32	30	36	33	32	25
Design	A2	Multi-functional ... beautifully crafted ... effortlessly simple to use	11	8	12	10	7	7	18
Design	A1	Craftsmanship with a personal touch	10	7	10	7	4	3	19
Design	A3	Beautifully designed ... so simple to operate	10	8	11	11	6	5	16
Design	A4	Limited edition...designer products	5	2	5	-2	3	-2	12
Style	B1	Improved service ... better features ... exquisite attention to details	10	8	10	4	1	17	13
Style	B4	Technologically sophisticated, yet elegantly understated	8	7	9	7	1	15	8
Style	B3	Features ergonomically superior design	6	7	5	5	-6	15	7
Style	B2	Created to be a style leader	5	8	4	6	-5	12	6
Experience	C1	Provides you with a richer life experience ... just try it	5	1	6	14	14	1	0
Experience	C3	An experience that can't be easily bought ... but still can be yours	3	2	3	13	7	-2	-1
Experience	C2	Feel your life in a more intense way	1	1	2	11	7	-3	-3
Experience	C4	Try it ... you may feel delight, even reverence	-1	-1	-2	7	6	-2	-9
Emotion	D1	As individual as a fingerprint	6	5	7	7	6	5	7
Emotion	D3	Problems solved instantly...making life more pleasant	5	5	5	3	2	4	8
Emotion	D2	Embrace it...feel the radiance and vitality of others who have done it	4	4	4	2	1	5	6
Emotion	D4	Suited for first-class taste	4	3	5	5	8	3	3
Exclusivity	E2	Delivers the ultimate level of personal touch and care	8	4	9	-6	12	13	7
Exclusivity	E4	Feel unique ... it can be customized to match your individuality	8	6	8	-1	14	9	6
Exclusivity	E1	Elevates you above the crowd	4	3	5	-6	12	9	0
Exclusivity	E3	Lifts you beyond the mass	1	1	1	-12	10	5	-3

Notes: T = Total panel, M = Males; F= Females, S1 = Segment 1 "It's the experience", S2 = Segment 2 "Exclusive fun", S3 = Segment 3 "Status and style" and S4 = Segment 4 "Craftsmanship"

Table A2   How elements about Authenticity and Value (Dimension 1) drive perception, as High End (high positive numbers in bold) or detract from perception of High End (low negative numbers in italics)

Silo		Element	T	S1	S2	US	UK	Italy	China
Number of participants			*369*	*196*	*173*	*99*	*94*	*90*	*86*
Baseline perception of future High End			**26**	**25**	**27**	**23**	**16**	**34**	**34**
Origin factor	A2	Made in … Italy/France/ Switzerland/UK/USA	**10**	**18**	**2**	**8**	**14**	**13**	**8**
	A1	Made in … a specific country of origin	*-2*	*7*	*-13*	*-3*	*0*	*-5*	*-2*
	A4	Made in …Japan	*-4*	*6*	*-16*	*-8*	*4*	*-2*	*-11*
	A3	Made in … India/Brazil/China	*-17*	*-4*	*-31*	*-18*	*-14*	*-26*	*-8*
Exclusivity factor	B3	outstanding service support	**9**	4	**13**	5	**6**	**10**	**14**
	B4	with exclusive mix of product design + functional features + service	**8**	1	**16**	3	**13**	5	**13**
	B2	exclusive technology	**7**	0	**14**	3	**13**	1	**10**
	B1	exclusive design	5	-1	**11**	2	**11**	5	1
Price factor	C2	exclusively priced	5	7	3	**6**	2	3	**7**
	C1	premium priced	5	7	2	**10**	2	-1	**8**
	C3	moderately priced	*-7*	*-1*	*-14*	*-4*	*-10*	*-7*	*-8*
	C4	very affordable	*-9*	*-3*	*-15*	*-5*	*-2*	*-9*	*-21*
Residual value factor	D2	will become a collector's item	**7**	-3	**18**	7	5	4	**10**
	D1	the value will increase over time	**6**	-2	**14**	6	**7**	2	**8**
	D3	resell value above purchase price	**4**	-5	**14**	**7**	5	1	2
	D4	not a purchase.. an investment	**4**	-5	**14**	**8**	5	2	1

Notes: T= Total panel, S1 = Segment 1 "Status seekers", S2 = Segment 2 "Connoisseurs"

Table A3 How elements about Design and Experience (Dimension 2) drive perception as High End (high positive numbers in bold) or detract from perception of High End (low negative numbers in italics)

Silo		Element	Total	S1	S2	USA	UK	Italy	China
Number of participants			*368*	*166*	*202*	*99*	*95*	*94*	*80*
Baseline perception of future High End			**30**	**29**	**30**	26	28	**31**	**34**
"Holistic" factor	A1	designed for a holistic experience	5	3	7	2	5	**8**	**8**
	A2	designed to capitalize on your vision of life	5	5	5	**8**	5	1	7
	A3	appealing before you own it	4	**6**	3	6	2	3	5
	A4	retains most of its value even when no longer functional	2	1	2	**8**	2	*-4*	2
"Craftsmanship" factor	B4	made with the world's finest materials	**13**	**21**	6	**10**	**13**	**17**	**11**
	B2	made with unmatched precision	**11**	**20**	4	6	**12**	**12**	**15**
	B1	exceptional hand-made craftsmanship	**11**	**19**	4	**12**	**13**	**11**	6
	B3	made by trained professionals	**8**	**18**	0	2	**12**	**12**	6
"Design leadership" factor	C2	produced by a maker reputed for great design	7	**12**	3	7	**8**	5	**8**
	C1	created by renowned star designers	7	**13**	2	6	7	**6**	**9**
	C4	created by designers whose opinions you admire beyond design	7	**13**	2	**9**	4	3	**11**
	C3	a design icon	2	**10**	*-4*	0	2	**6**	*-1*
"Inclusion" factor	D1	enables people to live according to new lifestyle choices	5	*-7*	**14**	2	*-3*	**10**	**11**
	D4	enables more diversity in the communities of use	*-5*	*-23*	**10**	*-11*	*-14*	3	4
	D2	enables senior citizens to live more comfortably	*-9*	*-28*	7	*-11*	*-19*	*-2*	*-2*
	D3	enables minorities to feel more integrated	*-12*	*-32*	4	*-20*	*-22*	*-9*	4

Notes: S1 = Segment 1 "Focus on product" and S2 = Segment 2 "Focus on people"

Table A4 How elements about Innovation and Leadership (Dimension 3) drive perception as High (high positive numbers in bold) or detract from perception of High End (low negative numbers in italics)

Silo		Element	Total	S1	S2	USA	UK	Italy	China
Number of participants			360	186	174	100	96	91	73
Baseline perception of future High End			32	34	29	19	24	50	35
Innovation factor	A1	with functional features that anticipate what you want	**6**	*-5*	**19**	**10**	**10**	-2	**9**
	A2	with technological features that anticipate what you want	**6**	*-3*	**16**	**10**	**6**	1	**9**
	A3	innovative in continuity with the earlier generation of the same product	5	*-7*	**18**	**9**	4	0	**6**
	A4	a natural extension of the current offer from its maker	3	*-6*	**13**	5	5	-1	3
Revolutionary factor	B4	completely changes the way you live	**9**	**13**	4	**8**	**7**	**9**	**12**
	B1	totally revolutionary	**7**	**9**	4	5	**9**	1	**13**
	B3	just creates a new product category	0	1	-2	-1	-2	-1	3
	B2	somewhat provocative	-2	3	*-7*	-2	-2	*-6*	3
"Partnership" factor	C2	offers multiple functions	**8**	**6**	**9**	**11**	**7**	1	**11**
	C3	combines benefits from different industries	**7**	**6**	**9**	**8**	**10**	1	**11**
	C1	intuitive to use	**6**	5	**8**	6	**8**	1	**11**
	C4	created thanks to a 'maverick CEO'	3	**7**	-2	2	-2	-1	**15**
"Thought leadership" factor	D3	comes from an authority I trust	2	**7**	-3	**8**	3	*-6*	3
	D2	one of the many creations of a public leader	-4	**6**	*-15*	-3	*-9*	*-6*	1
	D1	from an executive who is a public personality	*-7*	3	*-17*	*-6*	*-7*	*-9*	-4
	D4	from a creator with a seducing charisma	*-7*	4	*-18*	*-10*	*-7*	*-8*	-1

Notes: S1 = Segment 1 "Focus on leader" and S2 = Segment 2 "Functional innovation"

Table A5   How elements about Communication and Distribution (Dimension 4) drive perception as High End (high positive numbers in bold) or detract from perception of High End (low negative numbers in italics)

Silo		Element		Total	S1	S2	USA	UK	Italy	China
Number of participants				359	181	178	100	91	90	78
Baseline perception of future High End				28	28	27	23	18	35	35
Grassroots factor		A1	referred to me by a friend	**7**	4	**11**	7	9	7	**6**
		A4	created a buzz in a community I am part of	4	2	7	4	7	3	4
		A3	discovered through a non-conventional media	3	–1	7	2	2	2	7
		A2	positively reviewed in blogs and discussion groups	1	–4	7	0	4	0	3
Production values factor		B4	with top quality communication	6	3	9	1	4	5	**15**
		B3	with the associated colors that are beautiful to you	5	2	8	5	5	4	6
		B2	with the associated aesthetics that are beautiful to you	4	4	4	2	7	4	2
		B1	with the associated images that are beautiful to you	0	–1	0	–2	1	3	–2
Celebrity factor		C4	if you were a celebrity you would own this	–1	–4	2	–8	–1	–6	**14**
		C1	used by celebrities in their own life	–3	–6	0	–7	0	–12	**8**
		C3	with a celebrity brand spokesperson	–6	–11	–1	–13	–3	–10	4
		C2	with a celebrity testimonial used in advertising	–6	–9	–4	–11	–4	–8	–1
Placement factor		D1	with a superior point of sale	**9**	15	2	**12**	**9**	**10**	4
		D4	prominently displayed in a store	7	13	0	**12**	5	5	3
		D2	with the packaging that stands out on the shelf	6	12	1	**11**	7	4	3
		D3	exclusive on-line offer, not available in stores	1	9	–6	8	7	–3	–9

Notes: S1 = Segment 1 "Forms own opinions" and S2 = Segment 2 "Swayed by others"

Table A6   How elements about Sustainability and Simplicity (Dimension 5) drive perception as High End (high positive numbers in bold) or detract from perception of High End (low negative numbers in italics, none in this case)

Silo		Element	Total	S1	S2	USA	UK	Italy	China
Number of participants			365	196	169	100	93	90	82
Baseline perception of future High End			30	35	25	22	23	44	33
Green factor	A4	helps to save the environment in the long term	**10**	0	**22**	7	**10**	6	**18**
	A3	designed not to impact the environment	7	*−3*	**19**	5	**11**	6	8
	A2	Eco-friendly production process	7	*−4*	**19**	7	**10**	3	8
	A1	not polluting	6	*−3*	**16**	3	4	5	**11**
Society factor	B3	helps local communities to improve	6	7	5	**10**	7	3	3
	B4	improves the life of people in my own community	6	7	5	**11**	2	4	7
	B2	benefits the people in local communities producing it	5	6	3	7	6	2	3
	B1	produced respecting the local communities	5	6	3	6	6	2	4
Personal factor	C2	customizable to my own needs	8	9	6	7	5	7	**13**
	C3	helps me save time	7	7	8	6	8	8	9
	C1	can be upgraded over time	7	9	5	6	5	5	**12**
	C4	improves the quality of the space around me	5	5	5	6	3	5	6
Simplicity factor	D4	makes complex technology friendly to me	8	**15**	1	9	4	3	**18**
	D3	simplifies my life	6	**12**	*−1*	8	2	6	7
	D1	simple to use	4	**10**	*−1*	5	4	4	5
	D2	makes sense in my life	4	**12**	*−5*	8	0	3	6

Notes: S1 = Segment 1 "Personal simplicity" and S2 = Segment 2 "Sensitive"

General Predisposition to High End Perception

The additive constant or baseline perception of High End shows the general predisposition to label a future proposition or product as High End in the context of the specific dimension. Thus, the baseline is the best estimation of the starting point of the general attitude of participants towards High End. To this baseline you would add specific impact values. The sum provides you with a measure of the total "High Endedness" of the proposition.

Let's compare the baselines on country by country basis. You can see the baselines listed in Table A7, and presented graphically for more visual comparison in Figure A1.

Although each dimension was treated as an independent project with completely different set of participants, the baselines for the total across the dimensions are quite consistent (between +26 and +32). This means that the nature of the individual dimension does not drive participants to pre-judge a proposition as High End.

Table A7   **Magnitude of the baselines (predisposition to call a proposition High End), obtained from the five different RDE experiments, one for each dimension of the High End Charter**

Dimension	USA	UK	Italy	China	TOTAL
1: Authenticity & Value	23	16	34	34	**26**
2: Design & Experience	26	28	31	34	**30**
3: Innovation & Leadership	19	24	50	35	**32**
4: Marketing, Communication & Distribution	23	18	35	35	**28**
5: Sustainability & Simplicity	22	23	44	33	**30**
Average per country	**23**	**22**	**39**	**34**	**29**

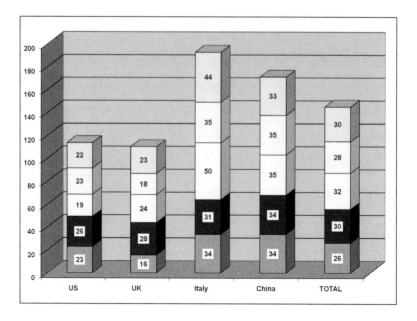

Figure A1   **Magnitude of the additive constant across the countries and dimensions. The taller stacks represent higher level of predisposition to consider a product to be High End**

In the absence of specific information about the proposition, respondents in the UK and the USA will be the least likely to expect a product or proposition to be High End in the near future, whereas consumers in China will be more predisposed to expect a proposition to be High End. Italians are most inclined to call a proposition "High End". Cultural and regional differences will be key to future High End success.

Table A8   **Cross-tabulation of the performance of the elements for High Net Worth Bank Experience Case study**

	T	S1	S2	S3	S4
Total					
Committed to providing clarity around the complex issues of wealth	7	8	9	2	9
Pay a fee for financial advice based on your total investments	−7	0	−10	−5	−7
Segment 1 – Make it easy and safe					
Easy to reach and easy to meet	3	**13**	6	1	−7
Wealth management made simple	1	**12**	−2	0	−2
We can help you with both your personal and business needs	1	**12**	3	0	−8
Choose a pricing option that suits you	1	**10**	−3	1	3
We provide a one stop shop for your wealth management needs	6	**−10**	13	7	3
We understand your needs, then develop and monitor a plan designed to meet your objectives	3	**−10**	5	−4	15
We provide banking services with extra features that meet your needs	0	**−10**	8	−7	1
A range of investment options ... to suit your risk appetite	3	**−12**	11	−2	7
Collaborate with your bank ... on investment decisions	0	**−13**	2	0	3
We select the appropriate investment options and the managers for your portfolio	0	**−24**	10	−3	3
You qualify for our affluent group program ... exclusive service	−3	**−28**	4	−3	2
Segment 2 – One stop shop					
We provide a one stop shop for your wealth management needs	6	−10	**13**	7	3
We provide consistency in our relationship that you'll want to recommend us to your family and friends	−1	−4	**12**	−18	3
We are local to you and you can reach us easily	2	7	**11**	−8	−5
A range of investment options ... to suit your risk appetite	3	−12	**11**	−2	7
Choose how you interact with us ... phone, mobile, online, face to face	3	5	**10**	−4	−1
A single point of contact ... for all your needs	4	4	**10**	−8	6
We select the appropriate investment options and the managers for your portfolio	0	−24	**10**	−3	3
Pay a fixed fee for planning your wealth strategy – and then only pay for investments you actually make	−4	0	**−10**	−2	1
Pay a fee for financial advice based on your total investments	−7	0	**−10**	−5	−7
Our fees are linked to the performance of your investments	2	−1	**−10**	16	5
Segment 3 – Pay for performance					
Our fees are linked to the performance of your investments	2	−1	−10	**16**	5

Table A8   *Concluded*

	T	S1	S2	S3	S4
Your retirement needs … plan with an expert	−1	−1	0	**−10**	10
We assign to you a personal relationship manager to better understand your needs	2	−7	5	**−11**	19
A relationship team that can look after your business needs and your personal wealth	−1	−2	3	**−12**	5
Access to a team of specialists coordinated by your relationship manager	−1	−5	5	**−13**	5
We provide consistency in our relationship that you'll want to recommend us to your family and friends	−1	−4	12	**−18**	3
We offer objective advice based on what is important to you	−3	−5	1	**−20**	14
Segment 4 – Personalize					
We assign to you a personal relationship manager to better understand your needs	2	−7	5	−11	**19**
Regular reviews with your financial advisor	−1	−4	−5	−9	**18**
We understand your needs, then develop and monitor a plan designed to meet your objectives	3	−10	5	−4	**15**
We offer objective advice based on what is important to you	−3	−5	1	−20	**14**
A financial plan to secure your future	1	−5	0	−5	**13**
Your retirement needs … plan with an expert	−1	−1	0	−10	**10**
We aim to be your trusted advisor	2	9	1	9	**−11**
Benefit from our solid expertise	−2	8	−1	−1	**−13**

Notes:

T = Total panel
S1 = Segment 1 "Easy and safe"
S2 = Segment 2 "One stop"
S3 = Segment 3 "Pay per performance"
S4 = Segment 4 "Personalize"

Table A9   Cross-tabulation of the performance of the elements for Passion for Art Case Study

	T	S1	S2
Total			
Art enhances our children and gives them the ability to become what is inside them	**12**	9	16
Art is an experience... to be enjoyed by all	**10**	7	16
You can even use your credit card to donate	**−10**	−12	−6
Segment 1 – Human fulfillment important			
Art enhances our children and gives them the ability to become what is inside them	12	**9**	16
Giving is a part of your family tradition	−6	**−10**	4
You can even use your credit card to donate	−10	**−12**	−6
Fulfilling a religious obligation to help others	−8	**−17**	9
Segment 2 – Art as an enriching experience			
Supporting an innovative project or addressing our most pressing artistic needs shows the vision of excellence across the past, present and future	8	3	**18**
Art is a touchstone...the colors, textures, smells and minutiae... It feeds your soul and anchors you	7	1	**18**
Art enhances our children and gives them the ability to become what is inside them	12	9	**16**
Art is an experience... to be enjoyed by all	10	7	**16**
Encouraging yourself and others to participate in a worthwhile project	7	2	**16**
What a gift to give... the appreciation to see what is around us everyday and to understand the intricacies of the web of life and how we are all bound together	8	4	**15**
Emphasizing interactive learning and a continuum of exposure, offering a scope and sequence ranging from a single museum visit to a semester-long art program in a school classroom	5	1	**14**
The diversity and myriad experiences of understanding art...keeps the America rich beyond our wildest dreams	4	−1	**13**
Donating time, money and effort makes a difference	3	0	**10**
Because you want to honor a loved one	−2	3	**−11**

Notes:

T = Total panel
S1 = Segment 1 "Human fulfillment"
S2 = Segment 2 "Art as enricher"

Index

sustainability and simplicity
161–3, **163, 164**
types of customers
identified 91, 92
WWF Luxury Initiative 151–2

Y
Yoox 103, 104

Yosimiya 7
Ypsilon, marketing campaign
for 137–9

Z
Zidane, Zinedine 34

Identity:
Transforming Performance through Integrated
Identity Management
Mark Rowden
Hardback: 978-0-566-08737-0

Memorable Customer Experiences:
A Research Anthology
Edited by
Adam Lindgreen, Joëlle Vanhamme and Michael B. Beverland
Hardback: 978-0-566-08868-1
e-book: 978-0-566-09207-7

The New Guide to Identity:
How to Create and Sustain Change
Through Managing Identity
Wolff Olins
Paperback: 978-0-566-07737-1

Visit **www.gowerpublishing.com** and

* search the entire catalogue of Gower books in print
* order titles online at 10% discount
* take advantage of special offers
* sign up for our monthly e-mail update service
* download free sample chapters from all recent titles
* download or order our catalogue